THE SACRED LITERATURE

THE SPIRIT OF BUDDHIST MEDITATION

THE SPIRIT OF BUDDHIST MEDITATION

INTRODUCED, TRANSLATED AND EDITED BY

SARAH SHAW

YALE UNIVERSITY PRESS
NEW HAVEN AND LONDON

For information about this and other Yale University Press publications please contact:
U.S. Office: sales.press@yale.edu yalebooks.com
Europe Office: sales@yaleup.co.uk www.yalebooks.co.uk

Typeset in Arno by IDSUK (DataConnection) Ltd
Printed in Great Britain by Hobbs the Printers Ltd, Totton, Hampshire

Library of Congress Control Number 2014944750

ISBN 978-0-300-19876-8

A catalogue record for this book is available from the British Library.

10 9 8 7 6 5 4 3 2 1

If there is any merit in this book, may it bring happiness and benefit
to my family, teachers and friends

CONTENTS

ACKNOWLEDGEMENTS

This book has been several years in gestation, and I realize that I have been greatly influenced by people I have met, whose advice, help, questions, or sometimes just an aside, I have found very useful. So I would like to thank the following for various different reasons.

Venerable Ashin Sitagu Sayadaw, Ato Rinpoche, Venerable Pa-Auk Sayadaw Ashin, Chris Collier, Ian Clarke, Dr Linda Covill, Dr L.S. Cousins, Ven Dr Khammai Dhammasāmi, Ven Dr Mahinda Degalle, Professor Florin Deleanu, Professor Halvor Eifrig, Dr Jas and Silvia Elsner, Professor Richard Gombrich, Dr Sanjukta Gupta, Professor Paul Harrison, Professor Peter Harvey, Dr Richard Hayes, Juin Hosen, Dr Jenny Kwek, Dr Jinwol Lee, Ven Dr Maha Laow, Dr John Maraldo, Dr Nina Mirnig, Peggy and Dr Teresa Morgan, Sarah Norman, Venerable Dr Pannyavamsa, Dr Dion Peoples, Deng Poonyathiro, Dr Ulrike Roesler, Kyozan Joshu Roshi, Dr Harold Roth, Alex and Annie Sevier, Dr Peter Skilling, Venerable Dr Sunil Sakya, Anne Schilizzi, Venerable Sudhiro, Dr Donald Swearer, Dr John and Deborah Taber, Professors Alan and Vesna Wallace, Jenny Wilkinson, and Professor Stefano Zacchetti. Thanks also to the OUDCE class, Oxford Centre for Buddhist Studies Buddhism classes and lectures, those that attended a summer school at the Bodhi Manda Zen Center in 2011, and US *samatha* meditators for all the helpfully forthright comments made discussing these texts. The librarians and colleagues at the Oriental Institute and Wolfson College have been kind and helpful. I am grateful to Malcolm Gerratt for asking me to do this book. An anonymous reader appointed by Yale made very helpful suggestions that I have tried to implement.

I practise – or try to – a traditional form of breathing mindfulness *samatha*, which has elements of *vipassanā* too. It is a type of practice that used to be very prevalent in rural Thailand and Southeast Asia, but is less so now in those regions. Fortunately it is taught in the UK and the States. So my thanks to Boonman Poonyathiro, and friends and teachers at the Samatha Association. Thanks also to old and new friends at the Oxford Buddha Vihāra and the OCBS.

My main thanks, as always, are to Charles, and our family.

CHAPTER ONE

INTRODUCTION

There is a story that one Buddhist school, the Chan, traces its lineage to the time of the Buddha. Trying to teach its first patriarch, then an aspirant meditator, the Buddha simply handed him a flower in silence. The Ven Kaśyapa, apparently, at that moment, smiled as he understood the nature of reality, and achieved awakening, freedom from rebirth. Clearly he needed to be of a certain disposition and level of experience to be taught, in just the right way, at just the right moment. The story raises, however, some interesting problems about writing on something like meditation in a book. How can the spirit of a tradition be communicated that has from its inception depended so much on oral/aural transmission, personal teaching and the learning of meditation? A newcomer to class can watch how someone holds their hands in as they sit, straightens the back in a certain way, and can perhaps sometimes sense a tone of levity in a particular instruction or piece of advice, or a tone of urgency. How is this, and the quality of its occasional stillness, transmitted on paper? Fortunately for us, the texts were designed to be passed on, to travel and to be assimilated by the new groups of people, in different localities: from the outset, Buddhism seems to have been geared to do these things. As stressed in this book, however, a good tradition, teacher and friends, along with texts, are the best way of finding out about meditation for oneself.

The underlying theme of this book will be to explore the way meditation was described and taught in the early period, from around the third century BCE to the seventh century CE, in canon and commentaries. All the texts chosen are still regularly used and consulted as part of the living tradition. It includes some from the very earliest layers of the tradition.

These texts form the 'canon' and give some of the earliest known Buddhist teachings on the subject. There will also be some texts and stories about early meditators from the later commentaries, which from the start of the tradition transmitted and explained the texts to practitioners. There are other readings, such as extracts from the questions of King Milinda, a series of questions asked by the Bactrian king about Buddhist meditation and doctrine, and a few Sanskrit texts, to indicate early variation.

Most of the texts are translated from Pāli, an ancient Indo-Aryan language very close to the language the Buddha originally spoke. Because of this emphasis, the magnificent heritage of text and manuals in Sanskrit, Chinese, Japanese, Korean, Thai, Burmese, Tibetan and various languages employed where Buddhism has taken root cannot be represented. Buddhism is characterized by an immense variety of texts and practices, in many languages and regions, demonstrating an adaptability considered by many as one of its greatest strengths. The advantage of this selection is that it is possible to show, through our only complete collection of early Buddhist genres of texts, the great variety of *types* of teachings, including verses, early prose, commentaries and narrative traditions, all used to help the practice of meditation from early times, in one genus of Buddhism. Some could be called sacred, and even their written, chanted, sung or painted forms are revered as examples of the *dhamma*, the Buddha's teaching. Such texts are those categorized under three headings or 'baskets': *Suttas*, teachings for specific occasions, *Vinaya*, the monastic rules, and *Abhidhamma*, the 'higher' teaching. Others, including some later poems, guides and manuals, are honoured but used primarily for the advice and teachings they provide. Many refer to one another, as we shall see. So, when they are read together, we can obtain a flavour of how some ways quite different kinds of texts and teachings were and are seen to support one another, with differing methods, used for varied and specific purposes, people and times. To my knowledge, this is the first book to try to present this kind of overview. There will be some explanatory introduction, giving background and possible application for those interested in meditation now. Brief reference will also be made to modern meditative teaching methods, uses of terms and techniques.

This is not a scholarly edition, and because of considerations of length, there are only minimal notes. However, as there are now a number of practitioners who like to know the original terms used in translations and work out the best for themselves, technical words have been given in the original where possible.

Some historical background

The life of the Buddha is considered in Southern Buddhism as the best means of expressing the principles that lie behind his system of meditation.

The young prince Gotama, who became the historical Buddha, was raised in a palace, in the fifth century BCE, in Northern India. According to the stories, he was protected amidst all the luxury that such a life could offer at the time. After seeing four 'messengers' – an old man, a sick man, a corpse and an ascetic – he became dissatisfied with a life of protected pleasure and decided to leave the palace to find understanding and freedom from suffering. According to his own later accounts, he tried many practices: before then, as he says, there were many teachers, wandering ascetics, and sages of various kinds. Ancient India seems to have been filled with all kinds of practitioners of various forms of meditation, arduous physical exercises and gruelling practices. First he trained in formless meditations, which he felt were only partial in their effectiveness, but which he later integrated into his own meditative system. He then endured severe mortifications and self-denial, living in the wilderness and eating sometimes only one grain of rice a day.[1] But he found that just as sensory indulgence did not bring peace or wisdom, so these practices also did not lead to knowledge or happiness.[2]

A legend popular in Southeast Asia describes Gotama's conversion from a path leading to self-destruction. Sakka, the king of the gods of a realm called the Heaven of the Thirty-Three Gods, sees the sufferings of Gotama and realizes that he is near death. So he comes down to the realm of humans as Gotama lies severely ill, and plays a lute with three strings. One of these is too taut, and makes a harsh, scratching sound. Another is too lax, and sounds off-key. The last string, however, is evenly tuned, and produces a beautiful note. On hearing this, Gotama senses the possibility of a way of practice that involves neither excessive self-gratification nor punishing austerities.[3] He remembers a simple and joyful meditation he had found for himself as a child, the first *jhāna*, and asks himself if this instead might be the way to peace and liberation. Taking food, he practises this meditation, and others, and becomes awakened. On the night of the enlightenment, seated under a Bodhi tree, he eradicates the roots of the attachments that bring suffering, and free from the burden of wanting and rejecting, is released from all the defilements which had clouded his mind. After that, he develops his teaching of the eightfold path, of right view, right intention, right livelihood, right speech, right action, right effort, right mindfulness and right concentration. This path, which covers all areas of life, is based on the principle of the middle way, an ongoing balance and equipoise, which, perhaps above all of the single formulations of the Buddha's teachings, communicates the spirit of the way Gotama practised. A revolutionary and innovative thinker and practitioner, for forty-five years the Buddha passed on his own system of meditation, which included some earlier practices, but also incorporated some he developed himself, yet suitable for a wide variety of kinds of temperaments and people.

We can see in his life story a principle that is the single most obvious characteristic of the way the Buddha taught. In apparent contrast to the systems around at the time, the Buddha introduced a system of meditation and practice that was realistic, workable and applicable to all kinds of temperaments and types of people: it seems to find the 'note' from which practitioners, with guidance, can start to find their own way to liberation. His advice to meditators at different stages varies according to their needs and experience: it is, he said, a 'graduated' path. Indeed, through the accounts of the early texts we are presented with a meditation guide who was alert to individual problems, took account of different levels of experience and, using similes and analogies that would be familiar to those he was teaching, was prepared to tailor meditations according to people's needs. At the time of the Buddha, Indian religious traditions had placed great emphasis on external forms, rituals and sacrifices; the Buddha, however, put meditation, and its associated practices, at the heart of a comprehensive spiritual path, accessible to everyone. In a move that was radical at the time, he emphasized that it was volition (*cetanā*), not external forms, that provided the key to finding liberation and peaceful contentment in daily life and in meditation. Also unusually for the time, he taught everyone, of any class, both men and women. Ignoring the rigid caste and gender restrictions of most traditions, which maintained that only males of high caste could attain liberation, he taught meditation to all who asked, and, after deliberation, welcomed all within his own monastic orders.

The Buddha's system – or perhaps we should say systems – of meditation not only was adapted to individual temperament and level of experience and attainment, but seems to have survived for so long because it was also geared to being taught by his followers to others. From what we can tell from these early texts, people who wanted to learn meditation in ancient India would move from one teacher to another, staying where they felt they could get teachings helpful to them, debating with others about points of meditation and doctrine. The Buddha worked within this milieu, but encouraged his followers not only to follow a wide range of practices, but also to debate amongst themselves and to teach, sometimes in his presence, when he often approved what they had said. Early texts are filled with examples of his own disciples, both male and female, learning from him and then going on to teach others, who in turn teach the next generation. 'Reading' the tone of ancient texts is not easy: but a sense of communal practice, friendship, humour and mutual encouragement can be felt in these interchanges. Throughout, meditators are encouraged to look for guidance, to find 'good friends' in the teaching, and to ensure that contacts with other practitioners maintain the health and balance of a meditative teaching whose spirit is communicated by the very notion of a balanced and 'middle' way. These characteristics are still encouraged today.

From the earliest days of the tradition, Buddhism travelled and adapted. In contrast to contemporary mores, at a time when Indian society viewed much travel and all sea and boat travel as hazardous and polluting, travel is encouraged and indeed embedded into the very formulation of early Buddhist doctrine. So those who follow the teaching take a 'path', the same word used for any thoroughfare, and follow a system of training that is compared to a boat or a raft, that will take the person who uses it across the dangerous and perilous waters of *saṃsāra*, the endless wandering that is the lot of all beings. Even within the Buddha's lifetime the tradition rapidly moved from the regions around northern India where he initially taught. So, from its inception inherently mobile, it had to acquire from the outset flexibility to new circumstances, in various adjustments of theory, practice and understanding suitable for different terrains, kinds of people and the demands of the local situation. We can take a very concrete example of this, in some changes that took place in the centuries after the tradition had become established in many different settings. In the very early texts the Buddha himself did not promulgate vegetarianism, though it was suggested to him as a policy, on the grounds that he wanted his order of monks to eat whatever the laity chose to give them. But when the tradition travelled, by the first centuries CE, to China, then Korea and finally Japan, the idea of saving other beings moved into the codified practice, in some schools, of refraining from eating meat. When, much later, Buddhism travelled to Tibet, from both China and India, such policies could not be maintained: no meditator would survive in those regions without eating meat. In other creative and exploratory ways the tradition, particularly with regard to meditation practices, adapted and evolved in accordance with local customs, rituals, and doctrines. Buddhist meditative practices and doctrines have tended to promote adaptation to the culture to which they move, a feature which helps to explain the great success of Buddhism in China, for instance, where it evolved and was reformulated to complement the pre-existent schools of Confucianism and Daoism. The diffusion of Buddhism was and is wide: after the death of the Buddha, teachings were taken around India, to Sri Lanka and Southeast Asian countries, and up through the north to regions such as Parthia, around modern Iran, and along the Silk Road, as well as eastwards through sea routes coming from India, and by land to China, where it underwent significant transformations. From here, the traditions that had evolved in China based on Buddhist meditative practice moved to Korea and then to Japan. The first movement to the Himalayan regions around Tibet appears to have occurred in the sixth century, from India and China, and then in later waves, primarily from India.

During these movements, Buddhism necessarily evolved, as it did indeed in places where it became established, in a long process of acculturation and absorption. This anthology will also attempt to communicate this spirit of creative adaptability in the types of texts that are chosen. In the course of the movement of Buddhism, with various forms of the teaching travelling at different times to different regions, the practice of meditation, too, inevitably developed and changed in a number of ways.

For instance, in the centuries after the Buddha's death around 400 BCE, there was a general movement towards the devotional and the visual in all the religious traditions extant at the time. In Buddhism itself, many new practices were developed, often involving the visualized figure of the Buddha, and the various settings and idealized realms in which he was felt to have taught, and in some traditions, was thought still to be teaching. The idea of the Bodhisatta/Bodhisattva, the being dedicated to saving all beings from suffering, became increasingly popular, and many texts describe such beings, their realms, and their teachings, often through visualized images of various Bodhisattvas and their followers. These texts and practices were taken to other regions as Buddhism travelled, adapting sometimes to local images, gods and imaginary realms. In Tibet, for instance, where it seems that the Bon already had a heritage of gods, visual images and rituals, the Buddhist tradition, which arrived in waves from about the seventh century, started to place more emphasis on such elements, or adapt them from Indian counterparts, and new meditative traditions evolved. In Tibet, such practices assumed even greater importance than they had before, and were imbued with great significance and meaning, as local gods, rituals and images seem to have been integrated with the exercises, mantras and devotional exercises popular in India at the time. This emphasis on visualized images of deities, bodhisattvas and Buddhas has remained a prominent characteristic of Tibetan meditative practice, with grades and initiations for each stage and further development of the meditation. We can trace the origins of these practices in texts, some of which are included in this volume, that were composed in India in the centuries after the Buddha's death. The Buddhist traditions in which they arose have now been lost, as India ceased to have a large Buddhist practitioner base from around the time of the end of the first millennium, but the early texts describe practices that evolved and changed in what are known as the Northern Buddhist areas.

In some areas, where Buddhism travelled in an early period, such as the regions now known as Thailand, Burma, Sri Lanka, Laos, Cambodia and Thailand, meditative practices developed in other ways, with some increasingly visual and devotional elements, but of a different nature. Under the influence of the kind of Buddhism associated with the Mahāvihāra monastery in Sri Lanka, meditation tended to remain true to canonical models and spirit, though again with much local variety and adaptation. These traditions also retained elements found in the early texts, but perhaps kept closer to them in the way they developed and changed. This kind of Buddhism is known as Southern or Theravāda Buddhism.

In China, where Buddhism had arrived far earlier than in Tibet, new sorts of practices emerged, with the Tiantai and Huayan schools, but again took directions they had not taken in other regions. In China, Japan and Korea, Chan/Zen/Seon tradition made radical departures in its emphasis on the moment and the awakening power of *gongans/koans*. In other schools, walking practices connected with the visualized figure of the Buddha became particularly popular, and rituals, images and devotional offerings were associated with meditative practices that assumed forms influenced by local preoccupations and interests. The Pure Land schools, popular throughout the Eastern Buddhist regions of China, Korea and Japan, absorbed elements that had originally come from India, and changed them to accommodate quite different demands and interests of these regions. Peasants who had little time for sitting meditative practice were particularly attracted to chants and recollections of the Buddha and his teaching that they could practise in daily life, so the evolution of a singular formula of a chant that could be murmured internally while working in the fields became and still is popular in Eastern Asia, with a number of developments over the next two millennia. This then would bring a fortunate rebirth in a Pure Land heaven, described in visual and aural terms very like the visualized human and divine realms of other forms of Buddhism. This development in turn, with many other factors, gave rise to the chanting meditative traditions in Japan, such as Nichiren, Sokka Gokkai and Pure Land schools. It is always difficult to generalize about forms of Buddhism, over a period of more than two thousand years, in widely disparate regions. One of the greatest strengths of Buddhism is that it lacks a centralized authority and even a single body of core texts, containing many in a number of different languages in various regions. Some, perhaps most, of these traditions are partly rooted in a number of the texts that will be included in this anthology, and can trace some ancestry to elements that were developed right at the start of the tradition, or in India, in the centuries after the Buddha's death.

This is not a historical anthology, and will not attempt to give any more than a brief account of the way meditation practices have developed as the tradition travelled or indeed stayed within regions where it had been for centuries.[4] Some texts dating from the first centuries after the Buddha's death, however, have either particularly influenced, or show affinities to, the way meditation has developed in Northern, Southern and Eastern Buddhist regions, and this will be noted in the introductions. Western Buddhism, if we can still use directional categories for the complex interrelatedness of global cultures, will also be included.

The path to awakening

The text below is perhaps the most succinct summary of the Buddha's teaching, along with the first sermon, the 'Turning of the Wheel' (*Dhammacakkapavattana-Sutta:* S V 420–5), which describes the four noble truths: *dukkha*, dis-ease, tension or suffering, that is to be understood; the origin of suffering in craving, that is to be abandoned; the possibility of the freedom from suffering, cessation, that is to be realized; and the path leading to this, that is to be brought into being. The text rests on a central paradox of a path found by no 'travel', other than that provided by the verbs 'knows at peace' and 'longs no more'.

Rohitassa-Sutta

At one time the Blessed One was staying near Sāvatthī, in Anāthapiṇḍika's pleasure grove in the Jeta wood. Then, in the depths of the night, Rohitassa, the son of a deva, his surpassing radiance illuminating the whole of the Jeta wood, approached the Blessed One. When he arrived, having paid homage to the Blessed One, he stood to one side. As he was standing there he said to the Blessed One: 'Is it possible, sir, by travelling, to know or see or reach a far end of the world, where one is not born, does not grow old, die, pass away or take rebrth?'

'I tell you, sir, that it is not possible by travelling to know or see or reach a far end of the world, where one is not born, does not grow old, die, pass away, or take rebirth.'

'It is astonishing, sir, and marvellous, how well this has been stated by the Blessed One: "I tell you, bhante, that it is not possible by travelling to know or see or reach a far end of the world, where one is not born, does not grow old, die, pass away, or take rebirth." Once I was a seer named Rohitassa, a student of Bhoja, of great psychic power, one who could travel through the air. My speed was as fast as that of a light arrow shot across the shadow of a palm tree by a strong archer, well-trained, an old hand at shooting, a crack exhibition shooter.[5] My stride was such that it spanned as far as the east sea is from the west. To me, endowed with such speed and such a stride, this desire came: "I will go travelling to the end of the world." So I, with a one-hundred-year life, a one-hundred-year span, spent one hundred years travelling, apart from the time spent in eating, drinking, chewing and tasting, urinating and defecating, and sleeping to ward off exhaustion, but, without reaching the end of the world, I died along the way. So it is astonishing, lord, and marvellous, how well that has been said by the Blessed One: "I declare, sir, that it is not possible by travelling to know or see or reach a far end of the world where one is not born, does not grow old, die, pass away, or take rebirth."'

'I declare, sir, that it is not possible by travelling to know or see or reach a far end of the world where one is not born, does not grow old, die, pass away, or take rebirth. At the same time, I tell you that there is no bringing to an end of suffering without reaching the end of the world. Yet it is just within this fathom-long body, with its perception (*saññā*) and mind (*mano*), that I declare the world, the origination of the world, the cessation of the world, and the path leading to the cessation of the world, to be.

'By travelling, it cannot be reached, the end of the world, at any time.
'But without reaching the end of the world, there is no release from suffering.
'So therefore the one who is wise, the one who knows the world,
'Knowing the world's end, at peace,
'Longs no more for this world, or for any other.'

(A II 49)

CHAPTER TWO

MEDITATION AND THE EIGHTFOLD PATH

PRACTICE AND *BHĀVANĀ*

How does the Blessed One, with his eye of the Buddhas, see clearly?

The Blessed One considers the world with the eye of the Buddhas. He sees some beings with but little dust in their eyes, and some with a great deal of dust in their eyes. Some have sharp faculties, some dull, some are of good disposition, some of bad disposition, some of good intelligence, some of little intelligence, some living seeing a source of fear in another world, some not living seeing a source of fear in another world. It is as if in a lake of red lotuses, in a lake of white lotuses and in a lake of blue lotuses, some red or white or blue lotuses are born in the water, grow in the water and flourish while still immersed, while some red or white or blue lotuses are born in the water, grow in the water, and then remain at the surface of the water, and some red or white or blue lotuses are born in the water, grow in the water and emerge right above the water, unstained by the water. In this way, the Blessed One considers the world with the eye of the Buddhas, and he sees some beings with but little dust in their eyes, and some with a great deal of dust in their eyes. Some have sharp faculties, some dull, some are of good disposition, some of bad disposition, some of good intelligence, some of little intelligence, some living seeing a source of fear in another world, some not living seeing a source of fear in another world.

And the Blessed One knows this: this individual has a temperament based in desire (*rāgacarita*); this individual has a temperament based in hatred (*dosacarita*); this individual has a temperament based in confusion (*mohacarita*); this individual has a temperament based in applied thought (*vitakkacarita*); this individual has a temperament based in faith (*saddhācarita*); and this individual has a temperament based in wisdom (*ñāṇacarita*).

To the individual based in desire, the Blessed One gives a talk on the foul (*asubhakatha*).

To the individual based in hatred, the Blessed One explains the cultivation of loving-kindness (*mettābhāvanā*).

The individual based in delusion he gets to stay near teachers, so that he can ask questions at the right time, listen to *dhamma* at the right time, and have discussion about *dhamma.*

To the individual based in applied thought, he explains breathing mindfulness.

To the individual based in faith he explains signs that arouse confidence (*pasādanīyanimitta*): the Buddha and his noble awakening, *dhamma* and the noble law, the sangha, who have entered upon a noble way, and the precepts (*sīlāni*).

To the individual based in wisdom, he explains the signs that arouse insight (*vipassanānimitta*) into the self: the mark of impermanence, the mark of dis-ease and the mark of non-self.

Just as someone standing on the rocky peak of a mountain
Sees people all around, below;
So the one who is wise, all-seeing, ascends into his palace of the *dhamma,* and sees all around.
The one who is freed from sorrow sees below all the people of the world,
Immersed in sorrow,
Overcome by birth and old age.

(Nidd I 359–60)

One text says that the Buddha, after his awakening, seeing the subtlety of the teaching, deliberated as to whether others would be able to understand it. The lord of the meditative heavens, Brahmā Sahampati, in modern terms perhaps an intimation from his meditative experience of loving-kindness and compassion, shows the world for him to see with his divine vision. Here he sees that some beings, like lotuses above the water, have 'but little dust in their eyes', and could benefit from his teaching. But, as the passage above shows, the Buddha also recognized that people were of very different temperaments, abilities and wishes. What is important, he stressed, is that teaching is given at the right time, the right place, and for people who want and need it, according to their disposition. This chapter looks at some background considerations to meditation.

So what is *bhāvana*, the word so often used in texts to describe the meditative process? Translated in this volume 'meditation', it encompasses all sorts of activities, before, after or as well as meditation. *Bhāvanā* means development or cultivation, literally a 'bringing into being', and is associated with the verb used for the fourth noble truth, the path to awakening (*bhāveti*). This certainly includes sitting meditation, but involves the cultivation of other path factors too. The term is commonly used within early texts and modern practice to describe a range of activities: sitting meditation, walking meditation, discussion, guided thinking about a number of attributes intended to arouse specific qualities, as when the Buddha, his teaching and his community are brought to mind, listening to chanting and texts, and participation in investigative *dhamma* discussion. Discussion and investigation are also seen as particularly important *bhāvanā*, correcting strong views, encouraging refreshing debate or even overcoming boredom (*arati*) or lassitude. As Rahula said, even reading and thinking deeply about the teaching is *bhāvanā*.[1] Many meditations are not always sitting practices, though all can be. Indeed, it would be difficult to find some activity, where the precepts are kept, which is *not bhāvanā*. A mix of activities along with 'sitting practice' is the usual way of teaching and describing meditation in the texts. Changes of posture, types of activities and kinds of meditation are encouraged.[2] The many texts suggesting adaptive change indicate that for most people balance in meditation practice is derived from mixing one's activities, bodily, emotional and social, during the day, if this is needed. This was central and perhaps peculiar at that time to early Buddhist meditative procedure, in a context where extremes that test body and mind seem to have been highly prized. In modern practice also, listening or taking part in chant, ritual, listening to talks, change of posture, a good mix of collective and solitary practice, discussion about the teaching, and consulting the teacher for help in the next stage are frequent variations and accompaniments to the pursuit of sitting meditation. In many *suttas* to individual meditators the Buddha gives a number of practices, pursued collectively or singly, and in others suggests a number of postures, including walking.

The eightfold path and practice

The interdependence of path factors is taught as important for the development of each in a balanced way. The practice of appropriate generosity, moral conduct (*sīla*) and meditation for the purposes of calm or insight are all considered related and dependent on one another. They are usually placed in three groupings: conduct in the world (*sīla*), with right speech, action and livelihood; the development of wisdom (*paññā*), in right view and right intention; and meditation, in right mindfulness, effort and concentration (*samādhi*). U Pandita writes:

> These three steps are not to be practised one after the other, however. They are interdependent. Practising generosity will assure us of encountering favourable circumstances under which we will be able to lead moral lives and develop our minds. Generosity will also help us to be less rigid in our thinking. It will help us to wish for wellbeing, both for ourselves and for others. Moral conduct will also assure us of favourable circumstances and will make it possible for us to calm our minds, concentrate properly, and thereby observe the true nature of the conditioned world objectively. The better concentrated we are and the more we understand concerning the true nature of reality, the more we will be inclined to lead moral lives. If we cannot control our minds, it will be impossible to control our actions and speech.
>
> (Sayagyi U Chit Tin 1993: 3)

All of the texts in this book could be said to be associated with the process of meditation, whether they enjoin it, describe its purpose, explain how it is done, give practical advice on how to do it correctly, or suggest tips that can help the practitioner when it is not going well. But just listening to the texts themselves, both in terms of their meaning and as chanted exercises, is considered to be part of the meditative process too.

Devotion

For many people, devotional practices help meditation. A preliminary to meditation that is constantly enjoined by early commentators, as well as being encouraged by the Buddha, is the use of devotional offerings to a shrine, such as flowers or incense. Chants such as the recollection of the Buddha, *dhamma*, the teaching and sangha, the community, accompany this. The early commentator Buddhaghosa recommends this practice as a calm (*samatha*) practice described, in 'The Simile of the Cloth', in this anthology (pp. 77–8).

Ajahn Butda (1894–1994), a dearly loved monk who followed very traditional practices, used to prostrate himself before Buddha images several times a day. 'People whom he met in the course of his wonderings liked to watch him pay respects to a Buddha image, because Ajan looked so humble, serene and focused.' When asked why he did this so often, he explained that he prostrated to the Buddha three times in the morning before the almsround, again on his return, before he ate, and frequently during the morning and evening group chanting sessions. 'I use the prostrations to tame the mind. Once the mind knows its duty, it can stay focused. Without rigorous work to do, the mind will wander freely.' (Tiyavanich 2003: 77)

Sīla and friendship

The Buddha taught anyone, monastic or lay. He also recommended from time to time practices, codes and modes of behaviour for lay people. In one of the most famous texts on the subject, the *Sigalovāda-Sutta*, the Buddha finds a brahmin worshipping the six directions: east, south, west, north, below and above, as his father has taught him. The Buddha does not try to stop him continuing this family custom, an important feature of this *sutta*. Instead, he offers a different perspective on the young man's actions, with an emphasis on mental state and good behaviour as the crucial elements, rather than, but not in place of ritual. The young man should, he advises, become a 'guardian of the six directions' in a different way, and so be 'on the way to conquer both worlds, and is successful both in this world, and in the next'. To do this, he observes good behaviour to parents, teachers, wife and children, friends and associates, servants and employers, and to those following the holy life. If he cares for these people, at death, he will be reborn in a heavenly realm. For this kind of lay practice, a friend who points out what is good for you is described as one who:

1. Restrains one from doing bad things.
2. Encourages one to do good things.
3. Informs one of what one did not know before.
4. Points out the path to heaven. (D III 187)

Another text describes the good friend in the following way:

Monks, let a monk cultivate a friend whose attributes are seven.

What seven? The friend gives what is hard to give, does what is hard to do, endures what is hard to endure, reveals his own secrets, guards the secrets of others; he does not forsake one at times of need and does not despise one for any loss.

Indeed, monks, let a monk cultivate a friend whose attributes are of this kind.

He gives what is hard to give and does what is hard to do.
He endures what is hard to endure, and reveals his own secrets.
But he guards the secrets of others and at times of need
he does not forsake you, and when you are ruined does not condemn.
The one in whom these attributes are found: that is the friend to cultivate, if anyone needs a friend.

(A IV 30)

Teaching

One association that is considered essential in meditation is with the teacher. Throughout Asia the teacher is highly respected, and certain patterns of behaviour are expected on both sides. In some forms of Buddhism, however, the teacher acquires a particular role as the 'guru'. In some forms of Tibetan practice, for instance, the practitioner takes refuge in the teacher as well as in the Buddha, the teaching and the sangha, the community. Southern Buddhism expresses the relationship more as that of the 'good friend', rather in the manner indicated above.

Various traditions have different encounters between the teacher and the meditator. Where practice is conducted on retreats, and in some schools on a regular basis, interviews or 'reports' are considered essential for the meditation to develop well. The experienced teacher can often immediately spot difficulties or problems that may not be obvious to the practitioner, and help them with those. It is a truism, for instance, in Buddhist practice that the person who is convinced he or she is not working hard enough is often putting in far too much effort in the practice, as the text pertaining to Soṇa demonstrates (this anthology, pp. 24–7). Conversely, there are certain times when some prodding and encouragement to effort are needed. The teacher is also felt important in *samatha* practices when the mental image (*nimitta*) is starting to develop, so that developments or the absence of them is treated with friendliness and non-attachment (A III 316). In *vipassanā* practices, images tend to be discouraged, as they might be at certain stages in *samatha* practice where the faculties need balancing or if there is too much strain and tension. The teacher who understands the practice one is undertaking and the principles behind it is essential for the healthy development of most meditations; even a very inexperienced teacher can also be helpful, simply by being able to listen and to sense intuitively when there is an imbalance. In one text, the Buddha comments that someone stuck in the mud cannot usefully help another one who is also stuck (M I 46). Buddhaghosa's recommendations, however, are realistic and practical. The best person to learn from is someone who is enlightened. But he also says that in the absence of such a person, 'Therefore the Ancient Elders said three times: the one who is conscientious guards it' (Vism III 64). The underlying attitude is that it is important to have a teacher one can trust. An attitude of compassion is felt important in all traditions of Buddhism. The role of the teacher in early Buddhism, however, is perhaps best seen in the narrative and *sutta* examples, through the way the Buddha and his followers teach and interact with meditators. In this anthology the texts concerned with Soṇa as well as the brahmin Sundarika Bhāradvāja, the goldsmith's son, the scared meditators in the wood, and the meditator who could not progress, give an indication of how this relationship was felt to work in practice (this anthology, Chapter Five).

Listening

Listening to the teaching, in the spoken language of those present, in addition to hearing and participating in chanting, is also considered a kind of collective practice. In the text below, the first feature is explained as a reference to the continued creativity of the tradition, as the teacher finds new similes or ways of expressing things that have not been used before. 'Dispelling doubts' refers to the inspirational effect of a good talk; the 'straightening' of views describes the way that any 'crookedness' of perception about oneself and others is corrected. The final element refers to the calming and clearing of the heart and mind that might occur on hearing the text (Wonglakorn 2010: 248–9).

On hearing the teaching

Monks, there are these five advantages from hearing the teaching. What five?

He hears things that have not been heard before; he makes clear things that have been heard; he dispels doubt; he straightens his views; and his heart becomes calm.

Indeed, monks, these are the five advantages from hearing the teaching. (A III 248)

Guidelines for teachers

One aspect of early Buddhism is that followers of the Buddha teach others. The opening of the *sutta* on 'Breathing Mindfulness', for instance, describes those expert in many different meditative skills, teaching others, who then are teaching others, in groups (M III 78–80). Most forms of Buddhist practice offer *dhamma* talks: on meditation courses there is usually one in the evening, and sometimes in the morning; sometimes a large part of the day is devoted to teaching. By convention, people become teachers when asked. One early text describes the Buddha giving advice on how to do this. The word used for the second item, *pariyāya*, has a number of meanings.[3] It translates literally as 'going around' and refers here to a kind of teaching found in the *suttas*, whereby figurative language, concrete example and direct simile apply the teaching discursively to a specific situation and people, as opposed to the *Abhidhamma* method, in which the teaching is communicated as principle, manifest in descriptions of the momentary mind. As this anthology demonstrates, simile, metaphor and anecdotal teaching, often fitted to the person, feature prominently in early Buddhism, as they do in modern Buddhist schools too.

Once when the Blessed One was dwelling near Kosambī in Ghosita Park, the Venerable Udāyin was seated teaching the *dhamma,* surrounded by a large gathering of laypeople.

Now the Venerable Ānanda saw the Venerable Udāyin, seated teaching the *dhamma,* and then went to the Blessed One, paid his respects and sat down to one side. Seated, he said to the Blessed One:

'Sir, the Venerable Udāyin teaches the *dhamma,* surrounded by a large gathering of laypeople.'

'Truly, Ānanda, it is not easy (*sukaraṃ*) to teach *dhamma* to others. In teaching *dhamma,* Ānanda, arouse in yourself five things, and then teach *dhamma*. What five?

'Teach others *dhamma,* having in mind, "I will give a talk that has gradual stages (*anupubbakatha?*)". Teach others *dhamma,* having in mind, "I will give a talk appropriate to the situation (*pariyāyadassāvī*)".

'Teach others *dhamma,* having in mind, "I will give a talk that is founded in compassion (*anuddaya*)". Teach others *dhamma,* having in mind, "I will give a talk that is not a means for material gain".

'Teach others *dhamma,* having in mind, "I will give a talk that does not disparage myself or others".

'Truly, Ānanda, it is not easy to teach *dhamma* to others. In teaching others *dhamma,* Ānanda, arouse these five things in yourself; then teach others the *dhamma.*'

(A III 182–4)

The forty meditation objects

Usually when people start meditation today an object is given, such as breathing mindfuless or mindfulness of body, and the way it is taught varies greatly according to school and tradition. Indeed, there does not seem to be any description of what constitutes a meditation object in early texts; perhaps an overall category was not thought necessary. As the text that opens this section indicated, meditation objects are sometimes chosen carefully by the teacher, with the practitioner in mind. Meditators often attribute the wrong character type to themselves; sometimes, as in many Buddhist texts, a number of different practices are needed for a particular person. One meditator, Meghiya, convinced he could 'go it alone', needed careful advice and a number of different practices to progress, which he eventually did, but only when he took advice.[4] It is usual for meditation schools to suggest two or three practices at some stages, or on retreat, with some attention given to all aspects of the eightfold path. Buddhaghosa uses forty terms to describe what he calls a 'place of work' (*kammaṭṭhāna*), all described as means of producing calm. His categories, however, do not seem to be definitive or prescriptive and some are only rarely taught. In early Buddhist texts, the Buddha recommended these and some others, concerned with insight. Both are considered necessary at different stages.[5] Some meditations are mentioned in the canon only once, and not included in this list.[6] Some are considered only suitable for particular people at particular times (Vism III 104).[7] How they are assigned and taught varies with school, practitioner and teacher.

1–10: ten devices (*kasiṇa*):
earth, water, fire, air, dark blue/black, yellow, red, white, light, limited space

11–20: ten 'impure' meditations (*asubha*):
bloated corpse, blue-black corpse, festering corpse, corpse with cracked skin, corpse gnawn and mangled, corpse cut to pieces, corpse mutilated and cut to pieces, bloody corpse, corpse infested with worms, and the skeleton

21–30: ten recollections (*anussati*):
Buddha, *dhamma*, sangha, good conduct (*sīla*), generosity, *devas*, mindfulness of death, mindfulness of body, breathing mindfulness, and the recollection of peace

31–34: four divine abidings (*brahmavihārā*), immeasurables (*appamāṇā*):
loving-kindness, compassion, sympathetic joy, and equanimity

35–38: four formless spheres (*arūpa*):
sphere of infinite space, sphere of infinite consciousness, sphere of no-thingness, and sphere of neither perception nor non-perception

39: the perception of loathsomeness in food (*āhāre paṭikkūlasaññā*)

40: the defining of the four elements (*catudhātuvavatthānam*) that occur within the body:
earth, water, fire, and air

The first ten, *kasiṇas*, are the classic calm (*samatha*) objects, and involve taking a colour, or an element, and using it, with instructions as to how to maintain mindfulness, as a means of obtaining the meditations known as *jhānas*. The next ten, only taught in monastic settings, and under supervision, involve seeing corpses in stages of decay. The ten recollections include practices usually with others from that set. The *iti pi so*, as the Recollection of the Triple Gem (20–22) is known, is today often a single chanted practice, undertaken by most South and Southeast Asian Buddhists, sometimes before a sitting meditation, such as breathing mindfulness (29).[8] It is intended to arouse cheerfulness, confidence, and a sense of direction in practitioners. The divine abidings and the formless realms are concentration practices: the first divine abiding, loving-kindness, is particularly emphasised today. The last two objects (39–40) are given only occasionally, for specific types of people. Elements from these forty form the basis of many systems of meditation as Buddhism travels: the divine abidings and breathing mindfulness have always been influential and feature in most early systems. All sorts of variation occur in schools regarding the sitting practice, and most have their ways, for instance, of suggesting different practices if needed and types of posture.

Walking

Mention should also be made of the many kinds of practices involving other postures during the day. Walking practices, for instance, often balance sitting meditation. There are many varieties in these now, emphasizing either calm, in associating the rhythm of the walk with a feeling of well-being, following the movement of the feet and body as the weight changes, or insight, through analysis of the stages of the process of lifting and moving the feet. Although walking practices are not described in detail in any canonical and commentarial material, stories describe meditators walking, often within the set limits of a *caṅkamana*, a term used both for the walking practice, and for the specifically designed walking grounds, are frequent.

Monks, there are these five benefits of walking meditation.
What five? One becomes strong for journeys. One becomes able to make an effort; one becomes healthy; what one has eaten, drunk and consumed and tasted is well digested. The concentration found through walking meditation is long-lasting.
These are the five benefits of walking meditation.

(A III 29–30)

But just going for a walk before or after meditation, being sure to be open to views, people and passing traffic, is good for mindfulness and for preventing the mind becoming strained. Since ancient times, centres for the practice of meditation have often been rural retreats, the better for allowing the mind to settle, and perhaps to build up reserves to have contact with the busy everyday world again.

The middle way and right effort

The life story of the Buddha is taken as the best guide to meditative practice: after living a life of great pleasure in the palace, and then going to various extremes of exertion, he comes to see that it is a balanced path, in which food is taken but not over-indulged, and effort is not excessive but sustained. This produces the ongoing dynamic of the middle way, summarized in the eight factors of the path, right view, right intention, right speech, right action, right livelihood, right mindfulness, right effort and right concentration. The last three are particularly associated with meditation.

In his first sermon, addressed to those who had been his companions in self-mortification, he finds his first followers through expounding the eightfold path. In the course of Buddhist history, and in early texts, the middle way is variously described: the mid-point between annihilationism and eternalism, that there is no survival after death, or an eternal being that lives on after death; between desire and hatred; or between the view that all exists, and the one that nothing does at all. The 'middle' lies at the heart of the meditative teaching, at all sorts of levels, from the middle way of effort to the middleness of the object in *samatha* meditation. Perhaps the most important from the meditative point of view is in its application in the area of right effort: this is of four kinds, in the avoidance of unskilful states, overcoming those that have arisen, the meditative development of skilful states, and the maintaining of them. In this regard it is not quite just a mid-point, but more a creative, continuing equipoise that does not fall into excess or view-making, of any kind. Wise attention (*yoniso-manasikāra*) avoids dwelling too much on the unskilful. As will be seen in the passage from Buddhaghosa, 'middleness' towards beings, events and one's own circumstances is to be cultivated while developing meditation and the seven factors of awakening (this anthology, pp. 210–11).

For meditators there may be other immediate concerns, in, for instance, how to find the middle way in the correct attitude towards the body and the posture. At what point should I move my legs when the knees are hurting? In this regard, schools and practices manifest a great deal of variety. An insight school might encourage investigation of the discomfort; a calm school might find pleasure and interest in the meditation object so that bodily pain can be overcome. Most would suggest a good practicable and comfortable solution. Neither would encourage excess, but rather a balanced and appropriate effort for the time, place and person.

This extract from a *sutta* summarises the spirit of the middle way in advice about the over-strained meditation of a meditator who is making too much wrong effort.[9] This, meditation teachers sometimes observe, is one of the most common problems for people starting meditation. Because Soṇa had bloody feet as a result of excessive walking practice, the story appears in the *Vinaya*, the Buddhist monastic code, as the incident that prompted the rule that monks could have a lining to their sandals! (Vin I 179ff).

The Simile of the Lute

Thus have I heard. On once occasion the Blessed One was staying at Rājagaha at Vulture's Peak. On that occasion the Venerable Soṇa was staying at Rājagaha in the Cool Wood. When Venerable Soṇa was sitting in seclusion, apart from others, this thought arose in him. 'Whatever disciples of the Blessed One that are strenuous: I am one of them! But my mind is not freed from the corruptions (*āsavā*) by not clinging. My family is rich: I can enjoy the wealth and do good things.[10] Why don't I give up the training and go to lower things? I would enjoy the wealth and do good things as well.'

Then the Blessed One, discerning in his own mind the thoughts of Venerable Soṇa, as a strong man might stretch his bent arm or bend his stretched arm, left Vulture Peak and appeared in the Cool Wood in front of the Venerable Soṇa. And when a seat had been arranged, he sat down. And the Venerable Soṇa paid his respects and also sat down, to one side. And the Blessed One said to him:

[375] 'Soṇa, did this thought not come up for you when you were sitting in seclusion and apart from others, 'Whatever disciples of the Blessed One that are strenuous: I am one of them! But my mind is not freed from the corruptions by not clinging. My family is rich: I can enjoy the wealth and do good things. Why don't I give up the training and go to lower things? I would enjoy the wealth and do good things as well.'

'Yes, it did, sir.'

'So what do you think, Soṇa: were you skilful in earlier times, when you lived at home, in the lute?

'Yes, sir.'

'And what do you think, Soṇa: when the strings of your lute were too tightly strung, was your lute beautifully tuned and easy to play?'

'No, sir.'

'And what do you think, Soṇa: when the strings of your lute were too loosely strung, was your lute beautifully tuned and easy to play?'

'No, sir.'

'So, in the same way, when the strings of your lute were neither too tightly nor too loosely strung, but adjusted to an even tension (*same guṇe*), was your lute beautifully tuned and easy to play?'

'Yes, sir.'

'In just this way, Soṇa, if effort is applied too forcefully if will lead to restlessness (*uddhacca*), and if effort is too lax it will lead to lassitude (*kossaja*). So, Soṇa, keep steady with balanced effort, penetrate to the balance of the faculties, and you will grasp the meditation object (*nimitta*).'

'Yes, sir.'

'And the Blessed One, after giving the Venerable Soṇa this advice, as a strong man might bend his arm backwards and forwards, left the Cool Wood and appeared on Vulture Peak.'

And another time the Venerable Soṇa was even in his effort, penetrated to the balance of the faculties, and grasped the meditation object. And, sitting in seclusion, apart from others, diligent, ardent and resolute, he soon realized the here and now, by his own direct knowledge, that unsurpassable goal of the holy life, for the sake of which sons of good family rightly go forth from the home to the homeless life, and, entering on it, he stayed there. And he knew: 'Exhausted is birth; the holy life has been fulfilled; what has to be done has been done; there is no more of existence here.' And the Venerable Soṇa became one of the arahants. (A III 374–6)

Right mindfulness

The mindful make effort:
They do not delight in a dwelling.
As geese leave a pool,
They give up any kind of home.
(Dhp 91: Roebuck 2010: 20)

The term 'mindfulness' is probably the most influential and frequently used term derived from Buddhism. The word *sati*, of which 'mindfulness' is the most common translation, is generally acknowledged and recognized as a key feature in arousing health in the mind, both by those who practise Buddhist meditation within the tradition, and by those who have borrowed the term, with a perhaps slightly different application and usage, within modern psychotherapeutic and psychiatric traditions.[11]

So is it possible to define it? What does it do? The original word is derived from the root 'to remember' (*smṛ*), and has some associations with what we normally think of by that term, but within the context of Buddhist meditation it is described and encompasses far more than this, including the notion of awareness, and being alert to events occurring in the present, whether in the body, the feelings, the mind or the interplay between all three.

Mindfulness is based in these four areas or fields, of which a simple, non-judgmental awareness is encouraged: body, feelings, the mind and *dhammas*, a largely untranslated term, which, in a Buddhist context, describes the teachings but also any events or phenomena as they occur. This last is seen as encompassing body, feelings and mind, directing attention where it is appropriate in any given situation. There are plentiful instructions to make us mindful of these four foundations throughout the early texts and later commentaries. They do not exclude one another, but are felt to be mutually supportive, so that, according to the *Mahāsatipaṭṭhāna-Sutta*, awareness goes where it is needed, when it is needed, in order that things can start to be seen, as they really are (*yathābhūtaṃ*). Each foundation involves the practitioner becoming aware of what is going on inside, what is going on outside, and awareness of both the inner and the external.

These four 'foundations' of mindfulness provide the basis of Buddhist meditative practice and are central to all Buddhisms: awareness of body, feeling, mind, *dhammas*. These four are the literal foundations of the list of the thirty-seven factors that contribute to awakening, found throughout all forms of Buddhism and often found enacted in the very structure of *stūpas*/chedis/pagodas, external representations of the Buddha's teaching.

As with so many terms in Buddhism, modern comment on the subject helps in a reading of the ancient texts. One highly regarded twentieth-century meditation teacher and scholar, Ven. Saddhatissa, wrote that body mindfulness, the first foundation, is always the starting point for meditation and often regarded as the most important, and can be undertaken as one gradually becomes more aware of the body's posture and sensations, and becomes aware of changes in them, in lying, sitting, standing and walking:

> Care must be taken to be neither too objective nor too subjective; we are not being asked to look at our bodies as 'things' moving puppet-like before the watching mind; nor are we asked to 'feel' very acutely every movement and gesture. What is required is that we try to live here and now 'in our bodies'. This might seem a bizarre request, but once we try and experience this state we realize how rarely in fact we are 'living in our bodies', how rarely we are aware of

the movements of our limbs and the interplay of our muscles. Mindfulness of the body can be practised too by watching the breath flowing in and out of the nostrils, by listening to sounds impinging on the ear, not pausing to name or judge them, but just noting their arising and passing away. We can learn to become aware of the taste and texture of food, not after the manner of a gourmet or a connoisseur, . . . but simply in order to intensify awareness, noting the order and intensity of sensations, the varieties of flavour, temperatures, colours, etc.

Saddhatissa notes that this can be tricky for the first time, particularly for thinking types. But he suggests a few minutes a day soon makes it simpler:

We forget about it, of course, maybe for hours on end, then suddenly the memory returns, and we begin again. 'Happy is he who dwells mindful of the body', it has been said. Whenever we become tense, nervous, exhausted, if we can remember the 'feel' of mindfulness of the body and re-establish it, the tension and weariness dissolve.

(Saddhatissa 1971: 54–5)

Modern techniques of teaching mindfulness vary, but most use to a greater or lesser degree the instructions suggested by the breathing mindfulness *sutta* and the *sutta* on mindfulness, the *Satipaṭṭhāna-Sutta*, which has influenced most forms of Buddhism. The basic injunctions included here, from the beginning of the text, are considered a kind of staple of meditative practice, for daily life and for practice in seclusion. The text opens with the instructions for breathing mindfulness and moves through basic bodily awareness and other practices associated with arousing mindfulness in daily life. The first four stages of the practice on breathing mindfulness are included under 'body'. Further exploration of breathing mindfulness involves twelve other stages, with one tetrad assigned to the other three foundations of mindfulness (see M III 78–88; this anthology, pp. 69–71).[12] After that, there is a return to normality and daily life. It is always worth remembering that one recurrent feature of Buddhist teaching is the art of putting down a meditation: it is not helpful to become too focused on the exercises when driving, or going across the road. This return to enjoyment of the everyday, as we shall see, is constantly emphasized in the texts, which encourage a simple awareness: of sights, sounds, movements, the feeling of the wind, and, in the body, the contact with the ground. During daily life, the practitioner is encouraged to be aware of surroundings and what is going on internally, externally and both of these. Body mindfulness includes knowing the ground on which you are walking, the people and cars that may be around you, and whether you are likely to bump into someone with your trolley in the supermarket.[13]

Body Mindfulness

And how, monks, does a monk practise contemplating the body in the body? Here, monks, a monk goes to a forest, or the roots of a tree or an empty place and sits, folding his legs in a cross-legged position, making his body straight, and sets up mindfulness in front of him. Mindful, he breathes in; mindful, he breathes out.

As he breathes in a long breath, he knows, 'I am breathing in a long breath', or, as he breathes out a long breath, he knows, 'I am breathing out a long breath'.

As he breathes in a short breath, he knows, 'I am breathing in a short breath'; or, as he breathes out a short breath, he knows, 'I am breathing out a short breath'.

He trains thus: 'Experiencing the whole body, I will breathe in'; he trains thus, 'Experiencing the whole body I will breathe out'.

He trains thus: 'Tranquillizing the bodily formation, I shall breathe in'; he trains thus, 'Tranquillizing the bodily formation, I shall breathe out'.

Just as a skilled turner or his apprentice, when making a long turn, knows, 'I am making a long turn', or, when making a short turn, knows,

'I am making a short turn', so, breathing in a long breath a monk knows, 'I am breathing in a long breath', and, breathing out a long breath he knows, 'I am breathing out a long breath'. He knows . . . short breath . . . conscious of the whole body . . . he trains thus, 'Tranquillizing the bodily formation, I shall breathe out'.

In this way, he practises, contemplating the body in the body, internally; or he practises, contemplating the body in the body, externally; or he practises contemplating the body in the body both internally and externally. He practises contemplating the arising of *dhamma*s in the body, the ceasing of *dhamma*s in the body, or he practises contemplating the arising and ceasing of *dhamma*s in the body. Or else mindfulness that 'there is a body' is established in him, just to the extent necessary for knowledge and mindfulness. And he practises independent, clinging at nothing in the world. In this way, monks, a monk practises contemplating the body in the body.

And again, monks, a monk, when walking, knows, 'I am walking'; when standing he knows, 'I am standing'; when sitting he knows, 'I am sitting'; when lying down he knows, 'I am lying down'; or, however his body is disposed, he knows it.

In this way he practises, contemplating the body in the body internally, externally and both internally and externally. . . . In this way too, monks, a monk practises contemplating the body in the body.

And again, monks, a monk acts with clear comprehension when going backwards and forwards. He acts with clear comprehension when looking ahead or behind, when bending and stretching, in wearing his robes and carrying his bowl, when eating and drinking, chewing and swallowing, when defecating and urinating, when walking, standing, sitting, falling asleep, waking up, talking and keeping silent.

In this way he practises contemplating the body in the body internally, externally and both internally and externally. . . . In this way too, monks, a monk practises contemplating the body in the body.'

(D I 290–3)

Some features of mindfulness in the *Abhidhamma*

A definition of mindfulness is given in this anthology from the opening passage of the first book of the *Abhidhamma* (this anthology, p. 151). In the commentary to this, mindfulness is said to be the remembering of the objects of the mind and the senses received at the sense-door – of which the mind is considered the sixth. It is said to have the characteristic of *'being present in'.* Because of this, it is a necessary 'faculty' of all meditation (*indriya*). Its characteristics are 'not drifting away', and acquirement of the object. The commentary gives a number of similes. Mindfulness evaluates resources: just as a royal treasurer reminds the king, the mind, to take note of and remember the royal possessions, it remembers mental states, and can offer to the mind the actions, thoughts and feelings it has experienced at any time (Asl 121ff.). The discriminatory power of mindfulness is shown by comparison to the king's adviser, who knows what is useful and valuable to him and what is not, just as the practitioner, with mindfulness, will intuitively perceive states of mind that are not useful and those that are. Later in this passage it said that mindfulness should be seen as a door-post, because it is firmly established in the object. And it is compared to salt, bringing out the flavour of everything with which it has contact (Asl 121–2). But perhaps the most commonly used simile is that of the door-keeper, guarding the doors of the senses. None of these images of course can say exactly what mindfulness is, or elicit it: but they suggest its character, purpose and function in establishing the mind at the beginning stages of meditation, helping it to sustain it during the meditation practice, enabling the practitioner to leave the practice, and keeping a light alertness going in daily life. Contemporary Buddhist teachers tend to follow the spirit of the *suttas* and hunt for new and sometimes funny similes for mindfulness: one modern teacher, Ajahn Amaro, for instance, has updated the tenor of these images. The mind, he says, is like a committee with all sorts of different voices and participants, all arguing their case, from the rebellious toddler to the grumpy grown-up. Mindfulness chairs these voices, and, when working, orchestrates them so that they work with rather than against one another, producing harmonious notes.[14]

Research on mindfulness

There has been considerable academic research conducted on the very notion of mindfulness: both how it can be defined and what it involves.[15] Buddhist practitioners are cautious in making any attempt at a quick definition, though it is clearly worth the try: 'an attentiveness directed towards the present' is one description sometimes used. Much that is encouraged in some schools of meditation, however, such as the deepening and strengthening of feeling and the pursuit of the divine abidings as a full meditation, is not necessarily easy to analyse in an academic setting. Some features may not be appropriate in secular therapeutic contexts. One longstanding Zen nun I know remained smilingly thoughtful during a highly technical group discussion on this interesting subject I attended. At the end, when people were leaving, I noticed she was writing something on the board:

Mindfulness is not mindfulness.
Mindfulness is mindfulness.

The point I think she was making, and it was really her engaging manner and timing that made it, is that some things just have to be experienced to be understood. Discussion is often useful, but just as an experienced musician or singer knows that there is no easy explanation of terms and practices they have worked on themselves, perhaps for decades, so many practitioners do not feel that a simple explanation can cover what it is *like* to experience mindfulness. The Tibetan lama Ato Rinpoche prefers the translation 'mind-awareness' for *sati*.

Mindfulness, as the first of the factors of awakening, is an essential starting point. Importantly, it is perceived to have a balancing property within meditation, guiding the mind away from the 'unskilful' (*akusala*) to the 'skilful' (*kusala*). According to the *Abhidhamma*, mindfulness is only present in those states of mind that have this health as their basis, and does not occur in states of mind that are 'unskilful': the word *kusala*, denoting health, skill and goodness of mind, involves an intuitive apprehension and even amused gravitation towards mindfulness. Rather as a spirit-level finds the straight, mindfulness tends to suppress the hindrances, the forces that undermine the health of the mind.

Ven Dhammasāmi (1965–) writes:

> Not excitement but an ordinariness is a challenge to the human mind. It is difficult to grasp and penetrate. There are enormous beauties in such ordinary activity we repeat every day of our life. Take, for example, walking, eating, washing, speaking, sleeping and so on. If we discover their beauties and enjoy them, we will then start living every moment of our life, no more feeling bored.
>
> There is no pressure in enjoying the beauties of ordinariness. You only need constant awareness, which is twofold; first the kind of awareness we try to develop through intensive practice of meditation, and general awareness, that we should have in daily life. Walking simply gives you a lot of joy. Going to work, driving back home, meeting the same people in your life, doing the same job, eating almost the same things, taking your children to school, earning and spending – they do not make you bored any more. You just enjoy every moment of doing your routine. This is the secret of happiness.
>
> (Dhammasāmi 2000: 54–5)

Right concentration

> Concentration is peaceful; concentration is beneficial; concentration is happy
>
> Patis I 269

An ancient pairing in Buddhist texts is that of mindfulness and concentration, eventually evolving into another distinction, between insight (*vipassanā*) and calm (*samatha*). These last two are described as 'yoked together' when the mind finds liberating insight.

But what is concentration? According to the *Abhidhamma* it is something we experience all the time, as the simple function that gathers together the mind in one locus of consciousness at any given moment (see Dhs 10; this anthology, p. 150). But in practice we all know the difference between a sense of being scattered and confused, where this feature is weak, and the collectedness (*ekaggatā*) or 'gone to oneness' of times when, without any apparent effort, our minds alight and settle on a single object, perhaps with a sense of deep joy and unification: a sea view, perhaps, an intensity of colour in a picture, or a thing like a candle flame. At such times concentration, in the meditative sense (*samādhi*), literally 'holding of oneness' or 'maintaining evenness', is strong, capable of being deepened and developed, with mindfulness, through meditation practice. Eventually, with training, the mind rests in 'right concentration', the state known as *jhāna*, the meditative state considered essential for the cultivation of all elements of the eightfold path in a balanced way. This state of unification is not a trance or a hypnotic state, and is described as possessing alertness and the faculty of wisdom as well as unification and stillness. The mind is trained through experiences described as blissful and peaceful, to be awake within them, and also to emerge from them, with the capacity to re-enter daily life refreshed and restored, or to cultivate further states of meditation and insight.[16] The state of *jhāna* finally unites with further wisdom in the attainment of liberation. As we see in one of the texts below, sometimes practitioners find concentration first, then wisdom; sometimes wisdom first and then concentration. Some balance both these factors throughout the stages of their meditative path. This depends on temperament, the meditative school in which one practises, and the particular stage one is at in meditation. Pa Auk Sayadaw (1934–), a leading Burmese *samatha* meditation teacher, says: 'Obtaining and applying the concentration of the *jhānas* allows the student to progress more quickly and deeply through the vipassanā portion of the Buddhist path. The *jhāna* practice itself, however, has its own inherent value as a path of purification, the same one undertaken by the Buddha himself.'[17] As always with meditation, taking advice from experienced teachers is important to establish the suitability of any practice at any time. One commentary describes the seven path factors of the eightfold path as the 'adornment' (*parikkhāra*) of concentration: it is possible, as with all the other path factors, to have concentration that is 'wrong', as when we try too hard at academic work or become over-focused; similarly mindfulness can be 'wrong' when it is too rigid or selective, and needs other path factors to keep it balanced.

The first text here describes the four *jhānas*, in which alert absorption in the object comes to settle, classically described in this way in the *Sāmaññaphala-Sutta*.[18] The first *jhāna* is a meditation described in Buddhist texts as characterized by five factors: initial thinking, discursive thought or examination, joy, happiness and one-pointedness, in a peaceful bodily, emotional and mental unification. This is the state that the life story of the Buddha says he remembered that prompted him to give up self-mortifications. Then, joy and happiness intensify as discursive thinking subsides. In the second, thinking is dropped and 'internal silence' is present: in the third, where joy is discarded, happiness, mindfulness and equanimity become strong. In the fourth, a state where feeling has been purified, the mind, untroubled by painful feeling and even excessively pleasant feeling, becomes fluid and flexible: the meditator is free to turn to insight, other meditations or psychic powers. These practices were used by the Buddha on the night of the enlightenment, and also recommended constantly after it. The states are considered highly distinct from one another, and all worth cultivating: 'Interestingly, each *jhāna* has a feel, a flavour, or an intuitive taste that is different from the other *jhānas*. With time and practice, you may learn to experientially distinguish which *jhāna* is present.' (Snyder and Rasmussen 2009: 78)

The Buddha often entered *jhāna* throughout his teaching career, and found it the best state for dying and leaving the body, when entering what is known as his *parinibbāna*, or final entrance into *nibbāna*. The fourth *jhāna* is seen as particularly important, traditionally regarded for its basis in equanimity and mindfulness as a kind of crossroads, after which meditators may pursue the stages of insight, or further skills in the development of concentration, in the higher knowledges, and the psychic powers, described below, and the formless realms, described in the text after that.

After the four *jhānas*, the exercise known as recollection and considered the highest expression of *samatha* practice, in the mastery of remembering, and so being able to enter and leave the meditation at will, is described.

Five-limbed concentration

'Monks, I will teach you how to cultivate the noble five-limbed right concentration. Listen carefully and pay attention: I will speak.'

'Indeed, sir,' they replied, and the Blessed One spoke:

'Monks, take the case of the monk who, quite secluded from sense desires, from unskilful states, enters and abides in the first *jhāna,* which is accompanied by initial thought and sustained thought, filled with the joy and happiness born of seclusion. He pervades, drenches, saturates and suffuses this very body with the joy and happiness born of seclusion, and there is no place in his entire body that is not suffused with this joy and happiness. Suppose a skilled bathman, or his assistant, were to sprinkle powdered soap into a metal dish, splash water all around it and knead it into a soap ball, so that the ball of soap would be taken up, permeated and steeped in moisture, inside and outside, yet would not trickle. In the same way, a monk pervades, drenches, saturates and suffuses this very body with the joy and happiness born of seclusion, and there is no place in his entire body that is not suffused with joy and happiness. This, monks, is how first to cultivate the noble five-limbed right concentration.

'Furthermore, with the subsiding of initial thought and sustained thought, a monk enters into and abides in the second *jhåna,* which is accompanied by internal peace, confidence and unification of the mind, is free from initial thought and sustained thought, and is filled with the joy and happiness born of concentration. He pervades, drenches, saturates and suffuses this very body with the joy and happiness born of concentration so that there is no place in his entire body that is not suffused with joy and happiness.

'It is as if there were a deep lake whose waters well up from below. It would have no inlet for water from the east, from the west, from the north or from the south, nor would it be replenished from time to time with showers of rain. Yet a current of cool water does well up from the depths of the lake and pervades, drenches, saturates and suffuses the whole lake, so that there is no place in the entire lake that is not suffused with cool water. In the same way, the monk pervades, drenches, saturates and suffuses this very body with the joy and happiness born of concentration, so that there is no part of his entire body that is not suffused with joy and happiness. This, monks, is how secondly to cultivate the noble five-limbed right concentration.

'Furthermore, with the fading away of joy, the monk, equanimous, mindful and clearly comprehending, experiences that happiness in the body about which the noble ones declare, "The one who is equanimous and mindful abides in happiness", and enters and abides in the third *jhāna*. He pervades, drenches, saturates and suffuses this very body with the happiness that is free from joy, so that there is no part of his entire body that is not suffused with happiness.

'It is as if there were in a lotus pond blue, white and red lotuses that have been born in the water, grow in the water, never rise above the water but are nurtured immersed in water. From the tips to the roots they are pervaded, drenched, saturated and suffused with water so that there is no part of the lotus that is not suffused with cool water. In this way a monk pervades, drenches, saturates and suffuses this very body with the happiness that is free from joy, so that there is no place in his entire body that is not suffused with happiness. This, monks, is how thirdly to cultivate the noble five-limbed right concentration.

'Furthermore, with the abandoning of happiness and pain and the disappearance of the earlier pleasant and unpleasant feeling, the monk enters into and abides in the fourth *jhāna*, which is beyond pleasure or pain, and is purified by equanimity and mindfulness. And he sits suffusing this very body with a purified and translucent mind so that there is no place in his body that is not suffused with a purified and translucent mind.

'It is as if a man were to sit enveloped from the head downwards with a white cloth, so that there would be no place in his body that was not enveloped with the white cloth. In this way, a monk sits suffusing his body with a purified and translucent mind, so that there is no place in his body that is not suffused with a purified and translucent mind.

This, monks, is how fourthly to cultivate the noble five-limbed right concentration.

'Or, the sign of recollection (*paccevekkhanānimitta*) is rightly grasped by the monk, rightly attended to, rightly reflected upon, rightly penetrated with wisdom. Monks, just as someone might look upon another person, as someone standing might look upon someone sitting, or when sitting might look upon another person lying down, in this way, the sign of recollection is rightly grasped by the monk, rightly attended to, rightly reflected upon, rightly penetrated with wisdom.[19] This, monks, is fifthly how to cultivate the noble five-limbed right concentration.

'Monks, when a monk has cultivated and practised frequently the five-limbed noble concentration, he can incline his mind to realize whatever state is so realizable by higher knowledge,[20] toward which he might incline his mind.

'It is as if, monks, a water jar, full to the brim so that a crow could drink from it, were placed on a dish. What do you think, monks – if a strong man were to come along and shake it backwards and forwards, would the water spill out?'[21]

'Yes, it would, sir.'

'So too, monks, when the noble five-limbed concentration has been cultivated and practised frequently in this way, then, as there is a suitable basis, he is capable of realizing any state realizable by higher knowledge, towards which he might incline his mind.

'It is as if, monks, there was on some even ground a four-sided pond, contained by banks, full of water up to the bank so that crows could drink from it. If a strong man were to remove the banks from each side, would water come out?'

'Yes, it would.'

'So too, monks, when noble five-limbed right concentration has been cultivated and practised frequently in this way, as there is a suitable basis, he is capable of realizing any state realizable by higher knowledge, towards which he might incline his mind.

'It is as if there was on even ground a carriage, harnessed with thoroughbreds, with a goad ready to hand, so that a skilled trainer, a driver of horses, could mount it and, taking the reins in his left hand and his goad in the right, he might drive out and come back wherever and whenever he liked. So too, monks, when noble five-limbed concentration has been cultivated and practised frequently in this way, then, as there is a suitable basis, he is capable of realizing any state realizable by higher knowledge, towards which he might incline his mind.

'And if he wishes, monks, "May I experience the various kinds of powers of the mind: having been one, may I become many, having become many, may I become one;[22] may I become visible or invisible; may I go unobstructed through a wall, through a city-wall, through a mountain as though through space; may I swim in and out of the earth as though it were water; may I walk on water without sinking as though it were earth; sitting cross-legged, may I travel in the sky like a bird; with my hand may I touch and stroke the moon and the sun, so powerful and strong; may I exercise mastery with the body as far as the Brahmā heaven": Then, as there is a suitable basis, he is capable of realizing any state realizable by higher knowledge, towards which he might incline his mind.[23]

'And if he wishes, monks, "May I, with the divine ear, purified and surpassing that of men, hear sounds both of devas and of men, both near and far": Then, as there is a suitable basis, he is capable of realizing any state realizable by higher knowledge, towards which he might incline his mind.[24]

'And if he wishes, monks, "May I know the minds of other beings, encircling them with my own mind", he knows a mind with desire as with desire (*rāga*), and a mind free from desire as free from desire; he knows a mind with hate as with hate ... a mind free from hate; he knows a deluded mind as deluded ... an undeluded mind; he knows a constricted mind as constricted ... a scattered mind as scattered; he knows a mind grown great as grown great ... a mind that has not grown great; he knows a surpassable mind as a surpassable mind ... an unsurpassable mind; he knows a concentrated mind as concentrated ... an unconcentrated mind; he knows a liberated mind as liberated ... an unliberated mind.[25] Then, as there is a suitable basis, he is capable of realizing any state realizable by higher knowledge, towards which he might incline his mind.

'If he wishes, "May I recollect manifold past lives, that is, one birth, two, three, four, five births, ten births, twenty, thirty, forty, fifty, a hundred, a thousand, a hundred thousand births, many aeons of world dissolution, world expansion, world dissolution and expansion, in this way: "there I was born with such a name, in such a family, in such a caste, my food was such, such my experience of pleasure and pain, such my lifespan. Falling away from there I arose there." In this way he remembers his various past lives, their circumstances, and details.[26] Then as there is a suitable basis, he is capable of realizing any state realizable by higher knowledge, towards which he might incline his mind.

'If he wishes, monks, "May I, with the divine eye, which is purified and surpasses that of men, see beings passing away and beings reborn, inferior and superior, beautiful and ugly, fortunate and unfortunate, and he knows how beings fare according to their *kamma,* in this way: "Certainly these beings who engaged in bad conduct of body, speech and mind, who reviled the noble, maintained wrong view, and made for themselves the bad *kamma* based on wrong view, with the breakup of the body, after death, have been reborn in an unhappy destination, in a lower world, in a hell. But these beings who engaged in good conduct of body, speech and mind, who did not revile the noble, who maintained right view, and made for themselves the good *kamma* based on right view, with the breakup of the body, after death, have been reborn in happy destination, in a heavenly realm.' In this way, may I, with the divine eye, which is purified and surpasses that of men, see beings passing away and beings reborn, inferior and superior, beautiful and ugly, fortunate and unfortunate, and know how beings fare according to their *kamma*."[27] Then, as there is a suitable basis, he is capable of realizing any state realizable by direct knowledge toward which he might incline his mind.

'And if he wishes, "May I, with the elimination of the corruptions, here and now, realize with my own direct knowledge freedom of the mind (*cetovimutti*) and the freedom based on wisdom (*paññāvimutti*) and may I, attaining that, abide there", then as there is a suitable basis, he is capable of realizing any state realizable by direct knowledge toward which he might incline his mind.'[28]

(A III 24–9)

The *Uposatha*

The *uposatha* day is the full moon, new moon and the quarter days, the first in particular traditionally the time for monks and laity to gather together, with laymen and laywomen often taking extra precepts, wearing white, offering food and eating with family and friends. All chant, practise meditation, listen to *dhamma* talks and, in *anumodana*, wish that the 'merit' involved can be transferred to friends and family, including the dead, and any beings of any kind in the locality around, so that they all can find safety and happiness. Meditation and listening to talks at this time is considered particularly auspicious.

This text is given to monks on such an occasion. It takes the first four *jhānas*, the four divine abidings (*brahmavihāras*) and the four formless realms as a grouping together, to give twelve different types of meditation practice.

The first four *jhāna*s have already been included in the last *sutta*. After them this text takes the divine abidings, of loving-kindness, compassion, sympathetic joy and equanimity. These, felt to include all appropriate responses to other beings, are also used as a basis for calming the mind. All beings can be perceived with loving-kindness, some invite compassion, when they are suffering, some invite delight in their delight, when they are happy, and all are heirs to their *kamma*, and create their own *kamma* themselves. The object of each of the divine abidings, all beings, is simple, dissolving usual boundaries, and all can be taken as a basis, with mindfulness and wisdom, to extend the mind beyond its usual confines on a limitless object so that it can enter *jhāna*. These *jhānas*, like the earlier ones, seem to restore the mind at its deepest levels: when the Bodhisatta, the Buddha in an earlier life, is a just, universal monarch and layman, he practises them in his *dhamma* palace (D II 185–7). The first three depend upon a strong basis of happiness, usually aroused by the *jhānas*; the last, like the fourth *jhāna*, represents the purification of all feeling, in what is described as limitless equanimity.

After the divine abidings the formless meditations are described. After the fourth *jhāna* some meditators choose to develop these attainments, rarefied concentration practice, in which the nature of the object, the meditation and the meditative mind that experiences the object are all explored, in successively more subtle degrees of *jhāna*. They are not taught as necessary for awakening, but are regarded as helpful as a means of loosening potential attachments to meditative states possible for *samatha* meditators, and worth exploring for their own sake, as the purest manifestation of a developed consciousness and its interaction with the world. They often feature as precursors to the process of awakening. They are perhaps the 'blue sky' areas of meditation: one teacher compares their practice to adventurous exploration of outer space.[29]

The Buddha said that he practised the last two before the enlightenment, so these two at any rate predate Buddhism.[30] That he incorporates the two into his meditation system is, however, significant: they and other formless realms, along with the exercise of higher knowledges and the psychic powers (*iddhi*), are frequently found described in *suttas* before the final eradication of the corruptions of the mind, in one of the stages of path. Many meditators at the time of the Buddha are described as developing such skills, as if they in some way arouse the mastery of mental states and flexibility in meditation needed to attain the final goal.

All formless meditations are described in the *Abhidhamma* as involving the same mental factors as the fourth *jhāna* (DhS 265–8). One modern teacher, Ven. Dhammadhāro, describes them as 'resting-places of the mind'.[31] That they are a natural progression from the simplicity of the beautiful object is implied by a canonical list, the 'releases' (*vimokkha*). Found frequently in the canon, this series describes the meditator first mastering the appearance of forms within his own body, then seeing them externally, and then, in the third 'release', of 'releasing the mind onto the beautiful', said by the commentaries to be the beauty of the *kasiṇa* object, though it could be loving-kindness too. After this he enters the four formless meditations, followed by the attainment of cessation (*nirodha-samapatti*), a meditative state experienced only by the enlightened.[32] So they act, for instance, as the crucial means of release for the meditator that ensures he is 'both-ways liberated' (See D II 55–7; this anthology, pp. 109–23).

In the first formless meditation, the sphere of infinite space (*ākāsānañcāyatana*), 'object'-ness itself is examined through an infinite and undifferentiated ground within which objects usually occur. It 'surmounts the perception of forms' present in form *jhāna*. In the second, the sphere of infinite consciousness (*viññāṇañcāyatana*), 'subject'-ness, or *nāma*, is explored in infinite extent; the meditation explores the mind that perceives the infinite object. The meditation on no-thingness (*ākiññcaññāyatana*) loosens attachment to any form or mental state, as not permanent or owned. Denoters or categories of 'subject', 'object', or 'thing'ness are dropped: Dhammadhāro says it is a 'focusing exclusively on a fainter or more subtle sense of cognizance that has no limit and in which nothing appears or disappears, to the point where one almost understands it to be *nibbāna*.' The meditation on neither-perception-nor-non-perception regards the mind at the arising of consciousness itself, before making differentiation or categories of 'space', 'consciousness', 'thing-ness' and 'nothingness', with, Dhammadhāro says, 'awareness, but with no thinking, no focusing of awareness on what it knows'.

Descriptions of their attainment are sparse in the canon, though extensively delineated by Buddhaghosa (Vism X). Usually associated with the *kasiṇa* practice, they can be undertaken on the basis of the divine abidings (see this anthology, pp. 81–6) and the breath. A wide range of objects lead to the first four *jhānas*; the first may be accessed by twenty-five of the forty objects that Buddhaghosa describes, the ten *kasiṇa,* ten *asubha*, four divine abidings and the breath. Each formless sphere, however, defines through one term object, state, and the sphere in which the mind of the practitioner enters and 'surmounts' the *jhāna* it supersedes. These are the only meditations in which object and state are not differentiated.

Their inclusion with the first four *jhānas* and divine abidings is interesting, in what is clearly regarded as a natural refinement of the range of possibilities for the specialist in concentration. The warm tone of the Buddha, found also in the 'Breathing Mindfulness' *sutta*, indicates the high esteem he holds for practitioners of all these twelve meditations. In early Chinese Buddhism, the idea of twelve gates to liberation, using any one of this set, was employed in the works of An Shigao.[33]

On one occasion the Blessed One was staying at Sāvatthī in Migāramātā's house[34] in the Eastern Park. Now at that time, on the *uposatha* day, he was sitting surrounded by the sangha of monks. Then, looking over the completely silent sangha of monks, the Blessed One addressed them.

'Monks, this assembly is free from chatter, this assembly is without chatter, pure; it is established in the uposatha day. Such a sangha of monks, such an assembly, would be hard to find anywhere in the world. Such a sangha of monks as this is worthy of gifts, worthy of hospitality, worthy of offerings, worthy of añjalis, an unsurpassed field of merit for the world.[35] Such a sangha of monks as this is an assembly to which even a little given is much, while much being given is even more. Such a sangha of monks is an assembly worth going many miles to see, even with a bag for food on one's shoulder. Such is the sangha of monks.

[184] 'There are monks abiding in this sangha who have attained the state of *devas*. There are monks abiding in this sangha who have attained the state of Brahmās. There are monks abiding in this sangha who have attained a state of imperturbability (*ānejja*). There are monks abiding in this sangha who have attained the state of the noble ones.

'And how has a monk attained the state of a *deva*?

'Here, secluded from sense pleasures, secluded from unskilful states, a monk enters and abides in the first *jhāna*, accompanied by initial and sustained thought, filled with the joy and happiness born from seclusion.

'With the stilling of initial and sustained thought, a monk enters in and abides in the second *jhāna*, which is accompanied by internal peace, confidence and unification of mind, is free from initial and sustained thought, and is filled with the joy and happiness born from seclusion.

'With the fading away of joy, a monk equanimous, mindful and clearly comprehending, experiences that happiness in the body about which the noble ones declare, "The one who is equanimous and mindful abides in happiness", and enters and abides in the third *jhāna*.

'With the abandoning of happiness and pain and the disappearance of the earlier pleasant feeling, a monk enters and abides in the fourth *jhāna*, that is beyond pleasure and pain, and is purified by equanimity and mindfulness.

'It is in this way that a monk has attained to the state of a *deva*.

'And how has a monk attained the state of a Brahmā?

'Here, a monk abides with a mind filled with loving-kindness, suffusing one quarter, likewise the second, likewise the third, likewise the fourth. So above, below, all around and everywhere, to all as to himself, he abides suffusing the whole world, in every direction, with a mind filled with loving-kindness, abundant, made great, immeasurable, free from hostility, free from ill-will.

'He abides with a mind filled with compassion, suffusing one quarter, likewise the second, likewise the third, likewise the fourth. So above, below, all around and everywhere, to all as to himself, he abides suffusing the whole world, in every direction, with a mind filled with compassion, abundant, made great, immeasurable, free from hostility, free from ill-will.

'He abides with a mind filled with sympathetic joy, suffusing one quarter, likewise the second, likewise the third, likewise the fourth. So above, below, all around and everywhere, to all as to himself, he abides suffusing the whole world, in every direction, with a mind filled with sympathetic joy, abundant, made great, immeasurable, free from hostility, free from ill-will.

'He abides with a mind filled with equanimity, suffusing one quarter, likewise the second, likewise the third, likewise the fourth. So above, below, all around and everywhere, to all as to himself, he abides suffusing the whole world, in every direction, with a mind filled with equanimity, made great, abundant, immeasurable, free from hostility, free from ill-will.

'It is in this way that a monk has attained to the state of a Brahmā.

'And how has a monk attained a state of imperturbability?

'Here, with the complete surmounting (*samatikkamma*) of the perception of material forms, by leaving behind perceptions of sensory impact and by not paying attention to perceptions of diversity, enter upon and abide in the sphere of infinite space, reflecting, "Space is infinite".

'With the complete surmounting of the sphere of infinite space, reflecting, "Consciousness is infinite", he enters upon and abides in the sphere of infinite consciousness.

'With the complete surmounting of the sphere of infinite consciousness, reflecting, "There is no-thing", he enters upon and abides in the sphere of no-thingness.

'With the complete surmounting of the sphere of no-thingness, he enters upon and abides in the sphere of neither-perception-nor-non-perception.

'It is in this way that a monk has attained a state of imperturbability.

'And how has a monk attained the state of the noble ones?

'Here a monk understands as it really is: this is suffering.
'He understands as it really is: this is the origin of suffering.
'He understands as it really is: this is the cessation of suffering.
'He understands as it really is: this is the path leading to the cessation of suffering.'[36]

It is in this way that a monk has attained the state of the noble ones. (A II 183–5)

Emerging from meditation and recollecting any state, with mindfulness, are considered very important skills for concentration practice, as the following texts suggest:

'Which five things are to be cultivated? Fivefold perfect concentration

1. Suffusion with joy
2. Suffusion with happiness
3. Suffusion with mind (*ceto*)
4. Suffusion with light (*āloka*)
5. The sign of recollection.

'These are five things to be cultivated.' (D III 278)

'What five things are to be made to arise? The fivefold knowledge of right concentration:

1. The knowledge arises that: "This concentration is both present happiness and productive of future resultant happiness".
2. The knowledge arises that: "This concentration is noble and free from physical desire".
3. The knowledge arises that: "This concentration is not practised by the unworthy".
4. The knowledge arises that: "This concentration is calm and choice, has attained tranquility, has attained unification (*ekodibhāva*); it is spontaneous, and cannot be denied or prevented".
5. The knowledge arises that: "I myself attain this concentration with mindfulness, and emerge from it with mindfulness".

'These are five things that are to be made to arise.'

(D III 279)

Calm and insight

This *sutta* follows a favourite Buddhist oral teaching device of four possibilities: a, b, neither a nor b, and both a and b, a method of approaching ideas found in philosophical and logic systems throughout the traditions. Here it is used to indicate the characteristically early Buddhist way of accommodating many different kinds of practitioner and routes to awakening.

The usual tendency in early Buddhist texts is that in practice, calm is taught before insight, but there are other models, particularly in recent times.

'There are these four kinds of people, monks, found existing in the world.

'What four?

'Here, monks, one kind of person has grasped internal calm of mind (*ajjhattaṃ cetosamatha*) but has not grasped insight into higher wisdom and the *dhamma (adhipaññādhammavipassanā)*.[37]

'Here, monks, one kind of person has grasped insight into the higher wisdom and the *dhamma*, but has not grasped internal calm of mind.

'Here, monks, one kind of person has neither grasped internal calm of mind nor insight into the higher wisdom and the *dhamma*.

'And then, monks, there is one kind of person who has grasped both internal calm of mind and insight into the higher wisdom and the *dhamma*.

'These four kinds of individuals are found existing in the world.' (A II 92)

The next two texts show that there may be times for meditators to practise in various ways, depending on the person, the stage of practice, the meditative school and the advice of the teacher. The exhaustion of the corruptions (*āsava*), or of the deepest taints or inclinations that lead to rebirth, is the final awakening. This is when calm and insight are both perfectly balanced, and the mind is liberated, with no further rebirth, in what is known as arahatship. Before arahatship there are three stages, all characterized by both calm and insight: stream entry, after which arahatship will be attained in seven lifetimes; once return, after which arahatship will be developed in one lifetime; and never return, when it will be attained in this lifetime. These stages successively weaken the fetters (*saṃyojana*) and latent tendencies (*anusaya*) that bind the being to continued existence.

On one occasion the Venerable Ānanda was staying at Kosambī in Ghosita's Park. Then the Venerable Ānanda addressed the monks.

'Friends! Monks!'

'Friend,' those monks replied. The Venerable Ānanda said this:

'Friends, whatever monk or nun has declared the attainment of arahatship in my presence has done so by these four paths, or by a particular one amongst them. What four?

'Here, a monk cultivates calm first before insight. As he is cultivating calm first before insight, the path is produced. He pursues this path, cultivates it and practises it frequently. As he is pursuing, cultivating and practising frequently, the fetters are abandoned and the latent tendencies are removed.

'Again, a monk cultivates insight first before calm. As he is cultivating insight first before calm, the path is produced. He pursues this path, cultivates it and practises it frequently. As he is pursuing, cultivating and practising frequently, the fetters are abandoned and the latent tendencies are removed.

'Again, a monk cultivates calm and insight yoked together. As he is cultivating calm and insight yoked together, the path is produced. He pursues this path, cultivates it and practises it frequently. As he is pursuing, cultivating and practising frequently, the fetters are abandoned and the latent tendencies are removed.

'Again, a monk is seized by restlessness about the *dhamma*. But there comes a time when his mind becomes internally steady, settled, unified and concentrated. Then the path is produced in him. He pursues this path, cultivates it and practises it frequently. As he is pursuing, cultivating and practising frequently, the fetters are abandoned and the latent tendencies are removed.

'Whatever monk or nun, friends, has declared the attainment of arahatship in my presence has done so by these four paths, or by a particular one amongst them.' (A II 157)

'Monks, these four times, rightly cultivated and kept on moving, arrive in gradual stages at the exhaustion of the corruptions. What four?

'A time for listening to *dhamma*, a time for discussion about *dhamma*, a time for calm, and a time for insight.

'These four times, rightly cultivated and kept on moving, arrive in gradual stages at the exhaustion of the corruptions.

'Just as, when it is raining and rain pours down in drops on a mountain top, the water flows down the mountainside and fills clefts, gullies and creeks; these, becoming full, fill up pools; these, becoming full, fill up lakes; these, becoming full, fill up rivers; and these, becoming full, fill up the great ocean.

'So too, these four times, rightly cultivated and kept on moving, arrive in gradual stages at the exhaustion of the corruptions.' (A II 140)

A SIMILE: THE CITY ON THE BORDERS

Early Buddhist *suttas* often use an extended single simile, with detailed exploration in relationship to the teaching. This one effectively demonstrates the need for, and difference between, calm and insight, that both need other path factors to support them too. Here an outpost city, on the borders, is used as an image for the 'body' of *dhamma*, which embodies a collectivity of disparate elements that need to work, live and play together, and sometimes face opposition from outside; the harmony of that condition is expressive of the harmony of an organism working well, with the parts supporting one another. The fuel sustaining the citizens of any city is food; here different kinds of food are related to the practice of the four *jhānas*, differentiated from one another by separate defining images. These support the way the *jhānas* are presented in the canon as a hierarchy that nonetheless involves distinctive qualities: the order involves an increased refinement; each is important for a varied and balanced diet.

The king's outpost city

Monks, when a king's outpost city on the borders is well guarded by seven requisites and can obtain easily, without difficulty and as it wishes, the four kinds of food:[38] such an outpost city on the borders, it is said, monks, cannot be undone by outside hostile forces or treacherous friends. And what are the seven requisites that make an outpost city well stocked up?

Here, monks, there is in this king's frontier city a deeply rooted[39] and dug in pillar, unmoving, and unshakeable. Through this first requisite for a city, the outpost city on the borders is guarded for the protection of those inside and the exclusion of those outside.[40]

Furthermore, monks, there is in this royal outpost city on the borders a deep moat, spread out wide. Through this second requisite for a city the outpost city on the borders is guarded for the protection of those inside and the exclusion of those outside.

[107] Furthermore, monks, there is in this royal outpost city on the borders a path on a rampart, high and wide. Through this third requisite for a city the outpost city on the borders is guarded for the protection of those inside and the exclusion of those outside.

Furthermore, monks, there is in this royal outpost city on the borders a great weaponry of arrows and missiles. Through this fourth requisite for a city the outpost city on the borders is guarded for the protection of those inside and the exclusion of those outside.

Furthermore, monks, in this royal outpost city on the borders there lives a large body of forces, namely mahouts, cavalrymen, charioteers, archers, standard-bearers, adjutants, quarter-master sergeants, mighty princes, great as elephants, heroes, warriors in leather armour and slave warriors. Through this fifth requisite for a city the outpost city on the borders is guarded for the protection of those inside and the exclusion of those outside.

Furthermore, in this royal outpost city on the borders there is a gate-keeper, shrewd, experienced and wise, who refuses entry to those he does not know and admits those he does.[41] Through this sixth requisite for a city the outpost city on the borders is guarded for the protection of those inside and the exclusion of those outside.

Furthermore, in this royal outpost city on the borders there is a rampart, high and wide, coated with plaster. Through this seventh requisite for a city the outpost city on the borders is guarded for the protection of those inside and the exclusion of those outside.

[108] With these seven requisites for a city it is very well protected.

And what are the four foods it can obtain easily, without difficulty and as it wishes?

Here in this royal outpost city on the borders, monks, there are plentiful reserves of grass, wood and water that have been stored up for the enjoyment, freedom from fear and worry, and comfort[42] of those inside, and for the exclusion of those outside ... there are plentiful reserves of rice and corn that have been stored up for the enjoyment, freedom from fear and worry, and comfort of those inside, and for the exclusion of those outside ... there are plentiful reserves of sesame, kidney bean, bean and other foods that have been stored up for the enjoyment, freedom from fear and worry, and comfort of those inside, and for the exclusion of those outside ... and plentiful medicines, that is to say, ghee, butter, oil, honey, raw sugar, salt, that have been stored up for the enjoyment, freedom from fear and worry, and comfort of those inside, and for the exclusion of those outside.

These are the four kinds of food that it can obtain easily, without difficulty, and as it wishes.

Indeed, monks, when a king's outpost city on the borders is well protected by seven requisites and can obtain easily, without difficulty and as it wishes, the four kinds of food: such an outpost city on the borders, it is said, monks, cannot be undone by outside hostile forces or treacherous friends. In just this way, monks, when the noble disciple is endowed with seven qualities and can obtain easily, without difficulty and as he wishes, four *jhānas,* concerned with higher consciousness and bringing a happy life in the here and now:[43] this noble disciple, monks, is not to be undone by Māra,[44] not to be undone by the bad one.

With what seven qualities is he endowed?

It is as if a deeply rooted and dug in pillar, unmoving, and unshakeable, the royal outpost city on the borders is guarded for the protection of those inside and the exclusion of those outside: in this way, monks, the noble disciple is confident, and has confidence in the awakening knowledge of the Tathāgata: 'By this reason the Blessed One is an arahant, fully awakened, perfect in knowledge and conduct, gone to happiness, the knower of worlds, incomparable leader of people to be tamed, teacher of gods and men, a Buddha, the Blessed One'. Confident,[45] monks, the noble disciple abandons the unskilful, brings into being the skilful, abandons the blameworthy and cultivates what is irreproachable[46]: he keeps himself pure.[47] With this first quality he is endowed.

It is as if, monks, in this royal outpost city on the borders there is a deep moat, spread out wide. Through this second requisite for a city the outpost city on the borders is guarded for the protection of those inside and the exclusion of those outside: in this way the noble disciple feels shame about wrong bodily, verbal and mental behaviour, feels shame about the cultivation of bad, unskilful states.[48] Full of self-respect, monks, the noble disciple abandons the unskilful, brings into being the skilful. He abandons the blameworthy and cultivates what is irreproachable. With this second quality he is endowed.

It is as if, monks, in this royal outpost city on the borders there is a path on a rampart, high and wide, guarded for the protection of those inside and the exclusion of those outside: just so monks, the noble disciple is scrupulous, and has scruples about wrong bodily, verbal and mental behaviour, has scruples about the cultivation of bad, unskilful states. Scrupulous, the noble disciple abandons the unskilful, brings into being the skilful. He abandons the blameworthy and cultivates what is irreproachable. With this third quality he is endowed.

It is as if, monks, in this royal outpost city on the borders there is a great weaponry of arrows and missiles and it is guarded for the protection of those inside and the exclusion of those outside: just so, monks, the noble disciple has listened to much and remembers what he has heard (*sutadhara*), stores up[49] what he has heard. Whatever teachings that he has heard that are beautiful in the beginning, in the middle and in their conclusion, which set out both the spirit and the letter (*sātthaṃ savyañjanaṃ*) that declares the holy life, perfectly fulfilled, pure: teachings of this kind are much listened to, remembered, learnt by heart, made familiar through discussion,[50] reviewed over in the mind, and well penetrated with right view. With learning as his armoury, the noble disciple abandons the unskilful, brings into being the skilful. He abandons the blameworthy and cultivates what is irreproachable. With this fourth quality he is endowed.

Just as, monks, in this royal outpost city on the borders there lives a large body of forces, namely mahouts, cavalrymen, charioteers, archers, standard-bearers, adjutants, quarter-master sergeants, mighty princes, great elephants, heroes, warriors in leather armour and slave warriors and it is guarded for the protection of those inside and the exclusion of those outside: just so, monks, the noble disciple lives set on vigour, for the abandonment of unskilful states, for the acquisition of skilful states, full of stamina, strong in effort, not putting down responsibility of skilful states. With a body strong in vigour, monks, the noble disciple abandons the unskilful, brings into being the skilful. He abandons the blameworthy and cultivates what is irreproachable. With this fifth quality he is endowed.

Just as, monks, in this royal outpost city on the borders there is a gate-keeper, shrewd, experienced and wise, who refuses entry to those he does not know and admits those he does and it is guarded for the protection of those inside and the exclusion of those outside: just so, monks, the noble disciple is mindful, endowed with the highest degree of mindfulness and care, remembering and recollecting things done long ago and said long ago. With mindfulness the gate-keeper, the noble disciple abandons the unskilful, brings into being the skilful. He abandons the blameworthy and cultivates what is irreproachable. With this sixth quality he is endowed.

Just as, monks, in this royal outpost city on the borders there is a rampart, high and wide, with a covering of plaster and it is guarded for the protection of those inside and the exclusion of those outside: just so, monks, the noble disciple is possessed with insight, is endowed with insight into rise and fall, with a noble penetration of the way to the utter destruction of all suffering. Having wisdom as a coat of plaster, monks, the noble disciple abandons the unskilful, brings into being the skilful. He abandons the blameworthy and cultivates what is irreproachable. With this seventh quality he is endowed.

With these seven qualities he is endowed. And what are the four *jhānas*, concerned with higher consciousness and bringing a happy life in the here and now, that he can obtain easily, without difficulty and as he wishes?

Just as in this royal outpost city on the borders, monks, there are plentiful reserves of grass, wood and water that have been stored up for the enjoyment, freedom from fear and worry, and comfort of those inside, and for the exclusion of those outside: in this way, monks, the noble disciple, secluded from the senses, secluded from unskilful states, with initial and sustained thought, joy and happiness, lives attaining the first meditation (*jhāna*) for his own delight, for his own comfort, leading to *nibbāna*.

Just as in this royal outpost city on the borders, monks, there are plentiful reserves of rice and corn that have been stored up for the enjoyment, freedom from fear and worry, and comfort of those inside, and for the exclusion of those outside: in this way, monks, the noble disciple, with initial and sustained consideration calmed, with peace, confidence and unification of the mind, is free from initial and sustained thought, and is filled with the joy and happiness born from concentration, enters and abides in the second meditation, for his own delight, for his own comfort, leading to *nibbāna*.

Just as in this royal outpost city on the borders, monks, there are plentiful reserves of sesame, kidney beans, beans and other foods that have been stored up for the enjoyment, freedom from fear and worry, and comfort of those inside, and for the exclusion of those outside: in this way, monks, the noble disciple lives with joy and dispassion, equanimous, mindful, clearly comprehending, and experiences the happiness in the body of which the noble ones declare 'the one who is equanimous and full of mindfulness abides in happiness', he lives attaining the third meditation, for his own delight, for his own comfort, leading to *nibbāna*.

Just as in this royal outpost city on the borders, monks, there are plentiful medicines, that is to say, ghee, butter, oil, honey, raw sugar, salt, that have been stored up for the enjoyment, freedom from fear and worry, and comfort of those inside, and for the exclusion of those outside; even so, the noble disciple, by putting away comfort and discomfort, and the disappearance of earlier pleasant and unpleasant feeling, abides and enters into the fourth meditation, that is beyond pleasure and pain, and is purified by equanimity and mindfulness, for his own delight, for his own comfort, leading to *nibbāna*.

These are the four meditations, concerned with higher consciousness and bringing a happy life in the here and now, he can obtain easily, without difficulty and as he wishes.

When, monks, the noble disciple is endowed with seven qualities and can obtain easily, without difficulty and as he wishes, four meditations, concerned with higher consciousness and bringing a happy life in the here and now: this noble disciple, monks, is not to be undone by Māra, not to be undone by the bad one. (A IV 106–13)

CHAPTER THREE

THE PRACTICE OF MEDITATION

This chapter gives some early *suttas* particularly associated with meditation and its development, including practices taught commonly at the time of the Buddha and today.

The Five Hindrances

This text explains the five hindrances to meditation, comparing the mind to a clear pool, obstructed and muddied by various disturbances. Saṅgārava, a learned brahmin, cannot remember the chanted texts that he would have learnt through recital as part of his family traditions. The *sutta* is applied, however, to the obstructions that can hinder meditation. All the hindrances are usually described with the same terminology in lists, though here passion for the senses (*kāmarāga*) is given as the first, a slight variation on the more usual longing (*abhijjā*) or wishing for the senses (*kāmacchanda*). The image is strikingly simple: it is worth noting that the 'clarity' of the mind free of hindrances is not coldly analytical, but a knowing that is without sense-desire, hatred, sloth and torpor, restlessness and worry and doubt. It does not judge, but sees without partiality. In the terms of early Buddhism, clarity of vision means that one of the 'divine abidings' of loving-kindness, compassion, sympathetic joy or equanimity will be present in the mind at the time. The hindrances are suppressed in states of concentration, but finally eradicated by insight, at various stages of path, when concentration is yoked with insight. The text also emphasizes the seven factors of awakening as achieving this (see this anthology, pp. 86–101).

At Sāvatthī.

Then the brahmin Saṅgārava approached the Blessed One. Having approached him, he greeted him, exchanged pleasantries and sat down to one side. When they had completed their greetings, seated at one side, Saṅgārava addressed the Blessed One.

'What is the reason (*hetu*) and cause (*paccaya*) why, Gotama, the chants that have been recited for many long days do not come back to me, not to say the ones that I have not recited? What is the reason and the cause why the ones I did not recite for many long days do come back to me?'

'At whatever time, brahmin, one lives with a mind possessed by passion for the senses (*kāmarāga*) and overcome by passion for the senses, and does not know, as it really is, the escape (*nissaraṇa*) from the sense desire and passion that has arisen, at such time one does not know or see, as it really is, one's own good, the good of others, or the good of both.[1] Then even those chants that have been recited for a long time do not come back to the mind, let alone those that have not been recited.

'It is as if, brahmin, there is a bowl of water, mixed with lac, turmeric, blue dye or crimson dye. If a man with good vision were to examine his own facial reflection in it, he would neither know it nor see it as it really is. So too, brahmin, when one lives with a mind possessed by passion for the senses, overcome by passion for the senses, on that occasion then even those chants that have been recited for a long time do not come back to the mind, let alone those that have not been recited.

'Again, brahmin, when one lives with a mind possessed by ill-will, overcome by ill-will, and one does not understand as it really is the escape from ill-will, at such time one does not know or see, as it really is, one's own good, the good of others, or the good of both. Then on that occasion even those chants that have been recited for a long time do not come back to the mind, let alone those that have not been recited.

'It is as if, brahmin, there is a bowl of water being heated over fire, bubbling up and boiling over. If a man with good sight were to see his own reflection in it, he would neither know it nor see it as it really is. So too, when one lives with a mind possessed by ill-will, overcome by ill-will, on that occasion even those chants that have been recited for a long time do not come back to the mind, let alone those that have not been recited.

'Again, brahmin, when one lives with a mind possessed by sloth and torpor, overcome by sloth and torpor, and one does not understand as it really is the escape from sloth and torpor, at such time one does not know or see, as it really is, one's own good, the good of others, or the good of both. Then on that occasion even those chants that have been recited for a long time do not come back to the mind, let alone those that have not been recited.

'It is as if, brahmin, there is a bowl of water covered with water mosses and algae. If a man with good sight were to see his own reflection in it, he would neither know it nor see it as it really is. So too, when one lives with a mind possessed by sloth and torpor, overcome by sloth and torpor, on that occasion even those chants that have been recited for a long time do not come back to the mind, let alone those that have not been recited.

'Again, brahmin, when one lives with a mind possessed by restlessness and worry, overcome by restlessness and worry, and one does not understand as it really is the escape from restlessness and worry, at such time one does not know or see, as it really is, one's own good, the good of others, or the good of both. Then on that occasion even those chants that have been recited for a long time do not come back to the mind, let alone those that have not been recited.

'It is as if, brahmin, there is a bowl of water ruffled by the wind, stirred up, turning and swirling around, rippling with waves. If a man with good sight were to see his own reflection in it, he would neither know it nor see it as it really is. So too, when one lives with a mind possessed by restlessness and worry, overcome by restlessness and worry, on that occasion even those chants that have been recited for a long time do not come back to the mind, let alone those that have not been recited.

'Again, brahmin, when one lives with a mind possessed by doubt, overcome by doubt, and one does not understand as it really is the escape from doubt, at such time one does not know or see, as it really is, one's own good, the good of others, or the good of both. Then on that occasion even those chants that have been recited for a long time do not come back to the mind, let alone those that have not been recited.

'It is as if, brahmin, there is a bowl of water that is stirred up, turbid and muddied, placed in the dark. If a man with good sight were to see his own reflection in it, he would neither know it nor see it as it really is. So too, when one lives with a mind possessed by doubt, overcome by doubt, on that occasion even those chants that have been recited over a long period do not come back to the mind, let alone those that have not been recited.

'This, brahmin, is the reason and the cause why chants that have been learned by heart for a long time do not come back to you, not to speak of those not learned in this way.

'But, brahmin, when one lives with a heart not possessed by passion for the senses, not overcome by passion for the senses, and one does understand as it really is the escape from passion for the senses, then even chants that have not been recited over a long period do come back to you, not to speak of those that have been recited over a long period.

'It is as if, brahmin, there is a bowl of water unmixed with lac, turmeric, blue dye or crimson dye. If a man with good vision were to examine his own facial reflection in it, he would know it and see it as it really is. So too, brahmin, when one lives with a mind not possessed by passion for the senses, not overcome by passion for the senses, then one knows as it really is the escape from passion for the senses that has arisen. At such time one does know and see, as it really is, one's own good, the good of others, and the good of both. Then on that occasion even those chants that have not been recited for a long time do come back to the mind, not to speak of those that have been recited for a long time.

'Again, brahmin, when one lives with a mind not possessed by ill-will, not overcome by ill-will . . . .

'It is as if, brahmin, there is a bowl of water not heated on the fire, not boiling up nor bubbling over. . . . If a man with good vision were to examine his own facial reflection in it, he would know it and see it as it really is. So too, brahmin, when one lives with a mind not possessed by ill-will, not overcome by ill-will, then one knows as it really is the escape from ill-will that has arisen. At such time one does know and see, as it really is, one's own good, the good of others, and the good of both. Then on that occasion even those chants that have not been recited for a long time do come back to the mind, not to speak of those that have been recited for a long time.

'Again, brahmin, when one lives with a mind not possessed by sloth and torpor, not overcome by sloth and torpor . . . .

'It is as if, brahmin, there is a bowl of water not covered with water mosses nor algae. If a man with good vision were to examine his own facial reflection in it, he would know it and see it as it really is. So too, brahmin, when one lives with a mind not possessed by sloth and torpor, not overcome by sloth and torpor, then one knows as it really is the escape from sloth and torpor that have arisen. At such time one does know and see, as it really is, one's own good, the good of others, and the good of both. Then on that occasion even those chants that have not been recited for a long time do come back to the mind, not to speak of those that have been recited for a long time.

'Again, brahmin, when one lives with a mind not possessed by restlessness and worry, not overcome by restlessness and worry . . . .

'It is as if, brahmin, there is a bowl of water not ruffled by the wind, not stirred up, not turning nor swirling around, not rippling with waves. If a man with good vision were to examine his own facial reflection in it, he would know it and see it as it really is. So too, brahmin, when one lives with a mind not possessed by restlessness and worry, not overcome by restlessness and worry, then one knows as it really is the escape from restlessness and worry that have arisen. At such time one does know and see, as it really is, one's own good, the good of others, and the good of both. Then on that occasion even those chants that have not been recited for a long time do come back to the mind, not to speak of those that have been recited for a long time.

'Again, brahmin, when one lives with a mind not possessed by doubt, not overcome by doubt . . . .

'It is as if, brahmin, there is a bowl of water not stirred up, not turbid, not muddied, and placed in the light. If a man with good vision were to examine his own facial reflection in it, he would know it and see it as it really is. So too, brahmin, when one lives with a mind not possessed by doubt, not overcome by doubt, then one knows as it really is the escape from doubt that has arisen. At such time one does know and see, as it really is, one's own good, the good of others, and the good of both. Then on that occasion even those chants that have not been recited for a long time do come back to the mind, not to speak of those that have been recited for a long time.

'This, brahmin, is the reason, the cause, why even chants not long recited do come back to the mind, not to speak of those that have been recited for a long time.

'There are, brahmin, seven factors of awakening that are without hindrance, without let, without defilements of the mind (*anupakkilesā*), to be cultivated, and practised frequently, that lead to the realization of the fruits of knowledge and freedom. What seven? The factor of awakening that is mindfulness is without hindrance, without let, without defilement of the mind, and, if cultivated and practised frequently, leads to the realization of the fruits of knowledge and freedom. The factor of awakening that is investigation of *dhammas* . . . leads to the realization of the fruits of knowledge and freedom. The factor of awakening that is vigour . . . leads to the realization of the fruits of knowledge and freedom. The factor of awakening that is joy . . . leads to the realization of the fruits of knowledge and freedom. The factor of awakening that is tranquility . . . leads to the realization of the fruits of knowledge and freedom. The factor of awakening that is concentration . . . leads to the realization of the fruits of knowledge and freedom.

The factor of awakening that is equanimity . . . leads to the realization of the fruits of knowledge and freedom.

'These seven factors of awakening, brahmin, are without hindrance, without let, without defilements of the mind, and, if cultivated and practised frequently, lead to the realization of the fruits of knowledge and freedom.'

At these words, Saṅgārava, the brahmin, said to the Blessed One:

'Wonderful, sir Gotama! Wonderful, sir Gotama! Let the worthy Gotama accept me as a lay disciple, gone to his refuge, henceforth as long as my life lasts.' (S V 121–126)

Sāmaññaphala-Sutta
The fruits of recluseship

The extract taken here is from another classic text of Buddhist meditation, the great *sutta* delivered to the remorseful parricide King Ajātasattu, who asks the Buddha about the 'fruits' of meditation and what they are. The Buddha gives his greatest exposition of the various benefits and skills that come to the one who persists in calm (*samatha*) meditation.[2] In accordance with the style and spirit of the *suttas*, teachings given on specific occasions, it gives us more rounded, human and even lyrical illustrations of the way the various factors of meditation work for the practitioner. From the outset of the Buddha's reply – of which only a small part has been included here – it is the simple contentment of living with few wants that is emphasized. Keeping the precepts, five for laypeople, is considered to provide the basis that protects the mind of the practitioner in meditation: of refraining from harming others, from stealing, from harmful sexual behaviour, lying, or intoxication. Here the freedom of the bird communicates this. In the following text the idea of 'clear comprehension' (*sampajañña*) is also introduced. The commentaries describe this as not just to know what one is doing, but to be clear about intent and purpose.[3] To take a modern example, one can be in the supermarket, mindful of feet on the ground, where one is and what one is doing, but perhaps not have clear comprehension, the factor that ensures one is aware of what it is one has come into the supermarket to buy.

Guarding the senses and abandoning the hindrances

And how, great king, is a monk a gatekeeper for the faculties of sense? Here, a monk, seeing a visible object with the eye, does not grasp at the appearance nor does he grasp at its various details. Because harmful, unskilful states such as longing and discontent would assail him if he were to abide without restraint with regard to the eye faculty, he practises restraint, guards the eye faculty and achieves restraint over the eye faculty. Here, hearing a sound with the ear . . . smelling an odour with the nose . . . tasting a flavour with the tongue . . . touching a physical object with the body . . . apprehending an object with the mind, the monk does not grasp at the appearance nor does he grasp at the various details. Because harmful, unskilful states such as longing and discontent would assail him if he were to abide without restraint with regard to the faculty of mind, he practises restraint, guards the faculty of the mind and achieves restraint over the faculty of the mind. Endowed with this noble restraint over the faculties of sense, he experiences within himself an untainted happiness.

In this way, great king, a monk is a gatekeeper for the faculties of sense.

And how, great king, is a monk endowed with mindfulness and clear comprehension? Here, a monk acts with clear comprehension when walking backwards and forwards, in looking ahead or behind, when bending and stretching, in wearing his outer and inner robe and carrying his bowl, when eating and drinking, chewing and swallowing, when defecating and urinating, when walking, standing, sitting, falling asleep, waking up, talking and keeping silent. In this way, a monk is endowed with mindfulness and clear comprehension.

And how, great king, is a monk content? Here, a monk is content with his robe to clothe his body and his almsfood to fill his stomach. Wherever he goes he takes just these with him, just as a bird carries his wings as his only burden when he goes into flight. In this way, wherever a monk goes, he is content with his robe to cover his body and his almsfood to fill his stomach and takes just these with him.

In this way, great king, a monk is content.

Then he, endowed with this noble pile of virtues, this noble restraint of the sense faculties, this noble mindfulness and clear comprehension and this noble contentment, finds for himself a place of seclusion, the roots of a forest tree, a mountain cave or a mountain cleft, a burial ground, a jungle thicket, or a pile of straw in the open air. After he has returned from the almsround and eaten his food he sits, folding his legs in a cross-legged position, makes his body straight and sets up mindfulness before him.

Abandoning longing for the senses, he abides, with a heart free from longing, and purifies his mind of longing.

Abandoning ill-will and hatred, he abides with his mind purified of ill-will and hatred, and, compassionate, wishing for the welfare of all beings, he purifies his mind of ill-will and hatred.

Abandoning sloth and torpor, he abides free from sloth and torpor, and, perceiving light, mindful and clearly comprehending, he purifies his mind of sloth and torpor.

Abandoning restlessness and worry, he abides in calm, and, with a mind made inwardly peaceful, purifies his mind of restlessness and worry.

Abandoning doubt, he abides having crossed over doubt, and, without being troubled about what is or is not wholesome, he purifies his mind of doubt.

It is as if a man were to accrue a debt to start up an enterprise, and his enterprise prospered: he would then pay off his old debts and with what was left over would be able to support a wife. Then he would think, 'Before this I got into debt to start up an enterprise, but now it has prospered and with what is left over I am now able to support a wife'. And for that reason he would be glad and rejoice.

It is as if a man were to become ill, in pain, terribly sick, so that he could not enjoy his food and had no strength in his body. After some time, he would be free of that illness, enjoy his food and recover his bodily health. Then he would think, 'Before this I was ill . . .' And for that reason he would be glad and rejoice.

It is as if a man were confined in prison. After some time, he would be released from prison, safe and without any loss, and with no diminishment of his property. Then he would think, 'Before this I was in prison . . .' And for that reason he would be glad and rejoice.

It is as if a man were a slave, without independence, subject to another, unable to go where he wanted. After some time, he would be released from slavery and gain his independence, he would no longer be subject to another, able to go where he wanted. Then he would think, 'Before this I was a slave . . .' And for that reason he would be glad and rejoice.

It is as if a man, with wealth and possession, were to undertake a journey on a road through a wilderness, where food was scarce and there were many perils. After some time, he would get through the wilderness and, safe and secure, reach the outskirts of a town. Then he would think, 'Before this I was undertaking a journey . . .' And for that reason he would be glad and rejoice.

In this way, great king, a monk sees that when these five hindrances have not been abandoned in him, it is like debt, sickness, imprisonment, enslavement and a wilderness road. But when he sees that these five hindrances have been abandoned in him, it is like freedom from debt, good health, release from prison, freedom from slavery, and a place of safety. When he sees these five hindrances have been abandoned in him, gladness arises. In the one who is glad, joy arises. The body of the one who is joyful becomes tranquil. The one who is happy concentrates the mind.[4]

(D I 70–3)

Breathing Mindfulness

One practice that has proved particularly popular in recent times is that of breathing mindfulness. In the *Mahāsaccaka-Sutta*, the Buddha gives some rare autobiographical recollection, describing the turning point of his abandonment of the mortifications as the memory of practising *jhāna* as a boy during the ploughing festival, when left for a while by his father under the shade of a rose-apple tree. An early 'biography' we have of the Buddha, the *Jātaka-nidāna*, describes the practice he undertook at that time as meditation on the breath (Ja I 58). Whether or not the attribution of breathing mindfulness is correct, that such an early source regards the practice as crucial in Gotama's decision to take food and to put aside fear of 'the joy that is free from sense desires' (M I 246–247) in his search for awakening shows the centrality of this practice in early and modern Buddhist meditation. The Buddha frequently recommended breathing mindfulness, describing it as a 'complete method for attaining *nibbāna*' (S V 326), praising it as the noble abode (*ariyavihāra*), the divine abode (*brahmavihāra*) and the Buddha abode (*Tathāgatavihāra*). In a famous incident in which a group of monks become severely unbalanced as the result of unwise attention to the foul (*asubha*), a practice not usually taught outside monastic settings, the Buddha resorts to breathing mindfulness as a calm meditation to restore their health of mind: 'It is just as if, monks, in the last month of the hot season, when the dust and dirt fly up, a great rain cloud out of season were to disperse and settle them. In just this way, monks, concentration by means of breathing mindfulness, when cultivated and practised frequently, is peaceful and choice: it is a sublime and happy abiding too, that disperses and settles harmful states of mind whenever they arise' (S V 322).

The breathing mindfulness discourse, or *Ānāpanasati-Sutta* (M III 78–88), describing all sixteen stages of the practice, is one of core texts of the Pāli canon and the subject of extensive commentary.[5] As Buddhism travelled, both practice and text remained important: one version of the *sūtra* is amongst the earliest extant Buddhist text we have, introduced to China by An Shigao around 148 CE. Indeed, breathing practices appear to have remained popular, though subject to a number of modifications within different doctrinal and ritual frameworks: many schools of Buddhism employ some breathing techniques as part of, or as, a preliminary to other practices.

Within Southern Buddhism, however, breathing mindfulness techniques, text and practice are notably central. An early commentator, Upatissa, supposedly an arahat, recommends them in this way: 'Why is air contact pleasant? Because it calms the mind. It is comparable to the soothing of a heavenly musician's (*gandhabba*) mind with sweet sounds. By this, discursive thinking is suppressed. And again, it is like a person walking along the bank of a river. His mind is collected, directed towards one object and does not wander. Therefore in mindfulness of respiration [breathing mindfulness], the suppression of discursive thinking is taught.'[6] The following extract shows the basic instructions for the practice. So, the *sutta* shows the breath as an object for calm and insight; as a way of entering *jhāna* and final liberation. Schools vary greatly in how the practice is taught. Each tetrad corresponds to one of the four foundations of mindfulness (see this anthology, pp. 27–34). After a warm greeting to his community, the Buddha starts to teach breathing mindfulness to a select gathering of monks, on the full moon of Komudī, the white lotus.

There are, monks, in this community of monks those who live dedicated to the cultivation of breathing mindfulness. When breathing mindfulness is cultivated and practised frequently, it is of great fruit and great reward. When breathing mindfulness is cultivated and practised frequently it fulfils the four foundations of mindfulness; when the four foundations of mindfulness are cultivated and practised frequently they fulfil the seven factors of awakening. When the seven factors of awakening are cultivated and made much of they fulfil knowledge and release.

And how, monks, is breathing mindfulness cultivated? How is it frequently practised? How is it of great fruit and great reward? Here, monks, a monk goes to a forest, or the roots of a tree or an empty place and sits, folding his legs in a cross-legged position, making his body straight and sets up mindfulness in front of him.

Mindful, he breathes in; mindful, he breathes out.

1. As he breathes in a long breath, he knows, 'I am breathing in a long breath', or, as he breathes out a long breath, he knows, 'I am breathing out a long breath'.

2. As he breathes in a short breath, he knows, 'I am breathing in a short breath'; or, as he breathes out a short breath, he knows, 'I am breathing out a short breath'.
3. He trains thus: 'Experiencing the whole body [of the breath], I shall breathe in'; he trains thus, 'Experiencing the whole body [of the breath], I will breathe out'.
4. He trains thus: 'Making tranquil the bodily formation, I shall breathe in'; he trains thus, 'Making tranquil the bodily formation, I shall breathe out'.
5. He trains thus: 'Experiencing joy, I shall breathe in'; he trains thus: 'Experiencing joy, I shall breathe out'.
6. He trains thus: 'Experiencing happiness, I shall breathe in'; he trains thus: 'Experiencing happiness, I shall breathe out'.
7. He trains thus: 'Experiencing mind formations, I shall breathe in'; he trains thus: 'Experiencing mind formations, I shall breathe out'.
8. He trains thus: 'Making tranquil mind formations, I shall breathe in'; he trains thus: 'Making tranquil mind formations, I shall breathe out'.
9. He trains thus: 'Experiencing the mind, I shall breathe in'; he trains thus: 'Experiencing the mind, I shall breathe out'.
10. He trains thus: 'Gladdening the mind, I shall breathe in'; he trains thus: 'Gladdening the mind, I shall breathe out'.
11. He trains thus: 'Concentrating the mind, I shall breathe in'; he trains thus: 'Concentrating the mind, I shall breathe out'.
12. He trains thus: 'Releasing the mind, I shall breathe in'; he trains thus: 'Releasing the mind, I shall breathe out'.
13. He trains thus: 'Contemplating impermanence, I shall breathe in'; he trains thus: 'Contemplating impermanence, I shall breathe out'.
14. He trains thus: 'Contemplating dispassion, I shall breathe in'; he trains thus: 'Contemplating dispassion, I shall breathe out'.
15. He trains thus: 'Contemplating cessation, I shall breathe in'; he trains thus: 'Contemplating cessation, I shall breathe out'.
16. He trains thus: 'Contemplating letting go, I shall breathe in'; he trains thus: 'Contemplating letting go, I shall breathe out'.

Monks, this is how breathing mindfulness is cultivated and practised frequently, so that is of great fruit and great reward (M III 78–88, extract).

The *sutta* then applies the practice to the four foundations of mindfulness, to the seven factors of awakening, a list explored later in this book with regard to the breath (this anthology, pp. 96ff.), and knowledge and release. But Walpola Rahula here describes one way the breath is used as a secluded meditation practice:

You breathe in and out all day and night, but you are never mindful of it, you never for a second concentrate your mind on it. Now you are going to do just this. Breathe in and out as usual, without any effort or strain. Now, bring your mind to concentrate on your breathing in and breathing out; let your mind watch and observe your breathing in and out; let your mind be aware of your breathing in and out. When you breathe, you sometimes take deep breaths, sometimes not. This does not matter at all. Breathe normally and naturally. The only thing is that when you take deep breaths you should be aware that they are deep breaths, and so on. In other words, your mind should be so fully concentrated on your breathing that you are aware of its movements and changes. Forget all other things, your surroundings, your environment; do not raise your eyes and look at anything. Try to do this for five or ten minutes.

(Rahula 1967: 70)

The Gong

One characteristic of the breath as a meditation object is that it becomes more subtle as attention becomes refined, and mindfulness develops. The breath can become almost imperceptible. The *Paṭisambhidhāmagga* offers reassurance on these grounds, under the section on the culmination of the first tetrad, on making the breath tranquil and developing mindfulness of the body, in terms of the famous image of the gong: the breath is present, and the practice needs to be developed through an ever finer and more subtle attentiveness.

Like what? Just as when a metal gong is struck: at first gross sounds occur, and consciousness proceeds because the sign (*nimitta*) of the gross sounds is well grasped, well attended to, well maintained in the mind, and when the loud sounds have ceased, then afterwards fainter sounds occur and consciousness proceeds because the sign of the fainter sounds is well grasped, well attended to and well maintained in the mind. And when the fainter sounds have ceased, then afterwards consciousness proceeds because it has the sign of the fainter sounds as its object. So too, at first gross in-breaths and out-breaths occur and consciousness does not go to distraction, because the sign of the gross in-breaths and out-breaths is well grasped, well attended to and well maintained in the mind. And when the gross in-breaths and out-breaths have ceased, then afterwards fainter in-breaths and out-breaths occur and the consciousness does not go to distraction because the sign of the fainter in-breaths and out-breaths has ceased. Then after that, consciousness does not go to distraction because it has the sign of the fainter in-breaths and out-breaths as its object.

This being the case, there *is* the production of wind, and there *is* cultivation of the in-breaths and the out-breaths. There *is* cultivation of breathing mindfulness and there *is* the cultivation of concentration through breathing mindfulness. And as a result of this, the wise do enter into and emerge from that attainment. (Patis 185–6)

The following extract from the same section describes some of the hindrances that can arise when following the breath, and factors that support and help the attention.

What are the eight kinds of knowledge of obstacles and the eight kinds of knowledge of aids (*upakārā*)?

Longing for the senses is an obstacle to concentration, meditation (*nekkhamma*) is an aid to concentration.
Ill-will is an obstacle to concentration, loving-kindness (*abyapāda*) is an aid to concentration.
Sloth and torpor is an obstacle to concentration, the perception of light is an aid to concentration.
Restlessness is an obstacle to concentration, balance (*avikkhepa*) is an aid to concentration.
Doubt is an obstacle to concentration, reflection on the *dhamma* (*dhammavavatthāna*) is an aid to concentration.
Ignorance is an obstacle to concentration, knowledge is an aid to concentration.
Boredom (*arati*) is an obstacle to concentration, gladness (*pāmojja*) is an aid to concentration.
All unskilful states of mind are an obstacle to concentration, and all skilful states of mind are an aid to concentration.
These are the eight kinds of knowledge of obstacles and the eight kinds of knowledge of aids.

When the mind (*citta*) is straight and well-based it is established in the kinds of oneness (*ekattā*) and is purified of the hindrances.

What are these kinds of oneness? Meditation is oneness; loving-kindness is oneness; perception of light is oneness; balance is oneness; reflection on the *dhamma* is oneness; knowledge is oneness; gladness is oneness; all skilful consciousness is oneness.

What are these hindrances?

Desire for the senses is a hindrance; ill-will is a hindrance; sloth and torpor are a hindrance; restlessness is a hindrance; doubt is a hindrance; ignorance is a hindrance; boredom is a hindrance; and all unskilful states of mind are a hindrance. (Patis 162–3)

Buddhaghosa suggests eight stages of this practice, often used today: counting, following, touching, settling, observing, turning away, purification and recollection (Vism VIII 189ff.). The way these, or some of these, are taught varies. Many traditions do not describe their methods, but Buddhadāsa, a twentieth-century teacher, describes his in a now classic book on the subject.[7] Francois Bizot has also worked on extensive Pāli and vernacular traditions from recent times concerning the esoteric traditions of *samatha* practice, some involving the breath.[8] A number of practices are described encoded in calligraphic loops known as *yantras*, often on the amulets, tattoos, and lucky cloths beloved by Southeast Asians. Some amulets are purportedly empowered by being held under water by those practising the fourth *jhāna*, in which the physical breath is suspended for a while.[9]

Here are some more general guidelines for breathing practice:

Five things that help breathing mindfulness practice

Possessing five things, monks, a monk practising breathing mindfulness in no long time penetrates to the unshakeable (*akuppaṃ*).[10]
What are the five?
Here, monks, a monk undertakes little, has few duties, is easily supported, and well contented with the necessities of life.
He takes little food and is not devoted to filling his stomach.
He is not lazy and is devoted to watchfulness
He has heard much (*bahussuto*), remembers what he has learned, and sets store by what he has learned (*sutasannicaya*). And those things that are beautiful in the beginning, beautiful in the middle, beautiful in the end, which both in spirit and in the letter speak about the holy life that is entirely perfected and purified: these things are rightly grasped by the monk, rightly attended to, rightly reflected upon, rightly penetrated with wisdom.[11]
He recollects (*paccavekkhati*) the extent of the release of his mind.

Possessing these five things, monks, a monk practising breathing mindfulness in no long time penetrates to the unshakeable.

(A III 120)

DIVINE ABIDINGS: LOVING-KINDNESS, COMPASSION, SYMPATHETIC JOY AND EQUANIMITY

If, for as much as the lasting of a finger-snap, monks, a monk pursues a mind with loving-kindness: such a man is to be called a monk. His meditation is not empty of result. (A I 10)

The practice of loving-kindness is central at all stages of the Buddhist path, and is the single Southern Buddhist practice that perhaps most distils the Buddhist teaching. *Mettā* is felt to be the best foundation for daily dealings with others. Vajiriñāṇa says it 'is not an evanescent exhibition of emotion, but a sustained and habitual mental attitude of service, good-will, and friendship, which finds expression in word, thought, and deed'.[12] In meditation it is a preparatory and a central practice, and a means of arousing *jhāna*. But all four divine abidings (*brahmavihāras*), of loving-kindness, compassion, sympathetic joy and equanimity, are felt to balance one another and to provide a way of responding to all beings. The commentaries describe them as the highest or best meditations (*settha*: Asl 196). They are perhaps best seen working enacted in the many stories about practitioners, who benefit from them and practise them. The classic text on loving-kindness, the *Mettā-Sutta*, is included in one of these (see this anthology, p. 179). One of these qualities is always present in daily life as a skilful consciousness (*kusala citta*) in the *Abhidhamma* system: for instance, as an aspect of taking delight in someone's happiness, or in compassionate action, one may arise with other path factors too (see this anthology, pp. 146–8). Each one can also be developed to be a meditative divine abiding (*brahmavihāra*), leading to *jhāna*, whereby the object, all beings, becomes immeasurable. Recommendations for the practice vary. One method is to radiate, say, *mettā*, from the location where one is at the time, in all directions, as suggested in these texts. Buddhaghosa's helpful advice recommends, amongst other instructions, giving loving-kindness to oneself first, then other beings (Vism IX). Teachers leading this practice in a group often start it by stating the specific location where the group is meeting, and then extend loving-kindness outwards from there. Yet another perspective on this adaptive practice is offered by Śāntideva, in the last chapter of this anthology.

The Simile of the Cloth

In *suttas*, texts given at specific occasions, the Buddha deals with meditators and querents of various kinds, frequently bringing together the practice of the divine abidings with others. He often teaches a number of meditations and practices, like a doctor treating different aspects of the practitioners' needs. Here he teaches first morality (*sīla*) and faith, with the three recollections of Buddha, *dhamma* and sangha, whose formula is chanted daily by practitioners, often as a preliminary to meditation. Loving-kindness, compassion, sympathetic joy and equanimity are then taught as *jhāna* practice. After that, one hearer, a brahmin, addresses him and is told that this is the 'inner washing' that will liberate him from unskilfulness. The man goes away, and attains arahatship.

Thus have I heard. At one time the Blessed One was staying at Sāvatthī in the Jeta Grove in Anāthapiṇḍika's park. There he addressed the monks in this way: 'Monks'. 'Venerable Sir,' they replied. The Blessed One said:

'Monks, suppose a cloth were defiled and stained, and a dyer dipped it in some dye or another, either blue or yellow or red or crimson, it would look badly dyed and impure in colour. Why is this? Because of the impurity of the cloth. In this way, when the mind is defiled, then an unhappy destination may be expected. But, monks, suppose a cloth were pure and very clean, and a dyer dipped it in some dye or another, whether blue or yellow or red or crimson, it would look beautifully dyed and pure in colour. So too, when the mind is undefiled, a happy destination may be expected.

'What, monks, are defilements of the mind? Longing and unbalanced greed are a defilement of the mind. Knowing this, he abandons it. Ill-will is a defilement of the mind; knowing this, he abandons it.

Anger is a defilement of the mind; knowing this, he abandons it. Resentment (*upanāha*) is a defilement of the mind; knowing this, he abandons it. Contempt is a defilement of the mind; knowing this, he abandons it. Spite (*palāsa*) is a defilement of the mind; knowing this, he abandons it. Envy is a defilement of the mind; knowing this, he abandons it. Meanness is a defilement of the mind; knowing this, he abandons it. Deceit is a defilement of the mind; knowing this, he abandons it. Treachery is a defilement of the mind; knowing this, he abandons it. Stubbornness is a defilement of the mind; knowing this, he abandons it. Rivalry is a defilement of the mind; knowing this, he abandons it. Conceit is a defilement of the mind; knowing this, he abandons it. Arrogance is a defilement of the mind; knowing this, he abandons it. Vanity is a defilement of the mind; knowing this, he abandons it. Carelessness is a defilement of the mind; knowing this, he abandons it.

'When a monk has known that longing and unbalanced greed are a defilement of the mind and has abandoned it, when he knows ill-will is a defilement of the mind and has abandoned it (*and so on to carelessness*), then he is possessed of unwavering confidence in the Buddha:

'"The Blessed One is indeed called thus: a worthy one, completely and fully awakened, perfect in wisdom and conduct, one who has gone rightly, the knower of all worlds, the incomparable trainer of those ready for training, teacher of gods and men, awakened, the Blessed One."[13]

'He is possessed of unwavering confidence in the *dhamma*:

'"The teaching is well taught by the Blessed One, visible here and now, immediately effective, inviting inspection, leading onward, to be experienced by the wise, each for oneself."

'He is possessed of unwavering confidence in the sangha:

'"The community of the Blessed One's disciples is practising the good path, practising the straight path, practising the true path, practising the proper path, that is, the four pairs of people, the eight types of individual. This sangha of the Blessed One's disciples is worthy of gifts, worthy of hospitality, worthy of offerings, worthy of homage, an unsurpassed field of merit for the world."

'When he has given up, to the utmost, expelled, released from, abandoned and renounced the defilements, with the thought, "I am possessed of unwavering confidence in the Buddha", he finds delight in the goal, finds inspiration from the teaching, and finds gladness associated with the teaching. And in the one who is glad, joy arises. In one of joyful mind, the body becomes tranquil. In the one whose body is tranquil, happiness arises. In one who feels happiness, the mind becomes concentrated.[14]

'When he has given up, to the utmost, expelled, released from, abandoned and renounced the defilements, with the thought, "I am possessed of unwavering confidence in the *dhamma*", he finds delight in the goal, finds inspiration from the teaching, and finds gladness associated with the teaching. And in the one who is glad, joy arises. In one of joyful mind, the body becomes tranquil, In the one whose body is tranquil, happiness arises. In one who feels happiness, the mind becomes concentrated.

'When he has given up, to the utmost, expelled, released from, abandoned and renounced the defilements, with the thought, "I am possessed of unwavering confidence in the Sangha", he finds delight in the goal, finds inspiration from the teaching, and finds gladness associated with the teaching. And in the one who is glad, joy arises. In one of joyful mind, the body becomes tranquil. In the one whose body is tranquil, happiness arises. In one who feels happiness, the mind becomes concentrated.

'Monks, if a monk of such virtue, such a state of concentration, and such wisdom eats almsfood consisting of choice rice along with various sauces and curries, even that will not be an obstacle to him. Just as a cloth that is defiled and stained becomes pure and very clean, with the help of clear water, or just as gold becomes pure and bright with the help of the furnace, so too if a monk of such virtue, such a state of concentration and such wisdom eats almsfood . . . it will not be an obstruction to him.

'He abides suffusing one quarter with a mind filled with loving-kindness, likewise the second, likewise the third, likewise the fourth;

so above, below, all around, and everywhere, to all as to oneself, he abides pervading the entire world, in all directions, with a mind filled with loving-kindness, abundant, made great, immeasurable, free from hostility and free from ill-will.

'He abides suffusing one quarter with a mind filled with compassion, likewise the second, likewise the third, likewise the fourth; so above, below, all around, and everywhere, to all as to oneself, he abides pervading the entire world, in all directions, with a mind filled with compassion, abundant, made great, immeasurable, free from hostility and free from ill-will.

'He abides suffusing one quarter with a mind filled with sympathetic joy, likewise the second, likewise the third, likewise the fourth; so above, below, all around, and everywhere, to all as to oneself, he abides pervading the entire world, in all directions, with a mind filled with sympathetic joy, abundant, made great, immeasurable, free from hostility and free from ill-will.

'He abides suffusing one quarter with a mind filled with equanimity, likewise the second, likewise the third, likewise the fourth; so above, below, all around, and everywhere, to all as to oneself, he abides pervading the entire world, in all directions, with a mind filled with equanimity, abundant, made great, immeasurable, free from hostility and free from ill-will.

'He understands this: "This is so, this is inferior, this is superior, and beyond there is the supreme liberation from (*nissaraṇa*) the field of identification." When he knows and sees in this way, his mind is released from the corruptions associated with the senses, his mind is released from the corruptions associated with becoming, his mind is released from the corruptions associated with ignorance. When it is released, there is the knowledge: "Exhausted is birth; the holy life has been fulfilled; what has to be done has been done; there is no more of existence here." Monks, this monk is called one who is washed, with an inner washing.'

Now at that time the brahmin Sundarika Bhāradvāja was sitting not far from the Blessed One. And he addressed the Blessed One in the following way: 'But does the Blessed One go to Bāhuka River to bathe?' 'Why, Brahmin, to the Bāhuka River? What will the Bāhuka River do?'

'Gotama, sir, many people aver that the Bāhuka River gives liberation, the Bāhuka River gives wisdom, and many people wash away their wrong actions in the Bāhuka River.'

Then the Blessed One addressed the brahmin Sundarika Bharadvāja in verses:

'Bāhuka and Adhikakkā, Gayā and Sundarikā, Payāgā and Sarassati
And the Bāhumati River:
A fool may bathe there for ever,
But he will not purify wrong action.

'What will the Sundarikā do? What the Pāyagā? What the Bāhuka River?
They cannot purify the one who has done wrong,
The man who has done cruel and unlawful actions.

'The one who is purified lives perpetually in early Spring,
In the purified *uposatha* day.
The one who is pure in his action, and in himself,
Brings his good living to perfection.

'It is here, brahmin, that you should wash, make yourself a refuge for all beings.
If you do not speak falsely and if you do not harm a living being,
If you do not take what is not given, and if you live in faith, generous,
What need is there for you to go to Gayā?
For any source of water will be your Gayā.'

When he had said this, the brahmin Bharadvāja said this to the Blessed One:

'That is marvellous, Gotama, sir! That is marvellous, Gotama, sir! It is as if lord Gotama had turned upright what had been overturned, revealing what had been hidden, showing a road to one who was lost, or holding a light up for those with eyes to see forms. In this way, Gotama, sir, has made the teaching clear in all sorts of ways. I go to Gotama, sir, for my refuge; and to the teaching, and to the Sangha. I would receive the going forth from Gotama: I would receive the full ordination.'

And the brahmin Bharadvāja received the going forth under the Blessed One, and received the full ordination. [40] And soon, not long after his full ordination, living on his own, diligent, ardent, and resolute, the Venerable Bharadvāja, by realizing for himself with direct knowledge, here and now, entered on and remained in that supreme goal of the holy life, for the sake of which people of family rightly go forth from the home life into homelessness. He knew from his own experience: 'Exhausted is birth; the holy life has been fulfilled; what has to be done has been done; there is no more of existence here.' And the Venerable Bharadvāja became an arahat.

(M I 36–40)

Accompanied by loving-kindness: *Haliddavasana-Sutta*

This famous *sutta* introduces the divine abidings as leading to the formless attainments. It also associates them with the factors of awakening, an important list communicating progress in meditation, discussed later in this chapter. Indeed, it has been recently argued that the Buddha, so fluid in his teaching in comparison with the commentaries, regards the first two, loving-kindness and compassion, as themselves routes to awakening.[15] A *brahmavihāra* means, literally, a 'place to stay' that is heavenly, or like a heaven realm.

On one occasion the Blessed One was staying among the Koliyans, in a Koliyan town called Haliddavasana. Then, in the morning, some monks dressed, and taking their bowls and robes, entered Haliddavasana for alms. Then this thought arose for the monks: 'It is still too early to wander around Haliddavasana for alms. Let us go to the park of the followers of other sects.'

Then those monks went to the park of the followers of other sects. Going up to them, they exchanged greetings and chat, and sat down to one side. The followers then said to them: 'Friend, the ascetic Gotama teaches the *dhamma* to his disciples in the following way: "Come, monks, abandon the five hindrances, the defilements of the mind weaken wisdom, and dwell suffusing one quarter with a mind filled with loving-kindness, likewise the second, likewise the third, likewise the fourth. So above, below, all around and everywhere, to all as to himself, abide suffusing the whole world, in every direction, with a mind filled with loving-kindness, abundant, made great, immeasurable, free from hostility, free from ill-will.

'"Abide with a mind filled with compassion, suffusing one quarter, likewise the second, likewise the third, likewise the fourth. So above, below, all around and everywhere, to all as to himself, abide suffusing the whole world, in every direction, with a mind filled with compassion, abundant, made great, immeasurable, free from hostility, free from ill-will.

'"Abide with a mind filled with sympathetic joy, suffusing one quarter, likewise the second, likewise the third, likewise the fourth. So above, below, all around and everywhere, to all as to himself, abide suffusing the whole world, in every direction, with a mind filled with sympathetic joy, made great, immeasurable, free from hostility, free from ill-will.

'"Abide with a mind filled with equanimity, suffusing one quarter, likewise the second, likewise the third, likewise the fourth. So above, below, all around and everywhere, to all as to himself, abide suffusing the whole world, in every direction, with a mind filled with equanimity, abundant, made great, immeasurable, free from hostility, free from ill-will."

'We too, friends, teach the *dhamma* to our disciples in this way: "Come, monks, abandon the five hindrances ... abide suffusing the whole world with loving-kindness ... compassion ... sympathetic joy ... equanimity (same as above)." So what is the distinction here, the difference, between the ascetic Gotama and us, that is, regarding the one teaching and the other, with regard to the one manner of training and the other?'

Then the monks did not take delight in nor did they reject the words of those followers. Not taking delight, and not rejecting, they rose from their seats and left, thinking, 'We shall learn the meaning of these words in the presence of the Blessed One'.

Then, when those monks had gone for alms in Haliddavasana and had returned from their almsround, they went up to the Blessed One. Having paid homage to him, they sat down to one side and relayed the whole discussion between those followers and themselves.

The Blessed One replied:

'Monks, when followers of other sects speak in this way, they should be asked, "Friend, how is the release of the mind through loving-kindness developed? What does it have as its outcome (*gatika*), its highest expression (*parama*), its fruit and its final goal? How is the release of mind through compassion developed? What does it have as its destination, its highest expression, its fruit and its final goal? How is the release of the mind through sympathetic joy developed? What does it have as its destination, its highest expression, its fruit and its final goal? How is the release of the mind through equanimity developed? What does it have as its destination, its highest expression, its fruit and its final goal?" When asked in this way, the followers of other sects would not be able to reply and in addition, they will get into a state of great annoyance. For what reason? Because that would not be within their domain. I do not see anyone, monks, in this world with its gods, and Māra, and Brahmā, in this generation with its ascetics and Brahmins, its gods and humans, who could provide an explanation that would satisfy the mind with an answer to these questions, except the Tathāgata, or a disciple of the Tathāgata, or one who has heard it from them.

[119] 'And how, monks, is the release of the mind through loving-kindness developed? What does it have as its outcome, its highest expression, its fruit and its final goal? Here, monks, a monk develops the factor of awakening that is mindfulness, accompanied by loving-kindness, the factor of awakening that is investigation, accompanied by loving-kindness, the factor of awakening that is vigour, accompanied by loving kindness, the factor of awakening that is joy, accompanied by loving-kindness, the factor of awakening that is tranquillity, accompanied by loving-kindness, the factor of awakening that is concentration, accompanied by loving-kindness, the factor of awakening that is equanimity, accompanied by loving-kindness, based on seclusion, dispassion (*virāga*), cessation (*nirodha*), and letting go (*vossagga*).[16] If he wishes, "May I abide perceiving the repulsive (*paṭikūlasaññī*) in the unrepulsive", he abides there. If he wishes, "May I abide perceiving the unrepulsive in the repulsive", he abides there. If he wishes, "Avoiding both the unrepulsive and the repulsive, may I abide with equanimity, mindful and clearly comprehending", then he dwells there, with equanimity, mindful and clearly comprehending.

'Or else he enters into and abides in the release through the beautiful. Monks, the release of the mind through loving-kindness has the beautiful as its highest expression, I declare, for a monk who is wise in this system, who has not penetrated to a higher release.[17]

'And how, monks, is the release of the mind through compassion developed? What does it have as its outcome, its highest expression, its fruit and its final goal? Here, monks, a monk develops the factor of awakening that is mindfulness, accompanied by compassion, the factor of awakening that is investigation, accompanied by compassion, the factor of awakening that is vigour, accompanied by compassion, the factor of awakening that is joy, accompanied by compassion, the factor of awakening that is tranquillity, accompanied by compassion, the factor of awakening that is concentration, accompanied by compassion, the factor of awakening that is equanimity, accompanied by compassion, based on seclusion, dispassion, cessation, and letting go. If he wishes, "May I abide perceiving the repulsive in the unrepulsive", he abides there. If he wishes, "May I abide perceiving the unrepulsive in the repulsive", he abides there. If he wishes, "Avoiding both the unrepulsive and the repulsive, may I abide with equanimity, mindful and clearly comprehending", then he dwells there, with equanimity, mindful and clearly comprehending.

'Or, with the complete surmounting (*samatikkamma*) of the perception of material forms, by leaving behind perceptions of sensory impact and by not paying attention to perceptions of diversity, he enters upon and abides in the sphere of infinite space, reflecting, "Space is infinite". Monks, the release of the mind through compassion has the sphere of infinite space as its highest expression, I declare, for a wise monk who is wise in this system, who has not penetrated to a higher release.

'And how, monks, is the release of the mind through sympathetic joy developed? What does it have as its outcome, its highest expression, its fruit and its final goal? Here, monks, a monk develops the factor of awakening that is mindfulness, accompanied by sympathetic joy, the factor of awakening that is investigation, accompanied by sympathetic joy, the factor of awakening that is vigour, accompanied by sympathetic joy, the factor of awakening that is joy, accompanied by sympathetic joy, the factor of awakening that is tranquillity, accompanied by sympathetic joy, the factor of awakening that is concentration, accompanied by sympathetic joy, the factor of awakening that is equanimity, accompanied by sympathetic joy, based on seclusion, dispassion, cessation, and letting go. If he wishes, "May I abide perceiving the repulsive in the unrepulsive", he abides there. If he wishes, "May I abide perceiving the unrepulsive in the repulsive", he abides there. If he wishes, "Avoiding both the unrepulsive and the repulsive, may I abide with equanimity, mindful and clearly comprehending", then he dwells there, with equanimity, mindful and clearly comprehending.

'Or, with the complete surmounting of the sphere of infinite space, reflecting, "Consciousness is infinite", he enters upon and abides in the sphere of infinite consciousness. Monks, the release of the mind through sympathetic joy has the sphere of infinite consciousness as its highest expression, I declare, for a monk who is wise in this system, who has not penetrated to a higher release.

'And how, monks, is the release of the mind through equanimity developed? What does it have as its destination, its highest expression, its fruit and its final goal? Here, monks, a monk develops the factor of awakening that is mindfulness, accompanied by equanimity, the factor of awakening that is investigation, accompanied by equanimity, the factor of awakening that is vigour, accompanied by equanimity, the factor of awakening that is joy, accompanied by equanimity, the factor of awakening that is tranquillity, accompanied by equanimity, the factor of awakening that is concentration, accompanied by equanimity, the factor of awakening that is equanimity, accompanied by equanimity, based on seclusion, dispassion, cessation, and letting go. If he wishes, "May I abide perceiving the repulsive in the unrepulsive", he abides there. If he wishes, "May I abide perceiving the unrepulsive in the repulsive", he abides there. If he wishes, "Avoiding both the unrepulsive and the repulsive, may I abide with equanimity, mindful and clearly comprehending", then he dwells there, with equanimity, mindful and clearly comprehending.

[121] 'Or, with the complete surmounting of the sphere of infinite consciousness, reflecting, "There is no-thing", he enters upon and abides in the sphere of no-thingness. Monks, the release of the mind through equanimity had the sphere of no-thingness as its highest expression, I declare, for a monk who is wise in this system, who has not penetrated to a higher release.'

(S V 115–21)

THE FACTORS OF AWAKENING: MEDITATION AS A PROCESS (*BOJJHAṄGAS*)

'If the four foundations of mindfulness are practised persistently and repeatedly, the seven types of *bojjhaṅgas* will be automatically and fully developed.'

Because the Buddhist tradition was passed on orally for so many centuries, the teaching is repeatedly summarized in lists that sound like refrains throughout the early texts. They are easy to remember, and helpful when trying to work on the meditation practice for oneself. One list of mental factors particularly important as a way of understanding the meditative process is the seven factors of awakening (*bojjhaṅgas*). This has continued to be popular in Southern Buddhist regions, where it is felt that even hearing the chant of each one in turn is felt to be restorative and health-giving, as the text below suggests: tradition holds that reciting the list can cure those who are enlightened of any illness from which they might be suffering. The factors are sometimes called *saṃbojjhangas*, with a prefix meaning noble, or true.

Mindfulness: *sati*
Investigation of *dhammas*: *dhammavicaya*
Vigour: *viriya*
Joy: *pīti*
Tranquillity: *passaddhi*
Concentration: *samādhi*
Equanimity: *upekkhā*

The sequence of the seven factors of awakening is the penultimate in the seven lists that comprise the *Bodhipakkhiyādhamma*, the thirty-seven factors contributing to and supporting awakening. These are considered the body of factors needed for meditation. This grouping, common to all forms of Buddhism, can be seen embodied in a *stūpa*/*dagoba*: the four foundations of mindfulness, discussed at the beginning of this book, form the base, and the eightfold path the peak or the finial at the top.[18] There are many repetitions within this larger list. Oral literature, oddly enough, follows patterns familiar in an internet society: lists interleave, and words link into other lists, so many factors recur in many, with a different force or sustaining a different role. For instance, the four right efforts come under 'right effort' in the eightfold path, and are linked in early texts to the second faculty, of vigour, the second power, of vigour, the second basis for success, the third factor of awakening, and finally to the eightfold path (see this anthology, pp. 24ff.).[19]

The four foundations of mindfulness
The four right efforts
The four bases of success
The five faculties
The five powers
The seven factors of awakening

The eightfold path
Bojjhaṅga chant

The following is a translation of a Pāli text used as a protective chant in hospitals and where people are ill or dying in South and Southeast Asia.[20] It describes two arahants at the time of the Buddha who were very ill; the Buddha recited the seven factors and they became well again.[21] Used by practitioners of both *samatha* and *vipassanā*, the list of seven *bojjhaṅgas* describes the healthy and skilful (*kusala*) mind when it is working free from defilements, in daily life, or in deeper form, in meditation, and as indicated here, after enlightenment.

The factor of awakening called mindfulness, investigation of *dhamma*s too, and the factors of awakening vigour, joy and tranquillity, also the two remaining factors of awakening of concentration and equanimity. These seven were taught perfectly by the all-seeing teacher and, when cultivated and practised frequently, bring about higher knowledge, *nibbāna* and awakening. By the speaking of this truth, may you ever have safety!

On one occasion, when the king of the teaching (the Buddha) saw that Moggallāna and Kassapa were ill and in pain, he taught to them the seven factors of awakening. They felt delight in that and were at that moment freed from their sickness. By the speaking of this truth, may you ever have safety!

Once when the king of *dhamma* (the Buddha) himself was afflicted by an illness, he got elder Cunda to chant the same seven factors with devotion. He rejoiced and immediately arose from that disease. By the speaking of this truth, may you ever have safety!

Those diseases were abandoned by those three great teachers, just as the defilements destroyed by the path can arise no more. By the speaking of this truth, may you ever have safety.

Mindfulness (*sati*)

Mindfulness is the starting point of the thirty-seven factors contributing to awakening, as well as here the seven factors of awakening that can arise in daily life, moments of skilful consciousness and as the factors that direct the mind towards awakening. The four foundations of mindfulness are central to all Buddhisms: awareness of body, feeling, mind, *dhammas*. Mindfulness is also the first of five faculties that come into balance in *jhāna* meditation (the list goes: faith, strength, mindfulness, concentration and wisdom) and the first of the five powers. This involves the same elements as the faculties, but intensified, so each is called a power (*bala*) as each cannot be shaken by its opposite. Right mindfulness is also the seventh factor in eightfold path.[22]

Investigation of states (*dhammavicaya*)

The investigation of *dhammas* involves events, phenomena, 'things as they are', investigation of the teaching, and directing the mind to liberation. In skilful states of mind it arises when the ground has been cleared by mindfulness and the mind turns to investigate an object. In the *Abhidhamma*, this mental state (*cetasika*) is associated with 'wisdom' (*paññā*).[23] The term is found only rarely, and nearly always in the context of this list, but it may be seen as occupying the role of wisdom within the factors of awakening, as it is through this factor in particular that the mind, supported by the other six factors, obtains liberating insight.

Vigour (*viriya*)

Vigour has the characteristic of supporting (*upatthambana*), upholding (*paggahaṇa*) and sustaining (*ussahana*).[24] It is described as overcoming idleness. In this anthology it is compared to the pillars of an old house, or the reinforcement for an army. In the thirty-seven factors it features as the second faculty (*indriya*), the second power (*bala*) and the second of the four bases of success (*iddhipāda*). As was seen in the story of Soṇa, it is also associated with the four right efforts and the sixth factor of the eightfold path (*sammā vāyāma*):

1. The effort to ensure the non-arising of unskilful (*akusala*) states that have not yet arisen.
2. The effort to abandon unskilful states that have arisen.
3. The effort to arouse skilful (*kusala*) states that have not yet arisen.
4. The effort to maintain skilful states that have arisen.

Joy (*pīti*)

The word variously described as joy, zest or pleasurable interest is not a feeling, but its precursor, like someone seeing an oasis in a desert; happiness is like the feeling when one has drunk from it.[25] It arises in insight practice, but is especially encouraged in *samatha*, where strong interest in the object is developed. Buddhaghosa describes five kinds of joy in the commentaries: slight, momentary, descending, transporting, suffusing, and of increasing intensity (Vism IV 94–9). These can be manifested in the body in various ways, ranging from a tingling, or hairs going on end, to a powerful joy where the body shakes and quakes – like the early shakers and quakers – until the joy runs its course, purifying the mind and, as the texts in this chapter suggest, the body is made tranquil and very content.[26] Joy of course can arise in all sorts of states, not necessarily skilful. Where it arises in meditation, through interest in the object, such as the breath, it is described as skilful and 'free from sense desires', liberating the mind from hindrances. This factor is considered a kind of hallmark of development on the path.

Tranquillity (*passaddhi*)

Tranquillity is often described as relating to both mind and body, an indicator of its flowing and cohesive nature (see this anthology, pp. 146 and 154).[27] Its chief characteristic is described as being the peaceful allaying of passions (*kilesadarathavūpasama*), in the soothing of effort and excitement. It is compared to the cool shade of a tree to a person affected by the sun's heat and is an antidote to restlessness of mind (*uddhacca*).

Concentration (*samādhi*)

Concentration has been considered earlier: it is associated in the *Abhidhamma* with *ekaggatā* (literally 'gone to oneness'), the fifth *jhāna* factor. Present in insight practice to some degree, in this sequence it represents the various types of calm possible to the mind, in *samatha* practice and daily life, and their development.

Equanimity (*upekkhā*)

Like vigour, joy and concentration, equanimity may be present in unskilful or neutral consciousness: it can range from the neutral feeling of a mildly unskilful consciousness of dullness in daily life, or in its highest expression, act as the culmination of a process, as in the factors of awakening, or as the fourth of the divine abidings. In both these important lists it is the last factor, suggesting its superiority and mastery. It is the final perfection developed by the Buddha in his earlier lives on the Bodhisatta path (see this anthology, p. 157). In the *Abhidhamma* this is associated with *tatramajjhatā*: 'keeping balance here and there' (PED 295) or, literally, 'being right there in the middle'.

Factors of Awakening

As usual for the *suttanta* method, the list is usually seen as a process, with one factor naturally giving rise to the next. This can be undermined by obstructions to the mind, but the factors are also an antidote to the five hindrances to meditation, as seen in the *sutta* about Saṅgārava. The list may be applied to some degree in any situation where there is a skilful mind. Their role, in meditation and in daily life, can perhaps be best seen through the Buddhist method of simile. If one does something one enjoys, like a skill or craft, all seven may arise at various times. So if one happens to enjoy cooking, the stage of mindfulness can be compared to awareness of the ground, or the field in which one is working, and the intended recipients of the food, perhaps some friends. After considering this field for a while, and getting a feeling for what one is going to do, the next stage, of creative investigation, arises: what shall I cook? What foods are in season? What ingredients are fresh? What do people coming like? Is the cooker big enough to cope with the varied dishes? Then, vigour arises as one gets going with preparations, buying the food and starting to chop, peel and arrange. At some time, joy may arise: *joie de vivre*, essential to good cooking and much Buddhist meditation, inspires the process and seeing it through difficult patches. After some while, tranquillity arises as the processes are getting underway and things start to flow. Sometimes it is important to give time to let this happen. This then leads to concentration and focus, when it is near the time for people to arrive. Equanimity, the point of letting go of the creative work, is needed to get the job done and to be able to serve the food well, accepting its shortcomings. This simple analogy shows how the factors can work in a process: if there is skilful consciousness, skill in what you are doing and the intention is to make people happy with the product, then the process will go through to completion. Of course various obstacles often get in the way: bad temper at things not working, worry over some irrelevant detail, over-excitement about one dish and forgetting another. These are literally the same hindrances described obstructing the mind in meditation too, which encounters all the same problems and difficulties met in daily life.

This is a very simple example, and not only shows the way the process can work, but also indicates ways it might be blocked at any stage. Joy, for instance, can become over-excitement, so that if tranquillity does not arise, the process does not continue. If the mind and body become sluggish, more zest and vigour may be needed. The seven feature in most forms of Buddhism, regarded as key to the practice of both insight and concentration. Walpola Rahula noted, 'To cultivate these qualities the most essential thing is a genuine wish, will or inclination' (Rahula 1967: 75). They are examined in more detail by Buddhaghosa, suggesting ways they balance meditation (this anthology, pp. 205–12).

Clothes

Texts like the following show the rhythm and use of repetition that characterize many of the Pali collections. Following the spirit of this text, a modern Thai tradition links the factors to days of the week, with mindfulness on Monday leading to equanimity on Sunday; the day of the week one was born on suggests the one to cultivate.

On one occasion the Venerable Sāriputta was staying at Sāvatthī in the Jeta Grove, Anāthapiṇḍika's park. There, the Venerable Sāriputta addressed the bhikkhus in this way:

'Friends, bhikkhus!'

'Friend', they replied.

The Venerable Sāriputta said this:

'Friends, there are these seven factors of awakening. What seven? The factor of awakening that is mindfulness, the factor of awakening that is investigation of *dhammas*, the factor of awakening that is vigour, the factor of awakening that is joy, the factor of awakening that is tranquillity, the factor of awakening that is concentration, the factor of awakening that is equanimity. These are the seven factors of awakening.

'Whichever of these factors of awakening I want to dwell in for the morning, I dwell in that factor of awakening for the morning. Whichever factor of awakening I want to dwell in for the middle part of the day, I dwell in that for the middle part of the day. Whichever factor of awakening I want to dwell in for the evening, I dwell in that for the evening.

'If, friends, it is the factor of awakening that is mindfulness, in this case I know it is boundless in me, or that it has begun well in me, or if it is established, I know that this is so. Again, if it abates in me, I know it is because of this or that cause. If, friends, it is the factor of awakening that is investigation of *dhammas*, in this case I know it is boundless in me, or that it has begun well in me, or if it is established, I know that this is so. Again, if it abates in me, I know it is because of this or that cause. If, friends, it is the factor of awakening that is vigour . . . I know it is because of this or that cause. If, friends, it is the factor of awakening that is joy . . . I know that this is so. Again, if it abates in me, I know it is because of this or that cause. If, friends, it is the factor of awakening that is tranquillity . . . I know it is because of this or that cause. If, friends, it is the factor of awakening that is concentration . . . I know that this is so. Again, if it abates in me, I know it is because of this or that cause. If, friends, it is the factor of awakening that is equanimity, in this case I know it is boundless in me, or that it has begun well in me, or if it is established, I know that this is so. Again, if it abates in me, I know it is because of this or that cause.

'It is as if, friends, a king or a royal minister has a wardrobe, full of clothes of different colours. Whatever garments he would want to wear in the morning, he would wear in the morning. Whatever garments he would want to wear in the middle of the day, he wears in the middle of the day. Whatever garments he wants to wear in the evening, he wears in the evening.

'Whichever of these factors of awakening I want to dwell in for the morning, I dwell in that factor of awakening for the morning. Whichever factor of awakening I want to dwell in for the middle part of the day, I dwell in that for the middle part of the day. Whichever factor of awakening I want to dwell in for the evening, I dwell in that for the evening.

'If, friends, it is the factor of awakening that is mindfulness, in this case I know it is boundless in me, or that it has begun well in me, or if it is established, I know that this is so. Again, if it abates in me, I know it is because of this or that cause. If, friends, it is the factor of awakening that is investigation of *dhammas* . . . I know it is because of this or that cause. If, friends, it is the factor of awakening that is vigour . . . it is because of this or that cause. If, friends, it is the factor of awakening that is joy . . . I know it is because of this or that cause. If, friends, it is the factor of awakening that is tranquility . . . I know it is because of this or that cause. If, friends, it is the factor of awakening that is concentration . . . I know it is because of this or that cause. If, friends, it is the factor of awakening that is equanimity, in this case I know it is boundless in me, or that it has begun well in me, or if it is established, I know that this is so. Again, if it abates in me, I know it is because of this or that cause.' (S V 70–2)

The seven factors of awakening as a sequence

The seven can also be seen as working in a longer process of growth and maturation. When learning a musical skill like, for instance, playing the piano, mindfulness first applies in becoming aware of the foundations: the body's relationship with the instrument, seating, the keyboard, and how to feel well-placed in the seat. The investigative mind then gets to understand the feel of the keys, learns how notes go together, attempts to learn new pieces, and sometimes tries things out, always necessary at every stage. In learning the piano over a long period, it is important for there to be a balance of attention between focusing on bad habits and mistakes, so that they can be eliminated or avoided, and attending to good habits and good playing, so that they can be encouraged and increased: the balance taught to Soṇa earlier in this anthology effectively describes the even use of energy and vigour. This then becomes joy, essential to the success of the learning process, carrying the mind through difficult patches and challenges. This may transform in time into tranquillity, as a kind of serenity and flow coming into the playing with continued practice and experience, when the mind and body start to work as a unified whole, expressing the music as if they are an instrument too. Concentration is the intentness that the mind brings to bear on fine-tuning the detail of technique and areas of the music that need attention; the player who has made a commitment to the skill, brings it to the highest standards. Equanimity can be compared to the ability to stand back from the performance, and to find awareness of a whole, sometimes with great feeling, but without attachment or rejection to any single part. This is perhaps the stage where the music seems to play itself, and the sense of 'self' becomes larger and selfless. Hindrances can and do of course get in the way of this. But in learning to play a musical instrument, one can see the seven factors working as a larger process that may need any one of the others at a particular time to keep the skills, perhaps themselves like different 'notes', all working well.

A comparable development operates in meditation. The list is often applied to breathing mindfulness practice (see M III 78–88; this anthology, p. 71). To start work on a sitting practice, the practitioner needs to arouse some mindfulness: making sure body and posture are comfortably alert, with a good position on the floor, ground or cushion. Then he or she becomes aware of the sensation of the breath, and the relationship between the mind and the body. The breath is examined further: its movement, areas of constriction or unease, and any sense of flow and pleasant feeling. This in time arouses vigour and strength, as the effort is balanced and adjusted. Joy may then arise in the feeling of the breath as it moves in and out of the body. When this becomes settled, the breath and body become tranquil, while the mind becomes absorbed and focused on the object of the meditation. At the end of the practice, the object is gently relinquished, for a return to daily life and the world around. Over time, these stages of the process become integrated and understood and, from the occasional perspective of equanimity, the factor needed in meditation at any given time starts to become clear, simply through continued practice and experience.

In the following text, the seven factors are considered in such a way. Texts in this section, the *Bojjhaṅgasaṃyutta*, are grouped by themes, whereby those dealing with these seven factors are accompanied, as if in counterpoint, with those on the five hindrances. Factors of awakening are described as the 'food' or 'nutriment' of skilful states of mind; the hindrances as the food of unskilful. Wise attention (*yoniso-manasikāra*) arouses the factors of awakening; unwise attention, or attention that is inappropriate, excessive or unbalanced, arouses the hindrances.

Whatever monks, monks, are endowed with virtue, endowed with concentration, endowed with wisdom, endowed with freedom, endowed with the freedom of knowledge and vision, even the sight of these, I say, monks, is of great benefit.

And I also declare that even hearing of these monks is of great benefit.[28] And I declare that approaching such monks is of great benefit. And I declare that the visiting of such monks is of great benefit; the recollection of such monks is of great benefit, and to follow them in taking the going forth is of great benefit.

What is the cause of this? Hearing the teaching from such monks, one lives secluded in two regards, secluded with bodily seclusion and with seclusion of the mind. Such a person, living secluded in this way, recollects the teaching and puts his mind to it (*anuvitakketi*).[29] On such an occasion the factor of awakening that is mindfulness is established in that monk. On that occasion the factor of awakening that is mindfulness comes to fulfilment in that monk. On whatever occasion a monk cultivates the factor of awakening that is mindfulness, on that occasion the factor of awakening that is mindfulness, through his cultivation, comes to fulfilment.[30]

So he, mindful, living in this way, having applied wisdom,[31] puts his mind to, explores, and gets involved in thorough examination of the teaching.[32]

On whatever occasion, monks, one who is mindful, living in that way, having applied wisdom, puts his mind to, explores, and gets involved in thorough examination of the teaching, the factor of awakening that is investigation of *dhammas* is established in that monk. On whatever occasion, monks, a monk cultivates the factor of awakening that is investigation of *dhammas*, on that occasion the factor of awakening that is investigation of *dhammas*, through his cultivation, comes to fulfilment.

In the one who, having applied wisdom, puts his mind to, explores, and gets involved in thorough examination of the teaching, indefatigable vigour is established.

On whatever occasion, monks, the one who, having applied wisdom, puts his mind to, explores, and gets involved in thorough examination of the teaching, indefatigable vigour is established. On that occasion the factor of awakening that is vigour is established in the monk. And on whatever occasion, monks, a monk cultivates the factor of awakening that is vigour, on that occasion the factor of awakening that is vigour, through his cultivation, comes to fulfilment.

In the one who has established vigour, joy, free from sensual desire, arises.

On whatever occasion, monks, a monk establishes vigour, joy, free from sensual desire, arises. On that occasion the factor of awakening that is joy is established in the monk. And on whatever occasion, monks, a monk cultivates the factor of awakening that is joy, on that occasion the factor of awakening that is joy, through his cultivation, comes to fulfillment.

In the one whose mind is joyful, both the body and the mind become tranquil.

On whatever occasion, monks, the mind of the monk is joyful, both body and the mind become tranquil in that monk. On that occasion the factor of awakening that is tranquillity is established in the monk. And on whatever occasion a monk cultivates the factor of awakening that is tranquillity, on that occasion the factor of awakening that is tranquillity, through his cultivation, comes to fulfillment.

In one whose body is tranquil there is a happy mind, and the happy mind goes to concentration.[33]

On whatever occasion, monks, the body of the monk is tranquil, there is a happy mind, and the happy mind goes to concentration, on that occasion the factor of awakening that is concentration is established in the monk. And on whatever occasion, monks, a monk cultivates the factor of awakening that is concentration, on that occasion the factor of awakening that is concentration, through his cultivation, comes to fulfillment.

He whose mind has been calmed in this way, is now an all-round overseer of his mind.

On whatever occasion, monks, the monk whose mind has been calmed in this way is now an all-round overseer of his mind, on that occasion the factor of awakening that is equanimity is established. And on whatever occasion a monk cultivates the factor of awakening that is equanimity, on that occasion the factor of awakening that is equanimity, through his cultivation, comes to fulfillment.

With these seven factors of awakening, cultivated and practised frequently, monks, seven fruits and advantages are to be anticipated. What seven fruits and advantages?

He establishes realization (*aññā*), beforehand, even in this very life.[34]

And if he does not do so, beforehand, at the moment of death he establishes realisation.

And if he does not even in this very life, beforehand, nor at the moment of death, then, through wearing away the five lower fetters (*saṃyojana*) he attains *parinibbāna* in the beginning of his next life [in the Pure Abodes].

And if he does not . . . with the complete destruction of the five lower fetters, he becomes an attainer of *nibbāna* on taking the ground of his next existence.[35]

And if he does not . . . with the complete destruction of the five lower fetters, he becomes an attainer of *nibbāna,* without effort.

And if he does not . . . with the complete destruction of the five lower fetters, he becomes an attainer of *nibbāna,* with effort.

And if he does not . . . with the complete destruction of the five lower fetters, he becomes bound upstream, towards the realm of Streaming Radiance.

When, monks, the seven factors of awakening have been cultivated and practised frequently, these seven fruits and advantages are to be anticipated. (S V 67–70)

The universal monarch

For some, a symbolic language is a good way of understanding this list of seven. Just as there are seven factors of awakening, so there are said to be seven treasures that arise for the universal monarch, the king whose reign is dedicated to *dhamma*, generosity and meditation. Supposedly living for thousands of years – a favourite Indian metaphor for the sense of time associated with happiness – he represents a lay ideal, of marriage and worldly success, that because of its dependence on good *sīla*, behaviour in the world, generosity, justice and meditation, is like a heavenly realm in the human (*Mahāsudassana-Sutta*, D II 169–99). In many lives spent preparing for Buddhahood, the Bodhisatta was several times a universal monarch who protects his subjects and rules by *dhamma*, not force. His palace is set in a city, a mandala of the mind, and is made of the seven kinds of gems, as are his lotus ponds, the palace gates and their railings. In its innermost chamber he practices the divine abidings, suggestive that the four illimitables can be found in the lay life, and in lay leadership. His seven treasures can be found in many forms of Buddhism, as symbols of the supports for the awakened mind, dedicated to the service of others. For instance, geographical features symbolizing each of the seven treasures are identified around many Tibetan temples; visualisations of a teacher or deity are also sometimes accompanied by the seven treasures. At the end of this book an extract from the *Sukhāvativuyha-Sūtra* uses the same imagery in a Sanskrit text about the heavenly Land of Bliss (see this anthology, pp. 237–9). The use of any of the wealth of kingship as a metaphor for the 'treasures' of the awakened mind can be seen in the story about the slow meditator (this anthology, pp. 185–96). These feature in many schools of Buddhism.

Monks, with the manifestation of a universal monarch comes the manifestation of seven treasures. What seven? There comes the manifestation of the wheel treasure, the elephant treasure, the horse treasure, the jewel treasure, the woman treasure, the treasurer treasure and the adviser treasure.

With the manifestation of a Tathāgata, monks, an arahant, a perfectly awakened one, comes the manifestation of the seven treasures of the factors of awakening. What seven? There comes the manifestation of the treasure of the awakening factor of mindfulness, the treasure of the awakening factor of investigation of states, the treasure of the awakening factor of vigour, the treasure of the awakening factor of tranquillity, the treasure of the awakening factor of concentration, the treasure of the awakening factor of equanimity. With the manifestation of a Tathāgata, an arahant, a perfectly awakening one, comes the manifestation of the seven treasures of the factors of awakening. (S V 99)

CHAPTER FOUR

VARIOUS KINDS OF TEXTS AND MEDITATION

This chapter explores some different types of text that accompany, support, describe or encourage meditation: *suttas* aimed at arousing insight; the poetic compositions of early followers of the Buddha; the often collective practice of protective (*paritta*) chanting; and the *Abhidhamma*, the Buddhist tool for describing the mind.

Wisdom and insight practice

Some wisdom (*paññā*) is present in all rightly established *jhāna*, and may occur naturally in daily life, just as some concentration is present in insight practice and in moments of wisdom. The full cultivation of wisdom, and the discernment of the marks of impermanence, dis-ease and non-self, is often taught at the end of the practititioner's personal path, as some stories in this anthology demonstrate: the goldsmith's son, for instance, needs to cultivate great calm first (this anthology, pp. 181–3). There are some primarily insight-based texts, however, devoted to eliciting and describing wisdom and insight as the first two factors of the eightfold path, right view and right understanding. Just as some texts, such as the extended visualization *suttas* discussed in this chapter, have a *samatha* or calm feel, so these also take the listener or audience receiving the talk through stages of understanding, and the purification of views. The text itself becomes an extended practice, as views are successively posited, suggested and refuted, often in copious and exhaustive detail.

Bhikkhu Bodhi observes that it is not a list found elsewhere in the canon; his notes are particularly helpful in explaining the stages.[1] For those who are interested in the text as an aid to practice – or indeed for anyone who would like to find a flavour of the great depth of feeling and discursive range of Sri Lankan teaching – a modern Sri Lankan monastic teacher, Bhante Gunaratana, has given an hour long *dhamma* talk on this text, explaining it as a meditative aid.[2]

One notable feature of this text is the quiet contradiction, so characteristic of Buddhist discourse, of the frame story. This is a text comparing the path to a chariot-race. But in the story itself, people do not rush to meet others, or make hasty decisions, or fail to observe greetings, as this primary image might suggest. The leisurely deliberation with which the great elder elicits a *dhamma* talk from Puṇṇa, and the meeting between two people, one coming from Saketa and the other from Sāvatthī, is 'set up' in the most low-key way; Puṇṇa's teachings are discreetly elicited in private by the Venerable Sāriputta. This encounter provides a gentle but probing counterpoint to the simile of the relay chariots, whose urgent business, pressed by royal imperative, makes the greatest possible speed between Sāvatthī and Saketa. At the end the sympathetic joy of the two monks who have addressed each other equally as 'friend' seems central to its communication of the stages of wisdom. Buddhaghosa takes the stages, expressed through the image of the relay chariots, as the foundation of the seven stages of the *The Path of Purification (Visuddhimagga)*.

Rathavinita-Sutta
The Relay Chariots

Thus have I heard. At one time the Blessed One was staying at Rājagaha in the Bamboo Grove, the Squirrels' Sanctuary.

Then a number of monks from the Buddha's own country, who had spent the Rains retreat there, went to the Blessed One, and after paying respects, sat down to one side. The Blessed One asked them:

'Monks, who is there in my home-town [Kapilavatthu] who is highly esteemed, by the monks there, by his friends in the following way?

'Having few wants himself, he gives talks to the monks about fewness of wants; content himself, he gives talks to the monks about contentment; secluded himself, he talks to the monks on seclusion; unentangled himself, he gives talks to the monks on unentanglement. Having aroused vigour, he gives talks to the monks on arousing vigour. Having attained to virtue, he gives talks on endowment with virtues, endowed with concentration, he gives talks on becoming endowed with concentration, attained to wisdom, he talks on wisdom, Having attained release, he talks on attaining release. Endowed with the knowledge and vision of release, he gives talks to the monks on becoming endowed with the knowledge and vision of release. He is one who advises, imparts wisdom, instructs, urges, rouses and gladdens his companions in the holy life.'

'The Venerable Puṇṇa Mantāṇiputta, bhante, is highly esteemed in the Blessed One's home town by the monks there, his companions in the holy life.'

Now at that time the Venerable Sāriputta was seated near the Blessed One. Then it occurred to the Venerable Sāriputta: 'It is a gain for the Venerable Puṇṇa Mantāṇiputta, it is a great gain for him, that his wise companions in the holy life praise him, item by item, in the presence of the Tathāgata. Perhaps sometime we might meet up with the Venerable Puṇṇa Mantāṇiputta and converse with him.'

Then, when the Blessed One had stayed at Rājagaha as long as he wished, he set out to wander in stages to Sāvatthī. He eventually arrived at Sāvatthī, and there he stayed at the Jeta Grove, Anāthapiṇḍika's park.

The Venerable Puṇṇa Mantāṇiputta heard that the Blessed One had arrived at Sāvatthī and was staying at the Jeta Grove, Anāthapiṇḍika's park. Then the Venerable Puṇṇa Mantāṇiputta put his lodgings in order, and, taking his outer robe and bowl, set out to wander by stages to Sāvatthī. He eventually arrived at Sāvatthī and went to the Jeta Grove, Anāthapiṇḍika's park, to see the Blessed One. After paying respects to the Blessed One, he sat down to one side and the Blessed One instructed, urged, roused and gladdened him with a *dhamma* talk. Then the Venerable Puṇṇa Mantāṇiputta, instructed, urged, roused and gladdened by the *dhamma* talk, delighting and rejoicing in the Blessed One's words, rose from his seat, and, after paying respects to the Blessed One, circling him and keeping him to the right, went to the Blind Man's Grove to spend the day there.

Then a certain monk went to the Venerable Sāriputta and said to him: 'Friend Sāriputta, the Venerable Puṇṇa Mantāṇiputta, of whom you have always spoken well, has just been instructed, urged, roused and gladdened him with a *dhamma* talk from the Blessed One. Delighting and rejoicing in the Blessed One's words, he rose from his seat, and, after paying respects to the Blessed One, keeping him to the right, went to the Blind Man's Grove to spend the day there.'

Then the Venerable Sāriputta quickly picked up a sitting mat and followed close behind the Venerable Puṇṇa Mantāṇiputta, keeping his head in sight. Then the Venerable Puṇṇa Mantāṇiputta entered the Blind Man's Grove and sat down to spend the day there at the root of a tree. The Venerable Sāriputta also entered the Blind Man's Grove and sat down to spend the day there at the root of a tree.

Then, when it was evening, the Venerable Sāriputta rose from meditation, went to the Venerable Puṇṇa Mantāṇiputta, and exchanged greetings with him. When this polite and friendly talk was completed, he sat down to one side and said to the Venerable Puṇṇa Mantāṇiputta:

'Is the holy life lived under our Blessed One, friend?'

'Yes, friend.'

'But, friend, is it for the sake of purification of virtue that the holy life is lived under the Blessed One?'

'No, friend.'

'Is it for the sake of purification of mind (*citta*) that the holy life is lived under the Blessed One?' 'No, friend.'

'Is it for the sake of purification of view that the holy life is lived under the Blessed One?' 'No, friend.'

'Is it for the sake of purification by overcoming doubt that the holy life is lived under the Blessed One?' 'No, friend.'

'Is it for the sake of purification by knowledge and vision of what is path and what is not path that the holy life is lived under the Blessed One?' 'No, friend.'

'Is it for the sake of purification of knowledge of the way that the holy life is lived under the Blessed One?' 'No, friend.'

'Is it for the sake of purification by knowledge and vision that the holy life is lived under the Blessed One?' 'No, friend.'

'But friend! When asked, ". . . is it for the sake of the purification of virtue that the holy life is lived by the Blessed One . . .", you answered "no". When asked, "is it for the sake of the purification of mind that the holy life is lived by the Blessed One?" . . . you answered "no". When asked, "is it for the sake of purification of view . . . purification by overcoming doubt . . . purification by knowledge and vision of the way . . . purification by knowledge and vision of what is path and not path . . . is it for the sake of purification by knowledge and vision that the holy life is lived by the Blessed One?" you answered "No, friend".

'Friend, it is for the sake of final *Nibbāna*, without clinging (. . .) that the holy life is lived by the Blessed One?'

'But friend, is final *nibbāna*, without clinging purification of virtue?' 'No, friend.'

'Is purification of mind final *nibbāna*, without clinging?' 'No, friend.'

'Is purification of view final *nibbāna*, without clinging?' 'No, friend.'

'Is purification by overcoming doubt final *nibbāna*, without clinging?' 'No, friend.'

'Is purification by knowledge and vision of what is path and not path final *nibbāna*, without clinging?' 'No, friend.'

'Is purification by knowledge and vision of the way final *nibbāna*, without clinging?' 'No, friend.'

'Is purification by knowledge and vision final *nibbāna* without clinging?' 'No, friend.'

'Then is, friend, final *nibbāna* without clinging to be attained without these states?' 'No, friend.'

'But when you were asked, "But friend, is final *nibbāna*, without clinging, purification of virtue?" you replied, "No, friend". When you were asked: "Is purification of mind final *nibbāna*, without clinging?" You replied, "No, friend". When asked, "Is purification of view final *nibbāna*, without clinging? . . . Is purification by overcoming doubt final *nibbāna,* without clinging? . . . Is purification by knowledge and vision of what is path and not path final *nibbāna,* without clinging? . . . Is purification by knowledge and vision of the way final *nibbāna,* without clinging?. . . . Is purification by knowledge and vision final *nibbāna,* without clinging?" You replied, "No friend". But how, friend, should the meaning of these statements be understood?'

'Friend: if the Blessed One had described purification of virtue as final *nibbāna,* without clinging, he would have described something that is still accompanied by clinging as final *nibbāna,* without clinging. If the Blessed One had described purification of mind as final *nibbāna,* without clinging . . . purification of view as final *nibbāna,* without clinging . . . purification by overcoming doubt as final *nibbāna,* without clinging . . . purification by knowledge and vision of what is path and not path as final *nibbāna,* without clinging . . . purification by knowledge and vision of the way as final *nibbāna,* without clinging . . . purification by knowledge and vision final *nibbāna,* without clinging . . . he would have described what is still accompanied by clinging as final *nibbāna,* without clinging.

Conversely, if final *nibbāna,* without clinging, were to be attained without these attributes, then an ordinary person would have attained final *nibbāna*: but an ordinary person is without these attributes.[3]

In that regard, friend, I shall make you a simile, for some wise people understand the meaning of a statement by means of a simile. It is as if King Pasenadi of Kosala, while living at Sāvatthī, had some urgent business to see to at Sāketa, and that between Sāvatthī and Sāketa seven relay chariots were prepared for him. Then King Pasenadi of Kosala, leaving Sāvatthī by the inner door to the palace, would mount the first relay chariot. By means of the first relay chariot he would reach the second relay chariot. Then he would get down from the first chariot and mount the second. By means of the second relay chariot he would reach the third . . . by means of the third, he would reach the fourth . . . by means of the fourth, he would reach the fifth . . . by means of the fifth, he would reach the sixth . . . by means of the sixth, he would reach the seventh relay chariot. And by means of the seventh relay chariot he would reach the inner door to the palace in Sāketa. Then, when he had arrived at the inner door to the palace, his friends, acquaintances, relatives and extended family would ask him: "Sire, did you really come from Sāvatthī to the inner door of the palace by means of this relay chariot?" How, then, would King Pasanadi of Kosala reply in order to answer truthfully?'

'In order to answer truthfully, friend, he should reply in this way:

' "While staying at Sāvatthī, here, I had some urgent business to see to at Sāketa. Between here and Sāketa seven chariots were prepared. Then, leaving Sāvatthī through the inner door of the palace, I mounted the first relay chariot, and by means of the first relay chariot I reached the second. Then I got down from the first chariot and mounted the second. By means of the second chariot I reached the third ... by means of the third chariot I reached the fourth ... by means of the fourth chariot I reached the fifth ... by means of the fifth chariot I reached the sixth ... by means of the sixth chariot I reached the seventh chariot, and by means of the seventh chariot I reached the inner door to the palace at Sāketa." In order to answer truthfully, he should reply in this way.

'So in this way, friend, purification of virtue is for reaching purification of mind. Purification of mind is for reaching purification of view. Purification of view is for reaching purification by overcoming doubt. Purification by overcoming doubt is for reaching purification by knowledge and vision of the way. Purification by knowledge and vision of the way is for reaching purification by knowledge and vision of what is path and not path. Purification by knowledge and vision of what is path and not path is for the sake of purification by knowledge and vision. Purification by knowledge and vision is for the sake of reaching final *nibbāna,* without clinging. It is for the sake of final *nibbāna,* without clinging, that the holy life is lived under the Blessed One.'

When this had been said, the Venerable Sāriputta asked the Venerable Puṇṇa Mantāṇiputta: 'What is the venerable one's name, and how do his companions in the holy life know the venerable one?'

'My name, friend, is Puṇṇa, and my companions in the holy life know me as Mantāṇiputta.'

'It is wonderful, friend, it is marvellous! Each deep question has been answered, item by item, by the Venerable Puṇṇa Mantāṇiputta, as a learned disciple who had understood the dispensation correctly. It is a great gain for them that they have the chance to see and to accord honour to the Venerable Puṇṇa Mantāṇiputta. Even if, just by carrying the venerable Sāriputta on a cushion above their heads, his companions in the holy life would get the chance to see and honour him, it would be a gain for them, a great gain for them. And it is a gain for us, a great gain for us, that we have the chance to see and honour the Venerable Sāriputta!'

And so in this way the two great beings rejoiced in what the other had to say.

(M I 145–51)

Mahānidāna-Sutta
The Great Discourse on Cause

This text gives the classic exposition of the doctrine of dependent origination (*paṭiccasamuppāda*), crucial to Buddhist insight practice.[4] This teaching, sometimes known as dependent arising, is found in many forms of Buddhism, and, usually shown around a circle, delineates the stages by which the mind knows, experiences, feels and grasps on to any object presented to the six senses of body, taste, smell, sound, sight and mind, also considered a sense in early Buddhism. The list is taught as a meditative practice in Burma/Myanmar. The full order, that goes in the opposite direction of the *sutta*, which traces causes, is:

1. [Ignorance: *avijjā*]
2. [Formations: *saṅkhārā*]
3. Consciousness (*viññāṇa*)
4. Name-and-form (*nāma-rūpa*)[5]
5. [Six sense-base] (*saḷāyatana*)
6. Contact (*phassa*)

7. Feeling (*vedanā*)
8. Craving (*taṇhā*)
9. Clinging (*upādāna*)
10. Becoming (*bhava*)
11. Birth (*jāti*)
12. Old age and death (*jarāmaraṇa*)

Three do not occur overtly in this *sutta*. Ignorance and formations, later features to the list, can be seen implied in the concept of self, and the resting places of consciousness, the foundations of our existence as living beings; the sense-bases are implied in the link between name-and-form and contact.[6] Dependent origination is a comprehensively wide doctrine: but it is worth noting that Asian teachers are often surprised by the negative effect this teaching can have on Westerners. Many get round this by plenty of jokes about 'just one thing after another'. Taught in the Southern Buddhist regions, where the idea of an innate health of the mind is so strong (see this anthology, pp. 139–46), the negative terms of ignorance and craving do not sound depressing, but rather are seen as the 'visitors' or defilements of mind that prevent it experiencing its innate radiance. Dependent origination is thus taught as a liberating doctrine, with the links after feeling particularly associated with calm, and the first links particularly associated with insight. Indeed read aloud, in the right circumstances, this text inspires awe in the great web of conditions that surround all existence. Ānanda, the Buddha's attendant, did not become enlightened until after the Buddha's death, but he so often speaks for the heart and the common man. His cheerful confidence in the obvious nature of dependent origination must have needed disturbing: in this meditative text the manner of this occurring is magnificent, and something about his faith does not seem so wrong after all.[7]

At the end the way out and the means of release is revealed, in description of the monk who is 'released on both sides' (*ubhatobhāgavimutto*), who understands and is free from all rebirths, and has practised the releases (*vimokkha*). Richard Gombrich has explained this difficult passage as a twofold attainment through meditation and wisdom, that combines the achievements of the one who 'touches states with his body' (*kāyasakkhī*), the experienced meditator, and the one released by wisdom (*paññāvimutto*). He is freed after having had experience and mastery in meditation of all states, and by wisdom.[8] After the great netted mesh of dependent origination, this twofold liberation breaks the links of interdependency and provides the path for such release, the entrance to *nibbāna*. It is traditionally held that the doctrine of the four noble truths should always be taught in a complete way, without missing any one truth out. The scope of this text helps us to understand the first, and suggests the finding of the others as a real possibility. The Most Venerable U Kaccayāna, a Burmese Mogok teacher, recently noted that while the world of *saṃsāra* and dependent origination is beginningless, it does have an end: the state of *nibbāna*, however, has no end, but does have a beginning, in the completion of the Buddhist path to liberation.[9]

Thus have I heard. On one occasion the Blessed One was staying among the Kurus, in a town in that area called Kammāssadamma. And the Venerable Ānanda approached the Blessed One, paid respects to him, and sat down to one side. Seated, he spoke to the Blessed One.

'It is wonderful and marvellous, Venerable Sir, how this dependent origination is so deep and appears so deep, yet to me it seems as clear as clear can be!'[10]

'Say not so, Ānanda! Say not so, Ānanda. This dependent origination is deep and it appears deep. It is because of not understanding this teaching and not penetrating it, Ānanda, that this generation has become like a tangled skein, like a knotted ball of thread, like muñja grasses and reeds, unable to pass beyond *saṃsāra*, with its realms of misery, unhappy destinations and lower realms of existence.

'If you, Ānanda, were asked, "Are old age and death caused by a particular condition?" you should say, "they are". And, if you were asked, "And by what condition are old age and death caused?" you should say, "By the condition of birth old age and death are caused".

'If you, Ānanda, were asked, "Is birth caused by a particular condition?" you should say, "It is". And, if you were asked, "And by what condition is birth caused?" you should say, "By the condition of becoming birth is caused".

'If you, Ānanda, were asked, "Is becoming caused by a particular condition?" you should say, "It is". And, if you were asked, "And by what condition is becoming caused?" you should say, "By the condition of clinging becoming is caused".

'If you, Ānanda, were asked, "Is clinging caused by a particular condition?" you should say, "It is". And, if you were asked, "And by what condition is clinging caused?" you should say, "By the condition of craving clinging is caused".

'If you, Ānanda, were asked, "Is craving caused by a particular condition?" You should say, "It is". And, if you were asked, "And by what condition is craving caused?" you should say, "By the condition of feeling craving is caused".

'If you, Ānanda, were asked, "Is feeling caused by a particular condition?" you should say, "It is". And, if you were asked, "And by what condition is feeling caused?" You should say, "By the condition of contact feeling is caused".

'If you, Ānanda, were asked, "Is feeling caused by a particular condition?" you should say, "It is". And, if you were asked, "And by what condition is feeling caused?" you should say, "By the condition of contact feeling is caused".

'If you, Ānanda, were asked, "Are name and form caused by a particular condition?" you should say, "They are". And, if you were asked, "And by what condition are name and form caused?" you should say, "By the condition of consciousness name-and-form are caused".

'And so it is in this way, Ānanda, that by the condition of name-and-form, consciousness is caused; by the condition of consciousness, name and form are caused; by the condition of name and form, contact is caused; by the condition of contact, feeling is caused, by the condition of feeling, craving is caused; by the condition of craving, clinging is caused; by the condition of clinging, becoming is caused; by the condition of becoming, birth is caused; by the condition of birth, ageing and death are caused, and hence grief, [57] lamentation, suffering, painful feeling, and despair. Such is the origin of the whole mass of suffering. It was said, "By the condition of birth old age and death are caused". Now how this is so, Ānanda, is to be understood in the following manner. Were there no birth of any sort or kind, whatever, of anyone, anywhere, that is to say of *devas* to the state of being a *deva*, of *gandhabbas* into the state of being a *gandhabba*, of *yakkhas* into the state of being a *yakkha*,[11] of ghosts to the state of being a ghost, of humans to the state of being a human, of four-legged creatures to the state of being a four-legged creature, of birds to the state of being a bird, of insects to the state of being an insect: were there no birth of any sort or kind, anywhere, for every one of those classes of beings, then, there being no birth at all, owing to the cessation of birth, would old age and death be discerned?' 'No, Venerable sir.'

'Therefore, Ānanda, this is the root, the cause, the origin, and the condition for old age and death, that is, birth. It was said, "By the condition of becoming, birth is caused". Now how this is so, Ānanda, is to be understood in the following manner. Were there no becoming of any sort or kind, anywhere, that is to say, becoming in the sense-sphere, becoming in the form (*rūpa*) sphere, becoming in the formless sphere, then, in the complete absence of becoming, with the cessation of becoming, would birth be discerned?' 'No, Venerable sir.'

'Therefore, Ānanda, this is the root, the cause, the origin, and the condition for birth, that is, becoming.

'It was said, "By the condition of clinging, becoming is caused". Now how this is so, Ānanda, is to be understood in the following manner. Were there no clinging of any sort or kind, anywhere, that is to say, clinging to the senses, clinging to views, clinging to precepts and vows, clinging to the doctrine of self: then, in the complete absence of clinging, the cessation of clinging, would becoming be discerned?' 'No, Venerable sir.'

'Therefore, Ānanda, this is the root, the cause, the origin, and the condition for becoming, that is, clinging. It was said, "By the condition of craving, clinging is caused". Now how this is so, Ānanda, is to be understood in the following manner. Were there no craving of any sort or kind, that is to say, craving for visual forms, craving for sounds, craving for smells, craving for tastes, craving for physical contacts, craving for mental states: then, in the complete absence of craving, with the cessation of craving, would clinging be discerned?' 'No, Venerable sir.'

'Therefore Ānanda, this is the root, the cause, the origin, and the condition for clinging, that is, craving.

'It was said, "By the condition of feeling, craving is caused". Now how this is so, Ānanda, is to be understood in the following manner. If there were no feeling of any sort or kind, that is to say, feeling born of eye contact, feeling born of ear contact, feeling born of nose contact, feeling born of tongue contact, feeling born of mind contact: then, in the complete absence of feeling, the cessation of feeling, would craving be discerned?' 'No, Venerable Sir.'

'Therefore, Ānanda, this is the root, the cause, the origin and the condition for craving, that is, feeling.

'In this way, Ānanda, dependent upon feeling there is craving; dependent on craving there is seeking out (*pariyesanā*); dependent on seeking out there is gain; dependent on gain there is deciding (*vinicchaya*); dependent on deciding there is wishing for desire (*chandarāga*). Dependent on desire and passion there is attachment (*ajjhosāna*), dependent upon attachment there is possessiveness; dependent upon possessiveness there is meanness; dependent upon meanness there is guarding over things (*ārakkha*) and as a consequence of guarding over things many bad and unskilful situations arise: blows, wounds, conflicts, quarrels and disputations, slanders and lies.

'It was said, "as a consequence of guarding over things many bad and unskilful situations arise: blows, wounds, conflicts, quarrels and disputations, slanders and lies". Now how this is so, Ānanda, is to be understood in the following manner. If there were no guarding over things, of any sort or kind, anywhere, that is to say, in the complete absence of guarding over things, with the cessation of guarding over things, would these various bad and unskilful situations arise?' 'No, Venerable sir.'

'Therefore, Ānanda, this is the root, the cause, the origin and the condition for various bad and unskilful situations, that is to say, guarding over things. It was said, "dependent on meanness there is guarding over things". Now how this is so, Ānanda, is to be understood in the following manner. If there were no meanness of any sort or kind, anywhere, that is to say, in the complete absence of meanness, with the cessation of meanness, would guarding over things be discerned?' 'No, Venerable sir.'

'Therefore, Ānanda, this is the root, the cause, the origin and the condition guarding over things, that is to say, meanness. It was said, "dependent on possessiveness there is meanness". Now how this is so, Ānanda, is to be understood in the following manner. If there were no possessiveness [60] of any sort or kind, anywhere, that is to say, in the complete absence of possessiveness, with the cessation of possessiveness, would meanness be discerned?' 'No, Venerable sir.'

'Therefore, Ānanda, this is the root, the cause, the origin and the condition for meanness, that is to say, possessiveness. It was said, "dependent on attachment there is possessiveness". Now how this is so, Ānanda, is to be understood in the following manner. 'If there were no attachment of any sort or kind, anywhere, that is to say, in the complete absence of attachment, with the cessation of attachment, would possessiveness be discerned?' 'No, Venerable sir.'

'Therefore, Ānanda, this is the root, the cause, the origin and the condition for possessiveness, that is to say, attachment. It was said, "dependent on desire and passion there is attachment". Now how this is so, Ānanda, is to be understood in the following manner. If there were no desire and passion of any sort or kind, that is to say, in the complete absence of desire and passion, with the cessation of desire and passion, would attachment be discerned?' 'No, Venerable sir.'

'Therefore, Ānanda, this is the root, the cause, the origin and the condition for attachment, that is to say, desire and passion. It was said, "dependent on deciding (*vinicchaya*), there is desire and passion". Now how this is so, Ānanda, is to be understood in the following manner. If there were no deciding of any sort or kind, that is to say, in the complete absence of deciding, with the cessation of deciding, would desire and passion be discerned?' 'No, Venerable sir.'

'Therefore, Ānanda, this is the root, the cause, the origin and the condition for desire and passion, that is to say, deciding.

'It was said, "dependent on gain, there is deciding". Now how this is so, Ānanda, is to be understood in the following manner. 'If there were no gain of any sort or kind, that is to say, in the complete absence of gain, with the cessation of gain, would deciding be discerned?' 'No, Venerable sir.'

'Therefore, Ānanda, this is the root, the cause, the origin and the condition for deciding, that is to say, gain.

'It was said, "dependent on seeking out, there is gain". Now how this is so, Ānanda, is to be understood in the following manner. If there were no seeking out of any sort or kind, that is to say, in the complete absence of seeking out, with the cessation of seeking out, would gain be discerned?' 'No, Venerable sir.'

'Therefore, Ānanda, this is the root, the cause, the origin and the condition for gain, that is to say, seeking out.

'It was said, "dependent on craving, there is seeking out". Now how this is so, Ānanda, is to be understood in the following manner. If there were no craving of any sort or kind, that is to say, in the complete absence of craving, with the cessation of craving, would seeking out be discerned?' 'No, Venerable sir.'

'Therefore, Ānanda, this is the root, the cause, the origin and the condition for seeking out, that is to say, craving. In this way, Ānanda, these two aspects become united through feeling [their conditioning factor].[12]

'It was said, "by the condition of contact, feeling is caused" [62]. Now how this is so, Ānanda, is to be understood in the following manner. If there were no contact of any sort or kind, anywhere, that is to say, eye-contact, ear-contact, nose-contact, tongue-contact, body-contact, mind-contact: in the complete absence of contact, with the cessation of contact, would feeling be discerned?' 'No, Venerable sir.'

'Therefore, Ānanda, this is the root, the cause, the origin and the condition for feeling, that is to say, contact.

'It was said, "by the condition of name-and-form, contact is caused". Now how this is so, Ānanda, is to be understood in the following manner. If those attributes,[13] distinguishing features, signs, and indicators through which there is a concept (*paññatti*) of the physical body were all absent, would the designation "contact" (*adhivacanasamphassa*) be discerned in the physical body?' 'No, Venerable sir.'

'If those attributes, distinguishing features, signs, and indicators through which there is a concept (*paññatti*) of the physical body were all absent, would either the designation "contact" or the sensory impingement of contact[14] be discerned?' 'No, Venerable sir.'

'If those attributes, distinguishing features, signs, and indicators through which there is a concept (*paññatti*) of name and form were all absent, would contact be discerned?' 'No, Venerable sir.'

'Therefore, Ānanda, this is the root, the cause, the origin and the condition for contact, namely, name-and-form. It was said, "by the condition of consciousness, name-and-form are caused". Now how this is so, Ānanda, is to be understood in the following manner. If consciousness were not to descend into the mother's womb, would name and form take shape there?' 'No, Venerable sir.'

'If, after descending into the womb, consciousness were to depart, would name-and-form be brought into existence in this state of being?' 'No, Venerable sir.'

'If the consciousness of a young boy or girl were to be cut off, would name-and-form grow up, develop and reach maturity?' 'No, Venerable sir.'

'Therefore, Ānanda, this is the root, the cause, the origin and the condition for consciousness, that is to say, name-and-form.

'In so far only, Ānanda, as one can be born, or grow old, or die, or pass away, or re-arise, only to such an extent is there a pathway for designating things, to this extent only is there a pathway for explanation, to this extent only is there a pathway for concepts, to this extent only is there a domain for wisdom, to this extent only do we go round the round of life [64] up to our arising to being in this way [thusness]. In so far as this is the case, this is, so to speak, name-and-form together with consciousness.

'Now with regard to definitions about the self, Ānanda, how many such definitions are there? Either one defines the self as having form and being limited, saying, "My self has form and is limited"; or one defines the self as having form and being boundless, saying, "My self has form and is boundless". Or one defines the self as formless and limited, saying, "My self is formless and limited"; or one defines the self as formless and boundless, saying, "My self is formless and boundless".[15]

'And in each case, Ānanda, the one who defines the self as having form and being limited, makes the definition with regard to the present life, or the next, or else his idea is, "My self not being like that, I will aim for it to be so". This being the case, Ānanda, it is right to say that the view that the self has form and is limited lies latent in this.

'One who defines the self as having form and being boundless ... (formula repeated). One who defines the self as formless and limited.... One who defines the self as formless and boundless makes his definition with regard to the present life, or the next, or else his idea is, "My self not being like that, I will aim for it to be so". This being the case, Ānanda, it is right to say that the view that the self has form is limited lies latent in this. It is in these ways, Ānanda, that the one defining self defines it.

'Now with regard to non-definitions about the self, Ānanda, how many such non-definitions are there? Either one does not define the self as having form and being limited, saying, "My self has form and is limited"; or one does not define the self as having form and being boundless, saying, "My self has form and is boundless". Or one does not define the self as being formless and limited, saying, "My self is formless and limited"; or one does not define the self as being formless and boundless, saying, "My self is formless and boundless".

'And in each case, Ānanda, the one who does not define the self as having form and being limited, does not make the definition with regard to the present life, nor the next, nor is his idea, "My self not being like that, I will aim for it to be so". This being the case, Ānanda, it is right to say that the view that the self has form and is limited does not lie latent in this.

'One who defines the self as having form and being boundless . . . (formula repeated). One who defines the self as formless and limited. . . . One who does not define the self as formless and boundless does not make his definition with regard to the present life, or the next, nor is his idea, "My self not being like that, I will aim for it to be so". This being the case, Ānanda, it is right to say that the view that the self is formless and boundless does not lie latent in this.

'It is in these ways, Ānanda, that the one not defining self does not define it.

'And under how many aspects, Ānanda, does the one considering consider the self? The one considering considers feeling as self, "My self is feeling". Or, considering, he considers "My self is not feeling; my self is without the experience of feeling". Or he considers, "My self is not feeling, but my self is not without the experience of feeling. My self feels; my self is subject to feeling." Under such aspects as these the self is considered.

'In this connection, Ānanda, the one who says, "My self is feeling", should be asked, "Friend, there are three kinds of feeling: happy feeling, painful feeling and neither happy nor painful feeling. Of these three kinds of feeling, which do you consider self?"

'Ānanda, at the time when you experience a happy feeling you do not, at the same time, experience a painful feeling or a neutral feeling. At that time you just experience a happy feeling. At the time when you experience a painful feeling you do not, at the same time, experience either a happy feeling or a neutral feeling. You just experience a painful feeling. And at the time you experience a neutral feeling you do not, at the same time, experience either a happy feeling or a painful feeling. At that time you just experience a neutral feeling.

'Ānanda, happy feeling is impermanent, compounded, is the result of causes, liable to destruction, falling away, to fading and to ceasing.

[67] So too is painful feeling. So too is neutral feeling. If when experiencing a happy feeling someone considers "My self is feeling", at the cessation of that feeling he thinks "My self has gone!" So too when the feeling is painful, or neutral. So he who says "My self is feeling", considers self something that in this present life is impermanent, mixed with happiness and pain, liable to beginning and end. Therefore it is not fitting to maintain, "My self is feeling".

'Again, Ānanda, anyone who says, "My self is not feeling, and is without experience of feeling", should be answered, "Friend, where there is no feeling of anything, can you say, "I am"? 'You cannot, Venerable sir.'

'Therefore it is not fitting to maintain, "My self is not feeling, and does not experience feeling".

'Again, anyone who says, "My self is not feeling, but is not without the experience of feeling. My self feels and is subject to feeling", should be answered, "Friend, if feeling of any kind were to cease completely, and there being, through the cessation of any kind of feeling, no feeling, can you say, "I am"?' 'You cannot, Venerable sir.'

'Therefore it is not fitting to maintain, [68] "My self is not feeling, but my self is not without the experience of feeling. My self feels; my self is subject to feeling."

'Now where a monk, Ānanda, does not consider feeling as self, either as feeling, or as not experiencing feeling, or as experiencing feeling, then he, in this way refraining from such views, clings to nothing whatever in the world. And not clinging, he is not frightened, and not being frightened, he finally attains *nibbāna*. And he knows: "Exhausted is birth; the holy life has been fulfilled; what has to be done has been done; there is no more of existence here."

'And if anyone were to say of a monk whose mind is thus released (*vimuttacitto*), "The Tathāgata exists after death", that would be seen by him as a wrong opinion, and not fitting. Likewise, "The Tathāgata does not exist after death . . ., both exists and does not exist . . ., neither exists nor does not exist after death". Why so? Whatever designation and a pathway for designating things, whatever explanation and pathway for explanation, whatever concepts and pathway for concepts, whatever wisdom and domain for wisdom, whatever the round of life and how far the round is crossed: from all of these things, the monk is released with the higher knowledges (*abhiññāvimutto*). And if anyone were to say of a monk whose mind is thus released with the higher knowledges, "He does not know, he does not see, this is his view": they would be wrong.

'There are, Ānanda, these seven resting places for consciousness (*viññāṇaṭṭhiti*) and two spheres (*āyatana*). What are the seven?

[69] 'There are beings who are of differing bodies and of differing intelligence: for instance, human beings, some of the gods and some of those in the lower realms. This is the first resting place for consciousness.[16]

'There are beings who are of differing bodies but of uniform intelligence: for instance, the gods of the Brahmā heaven who are reborn by means of the first *jhāna*. This is the second resting place for consciousness.

'There are beings uniform in body and of differing intelligence, for instance the sixth Brahmā heaven. This is the third resting place for consciousness.

'There are beings uniform in body and of uniform intelligence, for instance the [ninth Brahmā heaven]. This is the fourth resting place for consciousness.

'There are beings who, by completely surmounting the perception of material forms, by leaving behind perceptions of sensory impact and by not paying attention to perceptions of diversity, enter upon and abide in the sphere of infinite space, reflecting, "space is infinite": this is the fifth resting place for consciousness.

'There are beings who, by completely surmounting the sphere of infinite space, reflecting "consciousness is infinite", enter upon and abide in the sphere of infinite consciousness: this is the sixth resting place for consciousness.

'There are beings who, by completely surmounting the sphere of infinite consciousness, reflecting "there is nothing", enter upon and abide in the sphere of nothingness: this is the seventh resting place for consciousness.

'And the two spheres are the sphere of beings without perception and the sphere of neither-perception-nor-non-perception.

'Therein, Ānanda, if one understands the first resting place of consciousness – the human beings, and some of the gods and some of those in the lower realms, of differing bodies and of differing intelligence – if one understands its origin, passing away, enjoyments, dangers, and the escape from it, is it appropriate to take delight there?' 'No, Venerable sir.'

'If one understands the remaining resting places of consciousness, the sphere of beings without perception and the sphere of neither-perception-nor-non-perception . . . is it appropriate to take delight there?' 'No, Venerable sir.'

'So, Ānanda, when a monk, having understood, as they really are, the origin, passing away, enjoyments, dangers, and escape, of these seven resting places of consciousness and these two spheres, such a monk is called one who has been freed by wisdom (*cetovimutti*).

'Now these, Ānanda, are the eight releases. What are they?

'Possessed of material form, he sees forms: this is the first release.

'Not perceiving material forms internally, he sees material forms externally: this is the second release.[17]

'He releases his mind onto the beautiful: this is the third release.[18]

'By completely surmounting the perception of material forms, by leaving behind perceptions of sensory impact and by not paying attention to perceptions of diversity, he enters upon and abides in the sphere of infinite space, reflecting "space is infinite": this is the fourth release.

'By completely surmounting the sphere of infinite space, reflecting "consciousness is infinite", he enters upon and abides in the sphere of infinite consciousness: this is the fifth release.

'By completely surmounting the sphere of infinite consciousness, reflecting "there is nothing", he enters upon and abides in the sphere of nothingness: this is the sixth release.

'By completely surmounting the sphere of nothingness, he enters upon and abides in the sphere of neither perception nor non-perception: this is the seventh release.

'By completely surmounting the sphere of neither-perception-nor-non-perception, he enters upon and abides in the cessation of perception and feeling: this is the eighth release.

'Ānanda, when a monk attains these eight releases in forward order, in reverse order, and in both forward and reverse order: when he attains them, and emerges from them, wherever he wants, in whatever way he wants and for as long as he wants, and when, through the waning away of the corruptions he, here and now, enters and abides in the release of mind that is without corruptions (*cetovimutti*), and the release by wisdom (*paññāvimutti*), having found realization for himself through direct knowledge: such a one is called a monk who is released on both sides (*ubhatobhāgavimutto*).[19] And, Ānanda, there exists no release on both sides that is higher or finer than this one.'

Thus spoke the Blessed One. The Venerable Ānanda, rejoicing, delighted in the Blessed One's words.

(D II 55–71)

Aditta-Sutta
The Teaching on Fire
('The Fire Sermon')

This teaching is recorded as the third discourse of the Buddha, as it is narrated in the *Vinaya* (Vin I 34–5), which says it was given to a group of matted-hair ascetics under the tutelage of the Kassapa brothers, renowned for their austere and secluded habits. Devoted to fire sacrifice, they came to Buddhist practice after a series of miracles performed by the Buddha – the usual way, in ancient India, by which teachers 'proved' their psychic skill and level of attainment. As Richard Gombrich's eloquent discussion of this text notes, fire is everywhere in India: used for cooking, offerings, purification, and considered sacred within the brahminic traditions. The Buddha, however, here transforms brahminic external practice into a multi-valent metaphor for mental state, negative and positive.[20] The *sutta*'s transformatory effect works through an internal, psychological message, for it is only the one who is noble, and heard much, who is actually *able* to see the effects so simply and evocatively described.

Poetry lovers will find the wording of the title familiar. T. S. Eliot's poem 'The Waste Land' (1922) is an allusive, complex poem; nonetheless, the music, language and rhythms of Indian and Buddhist texts may be seen at crucial stages, even to the point, it can be argued, of offering, at its conclusion, some dimly grasped harmony and resolution to the fractured and dispossessed shards of poetry that have made it one of the seminal twentieth-century texts. 'The Fire Sermon' section derives its title from this text. Eliot was an able student of Pali, studying with the great scholar C. R. Lanman at Harvard. Did Eliot ever hear the way this text is chanted? He certainly attended early Buddhist meetings in London, and so was familiar with hearing about Buddhist teaching and practice, but does not seem to have had contact with Buddhist chant. If he had, he might as a poet have responded to the music of its recital now, where key words are emphasized through a regular change of pitch.[21] One such key word is *nibbidā*, a disenchantment or turning away, meaning not a simple rejection, but rather a finding of the path that leads away from attachments. The word *nibbindati*, 'is disenchanted', has an attractive upbeat that, repeated so often, lifts the last part of the *sutta*. This text, by its very rhythms as well as its content, communicates a sense of urgency, yet joy in change.

Thus have I heard. On one occasion, the Blessed One was staying at Gayā at Gayā Head with a thousand monks. There the Blessed One addressed the monks in this way.

'Everything, monks, is on fire. And what, monks, is the "everything" that is on fire?

'The eye is on fire, visual forms are on fire, eye consciousness is on fire, eye contact is on fire, and whatever feeling arises with eye contact as its cause, whether pleasant or painful, or neither pleasant nor painful: that too is on fire.

'On fire with what? It is on fire with the fire of passion, on fire with the fire of hatred, on fire with the fire of delusion. It is on fire with birth, ageing and death; with sorrow, lamentation, suffering, painful feeling, with despair: this I say.

'The ear is on fire, sounds are on fire, ear consciousness is on fire, ear-contact is on fire, and whatever feeling arises with ear-contact as its condition is on fire, whether pleasant or painful, or neither pleasant nor painful: that also is on fire. On fire with what? On fire with the fire of passion, on fire with the fire of hatred, on fire with the fire of delusion. I declare that it is on fire with birth, ageing and death; with sorrow, lamentation, suffering, painful feeling, with despair.

'The nose is on fire, smells are on fire, nose consciousness is on fire, nose contact is on fire, and whatever feeling arises with nose contact as its condition is on fire, whether pleasant or painful, or neither pleasant nor painful: that also is on fire. On fire with what? On fire with the fire of passion, on fire with the fire of hatred, on fire with the fire of delusion. I declare that it is on fire with birth, ageing and death; with sorrow, lamentation, suffering, painful feeling, with despair.

'The tongue is on fire, tastes are on fire, tongue consciousness is on fire, tongue contact is on fire, and whatever feeling arises with tongue contact as its condition is on fire, whether pleasant or painful, or neither pleasant nor painful: that also is on fire. On fire with what? On fire with the fire of passion, on fire with the fire of hatred, on fire with the fire of delusion. I declare that it is on fire with birth, ageing and death; with sorrow, lamentation, suffering, painful feeling, with despair.

'The body is on fire, physical contacts too are on fire, body consciousness is on fire, body contact is on fire, and whatever feeling arises with body contact as its condition is on fire, whether pleasant or painful, or neither pleasant nor painful: that also is on fire. On fire with what? On fire with the fire of passion, on fire with the fire of hatred, on fire with the fire of delusion. I declare that it is on fire with birth, ageing and death; with sorrow, lamentation, suffering, painful feeling, with despair.

'The mind is on fire, mental states (*dhammā*) are on fire, mind consciousness is on fire, mind contact is on fire, and whatever feeling arises with mind-contact as its condition is on fire, whether pleasant or painful, or neither pleasant nor painful: that also is on fire. On fire with what? On fire with the fire of passion, on fire with the fire of hatred, on fire with the fire of delusion. I declare that it is on fire with birth, ageing and death; with sorrow, lamentation, suffering, painful feeling, with despair.

'Seeing in this way, monks, the noble disciple, who has heard much, is disenchanted with the eye and with forms, is disenchanted with the eye consciousness, is disenchanted with eye contact, with whatever feeling that arises with eye contact as condition, whether pleasant or painful, or neither pleasant nor painful: with this also he is disenchanted . . . is disenchanted with the ear and with sounds . . . is disenchanted with the nose and with smells . . . is disenchanted with the tongue and with tastes . . . is disenchanted with the body and with physical contacts . . . is disenchanted with the mind and its mental states, is disenchanted with mind consciousness, is disenchanted with mind contact, with whatever feeling that arises with mind contact as condition, whether pleasant or painful, or neither pleasant nor painful: with this also he is disenchanted.

'Experiencing disenchantment, he becomes dispassionate. Through dispassion his mind is released. Through release there is knowledge of release; and so he understands: 'Exhausted is birth; the holy life has been fulfilled; what has to be done has been done; there is no more of existence here.'

This is what the Blessed One said. Delighted, those monks rejoiced in the words of the Blessed One. And while this teaching was being given, the minds of a thousand monks were released from the corruptions through non-clinging.

(S IV 19)

The followers of the Buddha

There is a tradition that monks and nuns compose their own verses upon reaching awakening. These ancient verses, dating over a two-hundred-year period from during the time of the Buddha to after his death, bear testimony to the way the tradition was immediately practised.[22] Here we can see the individual creativity of the early elders demonstrated through diverse teachings, distilled biographies, autobiographies, tributes to teachers and friends, and delighted personal responses to the world around after awakening. Read all together, the canonical verses of the monks and, importantly, nuns too, give a many-layered arrangement, of many different voices, types of people and varied paths.

The monk Ramāṇeyyaka, for instance, speaks this verse on attaining enlightenment:

Amidst the sounds of chirping and the songs of birds, this mind of mine does not tremble, for delight in being at one is mine! (Th 49)

The monk Vimala says this:

The earth is sprinkled, the wind blows, and lightning flashes. My thoughts have found peace, my mind is well-concentrated. (Th 50)

Sunāga sums up the path:

One who is skilled in the images of the mind, knowing the sweet taste of solitude,
  Adept in meditation, fully mindful, attains to the happiness that is not of the senses.

Nuns are also eloquent. Jentī became enlightened after hearing the Buddha teach:

Whatever factors of awakening there are, paths for the attainment of *nibbāna*,
These have I cultivated, just as the Buddha taught them.
I have indeed seen the Blessed One; this is my last body.
Being born in *saṃsāra* is finished for me: there is no further rebirth for me now.

(Thī 21–2)

Visākhā expresses her awakening practically:

Follow the Buddha's teaching. If you do, you won't regret it.
So quickly, wash your feet; and sit down to one side. (Thī 13)

Some nuns experience great loss, grief and poverty before attaining awakening. One nun, Dhammā, apparently attained realization after falling down on her almsround:

I went around for alms, leaning on a stick and weak; with limbs trembling, I fell, right there on the ground.
Seeing peril in the body, my mind was completely released. (Thī 17)

Prose commentarial accounts, written in about the sixth to the seventh century CE from an earlier oral tradition, describe the circumstances that prompted the verses, often with a background tale of a vow made lifetimes ago. This is an example of one of the shorter ones, a nun who is helped by an old friend.

Vijāyā[23]

She too performed meritorious deeds under previous Buddhas and accumulated good *kamma* in various lives as a strong support for her release.[24] In the course of time she travelled through *saṃsāra* amongst gods and men, strengthened by her skilful roots.[25] In this time of a Buddha she took rebirth in the home of a certain good family in Rājagaha. When she reached maturity she was a friend of the elder nun Khemā, while she was a householder.[26] Hearing that Khemā had taken the going forth, she thought, 'So, that great queen will take the going forth! Well, why don't I too?' So, wishing to become a nun, she approached the elder Khemā. The elder, understanding her disposition, taught the *dhamma* to her so that, with her mind stirred with a sense of urgency about *saṃsāra*, she would have the deepest confidence in the teaching. Indeed, when Vijāyā heard the *dhamma* a great sense of urgency did arise in her, she gained faith, and she asked to take the going forth. The elder admitted her into the nuns' order. When she had taken the going forth she fulfilled all the preliminaries, established insight (*vipassanā*) and, through the maturing of the skilful roots, not long afterwards attained arahatship with the discriminatory knowledges (*paṭisambhidā*). She reviewed her own attainment and spoke these inspired verses (*udāna*):

Four times, five times, I went out from my temple;
I had not found peace of mind, nor mastery over my own mind.
I approached a nun and I honoured her; then I asked her questions.
She taught the *dhamma* to me: the elements and spheres,
The four noble truths, the faculties and the powers,
The factors of awakening, and the eightfold path, for the attainment of the highest goal.
I listened to what she said; I did what she advised.
In the first watch of the night, I remembered that I had been born before.
In the middle watch of the night, I purified the divine eye.
And in the last watch of the night, I tore apart the mass of darkness.
And then I abided, suffusing the body with joy and happiness:
On the seventh day, I stretched out my feet, having torn apart the mass of darkness.

(ThīA 159–60; Thi 169–74)

Long texts and collective practice

The Great Occasion: *Mahāsamaya-Sutta*

One can think of Buddhist meditation as being solitary and silent, but this is not always the case. As well as temple days, when people take precepts, eat, chant, and practise together, there is a large loosely defined category of local *bhāvanā*, involved in bigger festivals, chanting days and even theatrical performances of texts such as *Jātakas*, to which the whole village or community will contribute and participate.

The texts used for these are crucial, and have particular functions or modes, used for specific occasions and for various purposes. A number of these, such as the *Āṭānāṭiya-Sutta* (D III 194–206), and the *Mahāsamaya-Sutta* (D II 253–62) in particular, are very long narratives, interspersed with others of that type in the collection known as the *Dīghanikāya*: the 'Long Texts Collection'; chanting and listening to them, for their very length, reinforces a sense that they are meditative exercises. When J. R. R. Tolkien spoke of the effects of fabulous worlds that take us out of the 'real' events for a while, he employed an argument apt also for Buddhist texts. He cites one of their main functions as a process of recovery:

> Recovery (which includes return and renewal of health) is a re-gaining – regaining of a clear view, . . . seeing things as we are (or were) meant to see them. . . . We need, in any case, to clean our windows, so that the things seen clearly may be freed from the drab blur of triteness or familiarity – from possessiveness. Of all those faces, those of our *familiares* are the ones both most difficult to play fantastic tricks with and most difficult to see with fresh attention, perceiving their likeness and unlikeness. . . . They have become like the things which once attracted us by their glitter or their colour or their shape, and we laid hands on them, and then locked them in our hoard, acquired them and acquiring ceased to look at them. (Tolkien 1964/1975:59)

He argues that one function of myths and fairy tales is to take us out of our usual perception of events and see the world as if for the first time. This capacity to see the world afresh, or in Buddhist terms with mindfulness and attentive interest, usefully describes the way the long texts of the *Dīghanikāya* effect their teaching. Within a Buddhist context, they are intended to arouse factors contributing to awakening, such as mindfulness, investigation, vigour, joy, tranquillity, concentration and equanimity. The texts seem to represent different registers or modes in which the constructing part of the mind, under conditions such as a holy day gathering, is employed with the intent of purifying in the participants any defilements associated with it.

The ritual element is important as part of the process of ensuring mindfulness and attentiveness. At public festivals the adornment of shared spaces with decorations, lamps and incense makes the familiar appear fresh, so that it can be perceived in a new light when the festival has finished: usually, according to local practices, it is necessary that all the accoutrements of the festival should be cleared away or burnt after the festive temporal period has elapsed. L. S. Cousins has suggested that the *Dīghanikaya* evolved from night-time teaching, a feature that certainly characterizes much of their modern performative context.[27] This is also worth bearing in mind as a feature affecting content and intent. Like bardic epics, long meditation texts need time for a different kind of restfulness and quality of attention, aroused by, for instance, the withdrawal of the usual distracting visual and auditory features of a daytime landscape, and the diffuse resting of attention achieved through visual objects such as butter-lamps and flowers and the smells of the coconut oil and incense. The familiar space becomes a different kind of field when evening falls. Rhythmic repetitions, changes of tone and tempo, the dramatic chanting finales of some *suttas*, and the ritual of preparing and sustaining, for instance, a canopied chanting area (*mandapa*) for monks, all create a liminal world where the meditative effects of the chant may be felt more deeply, to refresh the mind afterwards.

In Southeast Asia and South Asia it is not necessarily the obviously accessible texts that are the most popular. The 'Great Occasion', the *Mahāsamaya-Sutta*, for instance, Rhys Davids said involved just a 'long list of strange names [that] awakes no interest', making it 'almost unreadable now'.[28] It simply describes the various kinds of gods and beings who come to pay tribute to the Buddha, and who may be visualized during the recitation. These include beings near enlightenment, attendant deities and other hierarchies of *devas* and protective spirits. This is the kind of composition that characterizes much oral literature in the epic traditions, such as the attributes of the shield in the Iliad, the ranks of angels and beings in *Paradise Lost*, and in a modern context, the lists of the *Lord of the Rings*.

But it shares many elements with subsequent visualization practices in other Buddhist traditions: the defining of a protected space or field through the presence of directional deities; a marking of these four directions; the establishment of a hierarchy of beings who occupy a three-dimensional field, often producing sound; a wide colour range, described in the different appearances of the various fabulous creatures such as the mythical enemies, serpents, *nāgas*, and *garuda* birds; some sonorous names and epithets evocative of grandeur; and a sense that the whole of the attention is engaged, aurally and visually, by beings occupying a protective role, who will chase away inauspiciousness. In this case the intrusion of harmful elements is articulated through the personification of the forces that threaten the stability of the locality or region or person. In this *sutta* this is enacted with demons, ghosts and unkind spirits, who are sent away. At the still centre of this organized and complex hierarchy of beings is the Buddha, in whose presence their particular properties and powers become harmonious and work together, keeping hostile elements at bay. The hearer or participant in the festival is encouraged to create in his or her mind's eye an assembly of deities in all four directions to protect the field or locality within which the *sutta* is chanted. Afterwards, deities are often invited to leave, the field dispersed, and the familiar world reestablished.

The meditation teacher Ajahn Mun Bhuridatta (1870–1949) is said to have chanted the *Mahāsamaya-Sutta* and the *Dhammacakkapavattana-Sutta* almost every night, citing them frequently in his talks.[29] In a Southeast Asian context, it is regarded as a blessing or *paritta*, a word derived from the Sanskrit *trā*, 'to rescue'. After the tsunami, it was chanted on the beaches at Phuket, being regarded as the most appropriate and therapeutic means of restoring the health and the complex balance of life of the local environment.[30] Perceived as a group meditation, it re-establishes protective powers associated with the deities, thus ensuring the future health, ecological balance and spiritual well-being of the environs. It is chanted at weddings and for new buildings. That the chant has often been used for these purposes is evinced by the way it changes tempo, momentum and pitch at different stages, being split into four distinct recitative modes. While we cannot know whether such fine-tuning was present from early days, this sophistication and nuance is a product of a performative chanting tradition built on considerable local practice and custom. Other *paritta* texts translated in this volume are the *Mettā-Sutta* and the *Mora-paritta*.

One area that should be mentioned briefly in this regard is the complex language of the heaven realms. Much of the drama of the very long texts, and many shorter ones in other collections, derives from the close proximity of the heaven realms to the human, and the significance of the way participants in different *suttas* visit heaven realms for advice, consolation, inspiration and discussion, as indeed the inhabitants of those realms visit the humans. Just as in Ancient Greece, this was and still is considered normal in some Southern Buddhist areas. Whatever the rationalist reader may think of this, scholars such as S. Collins and R. Gethin have noted the precise correspondence of the realms to meditative states.[31] The *Mettā-Sutta*, for instance, says of the practice of loving-kindness: 'This they say is a heaven realm, here in this world" (Sn.151: this anthology, p. 178); the Buddha frequently compares meditators to inhabitants of those realms (this anthology, pp. 45–6). So while these realms are considered to have independent ontological status, their occurrence in texts may be read as embodiments of what meditation does: they show that future rebirths, in this lifetime or the next, can be shaped by the freeing of the mind through collective and single practice. In *suttas*, when the Buddha visits Brahmā realms, the meditative heavens, for advice, his visit can be 'read' as a consultation of the meditation states themselves. When Sakka, king of the Heaven of the Thirty-Three, is involved, the state of heaven (*sagga*) of *sīla*, generosity, investigation and faith are being evoked.

As with all such texts, the presence of the Four Great Kings is crucial, establishing an awareness of the four directions, and underlying mindfulness, key to visualization texts throughout the Buddhist tradition. The Four Great Kings are said to occupy and protect those who take refuge in the Buddha, guarding them from harm. They also are linked to the practice of *sīla* and generosity, for it is on the basis of these qualities that beings are reborn in their realm. They are thought to guard the practitioner from the demons routed in this *sutta*, described as being without, but also within, in fears, impulses and irrational forces that may arise, threatening to engulf the mind of the person attempting to practise meditation.

Such *suttas* are central to understanding the evolution of Buddhist meditation: they anticipate many features found in subsequent visualized texts of the Northern and Eastern schools, demonstrate the use of the eidetic imagination in *samatha* practice, and show ways that collective practice, through chanting, listening to chanting and being in the presence of it, constitutes group *bhāvanā*, a basis for the practice of meditation. As the texts and local practice always indicate, coming back to the everyday world is very important too.

The Great Occasion

Thus have I heard. On one occasion the Blessed One was staying in the great forest at Kapilavatthu, amongst the Sakyans, with a vast retinue of five hundred of the community of monks, all of whom were arahats. Now from all the ten world systems *devatās* gather together at certain times to catch sight of the Blessed One and the community of monks. And so the thought then occurred to four *devatās* of the Pure Abodes.

'The Blessed One is staying in the great forest at Kapilavatthu, amongst the Sakyans, with a vast retinue of five hundred of the community of monks, all of whom are arahats. From all the ten world systems *devatās* gather together at certain times to catch sight of the

Blessed One and the community of monks. Let us all approach the Blessed One and, on arrival, let us each recite a verse in his presence!'

Then, just as a strong man might stretch his bended arm or bend his stretched arm, those *devatās* disappeared from the midst of the *devatās* of the Pure Abodes and reappeared before the Blessed One. Paying respects to the Blessed One, they stood to one side. As they were standing there, one recited this verse in the presence of the Blessed One:

'This is a great occasion in the forest!
The deva companies have assembled.
We have come to this dhamma meeting
To see the invincible order of monks!'

Then another *devatā* recited this verse in the presence of the Blessed One:

'The monks here have practised concentration,
They have made their minds straight.
Like a driver holding the reins,
The wise ones guard their faculties.'

Then another *devatā* recited this verse in the presence of the Blessed One:

'Having cut through barrenness, having cut through bars,
having uprooted Indra's boundary post,
They wander pure and unstained,
Young elephants, well-tamed, with their vision clear.'

Then another *devatā* recited this verse in the presence of the Blessed One:

'Those who have gone for refuge to the Blessed One:
They will not go to an unfortunate realm.
When they have left behind the realm of humans,
They will fill the hosts of the devas.'

Then the Blessed One addressed the monks:

'At certain times, devas from all the ten world systems gather together to catch sight of the Blessed One and the community of monks. Whoever, monks, in the past were pure ones, self-awakened ones: such devas, of this level of attainment, assemble then for these blessed ones too, just as they do now for me. Whoever, monks, in the future will be pure ones, self-awakened ones: such *devas*, of this level of attainment, will assemble then for these blessed ones too, just as they do now for me.

'I will declare, monks, the names of the hosts of the *devas*.
I will let it be known, monks, the names of the hosts of the *devas*.
I will teach, monks, the names of the hosts of the *devas*.
Hear this: pay careful attention. I will speak.'

'As you say, sir,' the monks assented to the Blessed One.
The Blessed One said this:
'I shall pay tribute to them in verse, those who live where the gods of the earth appear;
Those who have a resolute will and composed minds,
living in a mountain thicket,
They have overcome hair-raising fears,
Like hidden lions,
White-hearted, pure, clear-minded and serene.'

In the Kapilavatthu forest, the Blessed One recognized five hundred or more:
His disciples, delighting in his teaching. To them the Teacher spoke:

'The hosts of devas have gathered together; become aware of them, monks!'
They made a great meditative effort[32], hearing the teaching of the Buddha.
And in them, knowledge appeared, and heavenly vision.
Some saw a hundred, some a thousand, gods
Some saw seven thousand; with heavenly vision
Some saw boundless gods, filling all the directions.

[After delineating several ranks of *devas*, the Buddha describes then the Four Great Kings guarding the four directions]:

'The Eastern Direction, King Dhataraṭṭha rules: a magnificent king, Lord of the Heavenly Musicians, with a splendid following, he.
Sons he has: abundant and greatly strong, with minds like Indra,
Displaying wonderful powers, radiating splendour, beautiful, of shining renown.
Rejoicing, they have approached the monks: the meeting in the forest.

'The Southern Direction, King Viruḷha rules: Lord of the Kumbhaṇḍas
With a splendid following, he.
Sons he has: abundant and greatly strong, with minds like Indra,
Displaying wonderful powers, radiating splendour, beautiful, of shining renown.
Rejoicing, they have approached the monks: the meeting in the forest.

'The Western Direction, King Virūpakkha rules: a magnificent king, Lord of the nāgas,
With a splendid following, he.
Sons he has: abundant and greatly strong, with minds like Indra,
Displaying wonderful powers, radiating splendour, beautiful, of shining renown.
Rejoicing, they have approached: the monks meeting in the forest.

'The Northern Direction, King Kuvera rules: a magnificent king, Lord of the Yakkhas,
With a splendid following, he.
Sons he has: abundant and greatly strong, with minds like Indra,
Displaying wonderful powers, radiating splendour, beautiful, of shining renown.
Rejoicing, they have approached: the monks meeting in the forest.

'Dhattaraṭṭha from the Eastern direction, Viruḷha from the South,
Virupakkha from the West, Kuvera from the West:
These Four Great Kings, on all sides, in the four directions,
Stand, shining brilliantly, at Kapillavatthu, in the forest.
. . . .
'Those who forcibly alight on nāga kings,
Heavenly, twice-born, winged, with eyesight pure:
Garudas have come from the sky, to the middle of the forest,
Citra and Supaṇṇa their names.

'But the Buddha has made the Nāga kings without fear,
Made them safe from Supaṇṇa.
They speak to one another, with friendly words:
Nāgas and the supaṇṇas have taken refuge in the Buddha.
. . . .
'And when all these had arrived, with sense-sphere gods and Brahmās,
Māra came too. Now look at the Black One's foolishness, [saying]
"Bind them! Seize them! Tie them down with passion!
Encircle them on every side! Don't let anyone escape at all!"
Thus the war-monger incited the black army.
And he banged his fist right on the ground, making a terrible din,
[262] As when a storm-cloud bursts with thunder, lightning and heavy rain –
And then he retreated, angry, but without exerting power.'

Recognising all of this, The One with Vision, the Teacher, wished to call his monks, Delighting in the teaching, and addressed them:

'The armies of Māra have arrived. Be aware of this, monks!'
And they, exerting great effort, heard the teaching of the Buddha.
'The army left those who had no passion
And on whom no hair of their body had stirred.
Having all won the battle, with fear now in the past, of shining renown,
Along with all the spirits, and all the people, they rejoice!'

THE *ABHIDHAMMA*: HOW DO YOU DESCRIBE THE HUMAN MIND?

'This mind, monks, is radiant, but is defiled by impurities which come as visitors from outside.[33] But people who have not heard the teaching, ordinary people, do not understand how this is. Therefore, I say that for people who have not heard the teaching, the ordinary people, there is no development of the mind. This mind, monks, is radiant, but is freed from impurities which come as visitors from outside. The noble disciple, who has heard much, knows this as it actually is. Therefore, I say that for the noble disciple, who has heard much, there is development of the mind.'

(A I 10)

There has been a fruitful dialogue in non-Buddhist countries on the nature of mindfulness and in the use of techniques associated with its development. One area that has received less attention, however, is Buddhism's subtle and flexible system of human psychology, articulated through a genre found throughout Buddhism, the *Abhidhamma*. One of the three 'baskets' that also include *suttas* and the monastic rules, the system is regarded as the highest form of Buddhist teaching, indicated by the prefix 'higher' (*abhi*). According to the commentarial tradition, the Buddha's mother after death was reborn in the serenely happy *Tusita* realm, a sense-sphere heaven. After the awakening the Buddha taught her the full seven books of the *Abhidhamma* in the Heaven of the Thirty-Three Gods, the gods' meeting place, which he is described as ascending to on a jewelled ladder from the realm, one of the most popular depictions in Southeast Asian and South Asian temple art.[34] Based on the *mātikā*, the short lists formed during or shortly after the Buddha's lifetime, it is considered a slightly later formulation of doctrine, but has historically constituted a central part of most forms of Buddhism, and is still regarded as a living tradition within many. In this chapter we explore this means of understanding the human mind, found in a complete form only in the Pāli texts.

The *Abhidhamma* is a descriptive and psychological aid for examining consciousness in both daily life and the various stages of meditation.[35] It needs hard work to learn all the lists involved in describing its permutations of mental states (*cetasikas*) in consciousness and the mind or heart (*citta*), but the theory is central to understanding Southern Buddhism's highly sophisticated delineation of mental states and their possibilities. The system was adapted in various ways as Buddhism spread and evolved. According to the *Abhidhamma*, our mind is experiencing manifold thought-processes that arise in momentary form, in succession, and in these it is all the time interacting with *rūpa*, form, the matter that makes up our body and objects in the outside world. So the road (*vitthi*) of consciousness as it perceives, takes in and responds to objects in the world and in the mind is seen as involving a fluid, moving stream, with patterns like waves or undercurrents providing continuity from one moment to the next and one lifetime to the next. In Southern Buddhism, *Abhidhamma* is regarded as the most sophisticated means of understanding the fluidity and complexity of human experience, and of seeing 'non-self' (*anattā*). In its emphasis on movement through various mental states, and entry in and out of meditation, its methods ensure that no aspect of the mind or matter can be 'grasped' or made rigid. It does not, however, undermine a sense of continuity between one self and the next, and one moment and the next. The system has been particularly valued in Burma (Myanmar), where it is a living tradition used as subject for debate, a means of providing topics for meditation practice, and as a way of learning about the teaching. In Thailand it is also popular: the many regular classes on the subject in Wat Mahathat, Bangkok, for instance, are packed with monks, nuns, laymen and laywomen. The method taught by Nina van Gorkem, in which *Abhidhamma* is used as a means of arousing mindfulness and wisdom in daily life, has also been popular not only in Thailand but in other centres around the world: *Abhidhamma* is a way of understanding 'everything which is real'. She writes:

> As regards the *Abhidhamma*, this is an exposition of all realities in detail ... the form of this part of the *Tipiṭaka* [three baskets of teachings] is quite different, but its aim is the same: the eradication of wrong view and eventually of all defilements. Thus, when we study the many enumerations of realities, we should not forget the real purpose of the study. The theory (*pariyatti*) should encourage us to practise (*paṭipatta*), which is necessary for the realization of truth (*paṭivedha*). While we are studying the different *nāmas* [mind and mental states] and *rūpas* [forms] and while we are pondering over them, we can be reminded to be aware of *nāma* and *rūpa* appearing at that moment. In this way we will discover more and more that the *Abhidhamma* is about everything which is real, that is, the worlds appearing through the six doors.
>
> (Gorkem 1975: viii)

The theory underlying this offers a simple premise concerning the nature of consciousness. This is not the indisputable latent tendency of the mind to foster the three roots, of greed, hatred and ignorance, but an inherent radiance or luminosity, accessible sometimes in active consciousness (*kamma*) in life and meditation, and also in passive form (*vipāka*) when in deepest sleep. Skilful, or healthy and good *citta*, is found in passive form in most humans, as a kind of birthright, and is associated with skilful roots that also form the basis of a human birth: generosity, loving-kindness and, sometimes, wisdom. Actively cultivated in waking life, it brings into being (*bhāveti*) and fosters the eightfold path.

Skilful (*kusala*) consciousness forms, according to the *Abhidhamma*, the underlying basis or the continuum (*bhavaṅga*) of the mind, as the restorative state to which consciousness usually returns in deep sleep.According to the technicalities of the thought process, it also occurs just for a couple of moments at the end of each process of relating to any object of the senses of the mind, an after-image of the moment of skilful consciousness that is said to have arisen at our death in the lifetime before. It is not a substantial entity, and does not have kammic effect for the future, as it is result (*vipāka*), but it provides continuity for the being throughout this lifetime, until at the moment of death a new *bhavaṅga* emerges, which forms a continued basis for the next lifetime. It is as if, after apprehending any object, our minds momentarily return to be 'washed' at their base before returning to the next object received, investigated and acted upon by renewed consciousness. For us to be reborn as humans, and indeed to be considering the material in this book, involved as it is with investigation of the human condition and its meditative possibilities, we are likely, according to Southern Buddhism, to be the recipients of great good *kamma* coming from our last lifetime. Most humans, at the last active moment of their preceding death, had what is known as a relinking consciousness (*patisandhi-citta*) that took as its object a skilful or beautiful object: a thought of loving-kindness, or a sense of release (*cāga*), or of equanimity. Such a moment then forms the *vipāka-citta*, the resultant state, that provides the basis of the being that takes conception immediately afterwards and that is the natural state of mind to which we are said by the tradition to return when in dreamless sleep, or, for a few moments, between the apprehending of any object at the sense-doors. When people are dying in Southern Buddhist regions, monks may come and chant, and their friends and family remind them of good things they have done, such as making generous donations to the temple, so that there is a greater chance of a sense of willing release at the moment of death, and thus a happy rebirth in the next life.

This is an important teaching: many cultures in our increasingly global civilization have been deeply influenced, perhaps at a popular level with only a partial understanding, by psychological or religious theories that draw attention to the 'unskilful roots' of greed, hatred and ignorance, which clearly play a large part in our daily lives and fundamental make-up. The Buddhist path of practice is concerned not just with eliminating and understanding the unskilful, important though that is, but with encouraging and nurturing the healthy and restorative properties of the human mind too.

The following extract is part of a list describing the skilful mind (*kusala citta*) that opens the first of the seven books of *Abhidhamma*, the *Dhammasaṅgaṇī*, giving the mental states (*cetasikā*) present when the first skilful consciousness arises. It uses a characteristically *Abhidhamma* method. From ancient times a differentiation was made between the approaches of various types of texts. The *suttas* describe particular situations and discourses, and with heavy recourse to simile, metaphor and various kinds of analogies appropriate to the situation, describe stages of development and how certain qualities and meditations may be developed. So *suttas* start with the words 'At one time' or 'on one occasion' to denote a specific instance of the Buddha's teachings: their method is based on process, as demonstrated with the factors of awakening (this anthology, pp. 95–101). The *Abhidhamma*, however, by describing the mind in each moment, gives a universalized description with the process inferred through the succession of *cittas*. The words used in this *Abhidhamma* text are 'at that time': at any moment where skilful consciousness arises, particular factors are felt to be present. Again, because chanted and learnt through chant, many features derive from its orality, with repetitions, rhetorical questions and cues in the form of a familiar introduction to each mental state. So we can see this delineation from the *Dhammasaṅgani* as like a checklist of attributes to be found in the awake, skilful or what could be called the truly human mind, when acting in accordance with its full potential.

Although the *Abhidhamma* method takes each moment of consciousness as a discrete whole, it avoids reification by seeing each moment as working in constant 'thought-processes', which provide a moving picture of the movements of consciousness as it reaches out for, receives, examines and responds to objects of the senses (including the mind) before moving on to the next. So, if an object is perceived and desire or hatred arises, then the thought process will produce 'unskilful' *kamma*, bringing into play undercurrents of unskilfulness that may contribute to the volitional formations (*saṅkhāras*) at that time. If skilful, mindful consciousness arises, it will have good kammic effect, allowing the currents of volitional formations from earlier thought processes and lives to find an outlet and momentum. At the end of each succession of thought moments experiencing and reacting to any object, the mind returns to its natural, stable, but passive luminosity (*bhavaṅga*).

Such theory was deeply influential in the spread of Buddhism. Schools vary in their interpretation of the doctrine of an inherently luminous mind, but the idea that there is at any rate a predisposition to freedom from defilement characterizes most forms of Buddhist practice and may be seen implied in a number of doctrines, such as that of the *Tathāgatagarbha* notion, whereby the seeds of Buddha nature are attributed to all beings, or the idea of the *dharmadhātu*, the underlying basis from which consciousness arises. These doctrines, while radically different from Southern Buddhist positions in their analysis of the human mind, also suggest that the predisposition to defilement is superficial, or at any rate not the whole story. In many ways we might view one role of such doctrines as a kind of 'skill in means', a notion that itself helps to elicit particular qualities in the meditator, such as faith in the possibility of path, and that the individual has some chance of finding release from problems in daily life and practice. This is a position or a perspective on the mind that becomes present, realized or possible in meditation. This teaching is articulated in the text quoted at the opening of this chapter by the idea that the mind has defilements like 'visitors' from outside. The notion is further reinforced by the images of the craftsman smelting gold, for instance, that describe the mind purified of defilements (see S V 92). Whatever the 'truth' of this assertion about the mind, its effect is important: doctrines such as dependent origination (see this anthology, pp. 109–13), taught where there is an underlying acceptance of an inherent luminosity or brightness in the mind, do not arouse fear or guilt, a feature worth remembering when the doctrine is taught in the West.

This is technical material, and it is not the place here to discuss the whole system. In this extract the contents or mental factors (*cetasikas*) of the skilful *citta* are simply listed as they are given. There are eight types of skilful consciousness, some without the root of wisdom, some spontaneous, and some without 'spontaneity', that are instigated. Some have a basis in joy, others in equanimity. One of the eight is thought to form the underlying continuum of most human beings. One important point about the list here is its applicability at all stages of practice. From the *Abhidhamma* point of view, factors of the eightfold path are present in any moment of skilful consciousness, suggesting that the attainment of the path is a completion of an ongoing process rather than a 'goal'. This 'consciousness', or state of mind, can be present in many activities in daily life, so that at any time, when, say, someone acts self-lessly, for some moments there will be right action, right mindfulness, and right concentration: some, though not all, of the path factors come into play whenever the mind is clear, in meditation and when investigating the mind with loving-kindness. The factors here are exactly the same as in the *citta* that forms the basis for the first *jhāna*: this is described as an intensification of factors that can arise in sense-sphere interactions, but which, intensified, form the basis of meditative states too.

So if the mind experiences peacefulness, a sense of spaciousness, and a letting go of 'I' making for a while, seeing a magnificent mountain view, for instance, or in helping someone in trouble, skilful consciousness might arise. In meditation, this consciousness is brought to bear on the single object that forms the basis of the meditation, and that allows the mind to be transformed. In the fourth *jhāna*, joy or happiness is transcended, leaving a deep equanimity; so the consciousness is described in the same way as the skilful consciousness with equanimity. In meditation, the consciousness becomes more powerful, but is based on the consciousness that is there in daily life when skilfulness is present. Similarly at the moment of one of the stages of awakening, or liberation, all eight path factors come into being, which they cannot do before then: at that moment, in the presence of all path factors, completely developed, the mind is freed from defilements and the path becomes realized. The path is said to become a tenfold path, with two new factors: that of 'I shall come to know the unknown' (*anaññātaññassāmītindriyam*) comes in at the moment of stream-entry, with the eradication of doubt, and some defilements; at the second stage of awakening, when the first two hindrances have been greatly diminished, the factor of 'the knowledge that has been made perfect (*aññindriya*)' completes the basis of path for the practitioner. It is as if the human mind, so predisposed to unskilfulness, also has at its disposal access to the path itself, perhaps only momentarily, but which the practice of *bhāvanā* can develop and deepen until the goal is finally obtained.

Some features in the description appear several times, suggesting the conflation of a number of lists. The 'six pairs', for instance, are always present together in the mind and body in skilful consciousness in the sense-sphere: they can be understood as the experience of the physical body when skilful states are present.[36] Like other factors of the first skilful state of mind (*citta*), they are also found in the first *jhāna*.[37] Whether in daily life or in meditation, this state of mind is also always characterized by one of the divine abidings (31–3), of loving-kindness, compassion or sympathetic joy, which can be present in daily life or as aspects of *jhāna*.[38] If the fourth divine abiding, equanimity, is present, as consciousness may be skilful with neutral feeling, the factors of joy and pleasant feeling do not occur at that time: this can arise in daily life, but is described in exactly the same terms for the fourth *jhāna*, accompanied by equanimity, with the transcending of joy and happiness, and the formless realms.

The way factors like 'concentration' appear in many lists, such a common feature of oral literatures where there are no index systems or books to browse through, can be understood by the very precise and helpful analogy of the way we look things up on the internet now, which has evolved to follow a pattern oddly akin to early oral systems. If you want to look up something – say, 'concentration' – you would go to a *dhamma* website. You would look up the word, perhaps highlighted in blue, and find that it occurs within a manifold variety of lists: the path factors, the five faculties, the five powers, the seven universal *cittas* in the Pāli *Abhidhamma*. You can look up any of these lists and find it with or through this factor. In each list it may perform a slightly different role – but concentration is often the last, a key point in Buddhist lists, where an underlying sense of sequentiality lends the final feature a sense of pre-eminence: so it is the last in the path factors, the last of the five faculties and the last of the five powers. An example can be taken in this list, which says:

What at that time is unification of mind?
Whatever at that time is a resting place of the mind (*ṭhiti*), the abiding together of the mind (*saṇṭhiti*), the equilibrium (*avaṭṭhiti*), the composure (*avikkhepa*), the mind without peturbation (*avisāhaṭamānasatā*), the calm (*samatha*), the faculty of concentration, the power of concentration, right concentration – this, at that time, is unification of the mind (DhS 11).

Here concentration is described briefly, linked, however, to its purpose in calm meditation, then to its place in the list of faculties, powers and the eight path factors. It might seem formulaic, or even cold on the printed page: but each word would have great meaning to the one who hears and the one who chants such a list. Rupert Gethin writes:

To take but one example, 'faculty of concentration' (*samādhindriya*) may sound rather uninteresting and dry, but for the ancient monk – and his modern descendent – the faculty of concentration means the four meditations, and the four meditations mean four vivid and, in the right context, beautiful, and moving similes. And according to the *Dhammasaṅgani*, the seeds of these calm and comforting states of meditation are present in every moment of wholesome consciousness. Thus at this level, the mindful recitation of a text such as the *Dhammasaṅgani* acts as a series of 'reminders' of the Buddha's teaching and how it is applied in the *sutta*. The recitation operates as a kind of recollection of Dhamma (*dhammānussati*), a traditional subject of meditation. The lengthy repetitions themselves contribute to the majesty of the performance; the sheer vastness of the full recitation itself is awe-inspiring. Hearing it, one is in the very presence of the Dhamma that is 'profound, hard to see, hard to know, peaceful, subtle, outside the sphere of discursive thought, skilful, to be known by the wise' (Gethin 1992: 166).

The similes described can be found in this anthology (pp. 37–9).

One additional point is that the *Abhidhamma* classification defines the three skilful roots through a negative: as non-greed, or generosity and non-hatred, or loving kindness, non-delusion, or wisdom. These are the underlying roots of the skilful *citta*, and, as often is the case in Indic languages, the 'a', meaning 'not', suggests not just absence, but also presence: of something more than the negative of what is denoted. The doctrine of *anattā*, non-self, for instance, does not mean the absence of self, but a kind of selflessness. The doctrine of *ahiṃsa*, or non-harm, so popular in Indic religions, denotes not just an abstention, but an active force for good. So absence of hatred in *Abhidhamma* means loving-kindness. The same applies for the absence, or relief from, greed, associated with generosity. *Amoha*, or the absence of delusion, counters ignorance, and, as the list below demonstrates, is equated with insight (*vipassanā*), wisdom (*paññā*) and the first path factor, right view.

1. What are the states (*dhammā*) that are skilful?
At whatever time the sense-sphere mind (*citta*) has arisen, associated with pleasant feeling, and connected with knowledge, with an object that is visual form (*rūpa*) or sight, or smell, or taste or bodily contact, or an event (*dhamma*), on that occasion there is:
Contact, feeling, identification, volition, mind;
Thinking of, examining, joy, happiness, unification of mind;
The faculty of faith, the faculty of vigour, the faculty of mindfulness, the faculty of concentration, the faculty of wisdom and the faculty of mind, the faculty of pleasant feeling, the faculty of life;
Right view, right intention, right effort, right mindfulness, right concentration;
The power of faith, the power of vigour, the power of mindfulness, the power of concentration, the power of wisdom, the power of self-respect, the power of regard for consequences;
The absence of greed [generosity], the absence of hatred [loving-kindness], the absence of confusion [wisdom];
The absence of longing [generosity] and the absence of malevolence [loving-kindness];
Self-respect and regard for consequences;
Tranquillity of body, tranquillity of mind;

lightness of body, lightness of mind;
softness of body, softness of mind; pliable, flexible
manageability of body, manageability of mind;
healthiness of body, healthiness of mind;
straightness of body, straightness of mind;
Mindfulness, clear comprehension, calm (*samatha*), insight (*vipassanā*), grasp (*paggāha*), balance; whatever other non-material things at that time arise in dependence: these are the things that are skilful.

2. What, at that time, is contact (*phassa*)? Whatever at that time is the contact that is the touch, the touching, the state of having been brought in touch with: that, at that time, is contact.

3. What at that time is feeling (*vedanā*)?
Whatever at that time is the mental factor (*cetasika*) of pleasure, the mental factor of happiness, founded on the mind door element, born of contact, that is, the mind born of this contact, experiencing happiness, and the pleasant mind born of this contact, the feeling of happiness: this, at that time, is feeling.
(also for happiness (10) and the faculty of pleasant feeling (*somanassindriya*, 18)

4. What at that time is identification (*saññā*)?
Whatever at that time is the identification, the knowing and the fact of knowing, founded on the mind-door element, born of contact: this, at that time, is identification.

5. What at that time is volition (*cetanā*)?
Whatever at that time is the volition, the will, and the state of there being volition, founded on the mind-door element, born of contact: this, at that time, is volition.

6. What at that time is consciousness (*citta*)?
Whatever at that time is the consciousness, the mind, the state of mind, the heart, that which is clear, the mind, the mind sphere, the mind faculty, consciousness (*viññāṇa*), the aggregate of consciousness: this, at that time, is consciousness.
Also for the faculty of mind (*manindriya* 17)

7. What at that time is 'thinking of' (*vitakka*)?

Whatever, at that time, is the thinking, the thinking of, the intention, the taking up of an object, the applying of the mind, right intention: this, at that time, is 'thinking of'.

Also for right intention (*sammāsaṅkappa* 21).

8. What at that time is 'examining' (*vicāra*)?

Whatever, at that time, is the considering, the examining, the repeated examining, the close examining, the continual attentiveness of the mind: this, at that time, is examining.

9. What at that time is joy?

Whatever, at that time, is the joy, the gladness, the delight, the rejoicing, the merriment, the smiling merriment, the felicity, the exultation, the pleasedness of the mind: this, at that time, is joy.

10. What at that time is happiness?

The same as for feeling (2).

11. What at that time is unification of mind?

Whatever at that time is the resting place of the mind, the abiding together of the mind, the steadiness of the mind, the equilibrium, the balance,[39] the mind without perturbation, the calm, the faculty of concentration, the power of concentration, right concentration: this, at that time, is unification of mind.

Also for the faculty of concentration (15), right concentration (24), the power of concentration (28), calm (54) and balance (57).

12. What, at that time, is the faculty of faith?

What at that time is the faith, the trust, the steady assurance, confidence, the faith, the faculty of faith, the power of faith – this, at that time, is the faculty of faith.[40] Also for the power of faith (25).

13. What at that time is the faculty of vigour?

Whatever at that time is the mental factor of the arousing of vigour, the leaving behind (*nikkama*),[41] the exertion, the endeavour, the effort, the daring, the courage,[42] the stamina,[43] the steadfastness (PED 177), the unfaltering exertion, the sustained willingness, the unflinching endurance, and the taking of responsibility (*dhurasampaggaha*), the vigour, the faculty of vigour, the power of vigour, right effort: this, at that time, is the faculty of vigour.

Also for right effort (22), the power of vigour (26) and grasp (56).
14. What at that time is the faculty of mindfulness?
The mindfulness which at that time is a recollection (*anussati*),[44] a bringing back to mind; the mindfulness that is remembering, holding steady in the mind (*dhāraṇatā*), of not drifting away (*apilāpanatā*),[45] a not being bewildered (*asammussanatā*), the mindfulness that is the faculty of mindfulness, the power of mindfulness and right mindfulness: this, at that time, is the faculty of mindfulness.[46]
Also for right mindfulness (23), the power of mindfulness (27), and mindfulness (52).
15. What at that time is the faculty of concentration?
The same as for unification of mind (11), right concentration (24), the power of concentration (28), calm (54) and balance (57).
16. What at that time is the faculty of wisdom?
Whatever at that time is the wisdom, the discernment (*pajānanā*), the investigation, the search, the investigation of the teaching (*dhammavicaya*), the testing, the discrimination, the differentiation, the intelligence, the proficiency, the skill, the thinking over, the act of thinking, the examination, the understanding, the sagacity, the advising, the insight, the clear comprehension, the goad, wisdom, the faculty of wisdom, the power of wisdom, the sword of wisdom, the stronghold of wisdom, the light of wisdom, shining wisdom, the lamp of wisdom, the jewel of wisdom, the absence of confusion, investigation of the teaching, right view: this, at that time, is the faculty of wisdom.
Also for right view (20 and 37), the power of wisdom (29), the absence of confusion (34), clear comprehension (53), insight (55).
17. What at that time is faculty of mind?
The same as for consciousness (6).
18. What, at that time, is the faculty of pleasant feeling?
The same as for feeling (3) and happiness (10).
19. What, at that time, is the faculty of life?
Whatever, at that time, is the vitality of these non-material states, their continuity, their going on, their progress, their upkeep, their guarding, their life and their faculty of life: this, at that time, is the faculty of life.

20. What, at that time, is right view?
The same as for the faculty of wisdom (16), right view (37), the power of wisdom (29), the absence of confusion (34), clear comprehension (53), insight (55).
21. What, at that time, is right intention?
Whatever, at that time, is the thinking, the thinking of, the intention, the taking up of an object, the applying of the mind, right intention: this, at that time, is right intention.
The same as for 'thinking of' (7).
22. What, at that time, is right effort?
The same as for the faculty of vigour (13), the power of vigour (26), and grasp (56).
23. What, at that time, is right mindfulness?
The same as for the faculty of mindfulness (14), the power of mindfulness (27), and mindfulness (52).
24. What, at that time, is right concentration?
The same as for unification of mind (11), right concentration (24), the power of concentration (28), calm (54) and balance (57).
25. What at that time is the power of faith?
The same as for the faculty of faith (12).
26. What at that time is the power of vigour?
The same as for the faculty of vigour (13), right effort (22), and grasp (56).
27. What at that time is the power of mindfulness?
The same as for the faculty of mindfulness (14), right mindfulness (23), and mindfulness (52).
28. What at that time is the power of concentration?
The same as for unification of mind (11), the faculty of concentration (15), right concentration (24), calm (54), and balance (57).
29. What at that time is the power of wisdom?
The same as for the faculty of wisdom (16), right view (20 and 37), the absence of confusion (34), clear comprehension (53), insight (55).
30. What at that time is the power of self-respect?
Whatever at that time is the self-respect, felt at the time when there

should be self-respect, the scruple at attaining to bad and destructive states, this, at that time, is the power of self respect.
Also for self-respect (38).
31. What at that time is the power of scrupulousness?
Whatever the sense of scrupulousness at the time when there should be a sense of scrupulousness, a sense of scrupulousness in attaining to bad and destructive states, this at that time is the power of scrupulousness.
Also for scrupulousness (39).
32. What at that time is the absence of greed?
Whatever, at that time, is the absence of greed, of being greedy, of greediness, the absence of infatuation, the feeling and being infatuated, the absence of longing, the absence of greed, the skilful root: this at that time is the absence of greed.
Also for absence of longing (35).
33. What at that time is absence of hatred?
The absence of hate, hating, of hatred, the absence of malevolence, the relief from spleen, the skilful, healthy root: this at that time is the absence of hate.
Also for absence of malevolence (36).
34. What at that time is the absence of confusion?
The same as for the faculty of wisdom (16), right view (20 and 37), the power of wisdom (29), clear comprehension (53), insight (55).
35. What at that time is the absence of longing (*anabhijjhā*)?
The same as for the absence of greed (32).
36. What at that time is the absence of malevolence (*avyāpāda*)?
The same as for the absence of hatred (33).
37. What at that time is right view?
The same as for the faculty of wisdom (16), right view (20), the power of wisdom (29), the absence of confusion (34), clear comprehension (53), insight (55).
38. What at that time is self-respect?
The same as the power of self-respect (30).
39. What at that time is scrupulousness?

The same as the power of scrupulousness (31).

40. What at that time is tranquillity of body?

At that time the tranquillity, the full tranquillity, the composure and the collectedness of the aggregate of feeling, of the aggregate of identification and of the aggregate of formations – this, at that time, is tranquillity of body.

41. What at that time is tranquillity of mind? At that time the tranquillity, the full tranquillity, the composure and the collectedness of the aggregate of consciousness – this, at that time, is tranquillity of mind.

42. What at that time is lightness of body? At that time the lightness of body which is there on that occasion, the lightness in changing state, the absence of sluggishness, or inertia of the aggregate of feeling, of the aggregate of identification and of the aggregate of formations – this, at that time, is lightness of body.

43. What at that time is lightness of mind? At that time the lightness which is there on that occasion, the lightness in changing state, the absence of sluggishness, or inertia of the aggregate of consciousness – this, at that time, is lightness of mind.

44. What at that time is softness of body? At that time the softness, the gentleness, the absence of harshness or stiffness of the aggregate of feeling, of the aggregate of identification and of the aggregate of formations– this, at that time, is softness of body.

45. What at that time is softness of mind? At that time the softness, the gentleness, the absence of harshness or stiffness of the aggregate of consciousness – this, at that time, is softness of mind.

46. What at that time is manageability of body? At that time the manageability, the manageability for use, the state of being manageable of the aggregate of feeling, of the aggregate of identification and of the aggregate of formations – this, at that time, is manageability of body.

47. What at that time is manageability of mind?

At that time the manageability, the manageability for use, the state of being manageable of the aggregate of consciousness – this, at that time, is manageability of mind.

48. What at that time is proficiency of body?
At that time the proficiency, the healthiness, the proficient state of the aggregate of feeling, of the aggregate of identification and of the aggregate of formations – this, at that time, is proficiency of body.
49. What at that time is proficiency of mind?
At that time the proficiency, the healthiness, the proficient state of the aggregate of consciousness – this, at that time, is proficiency of mind.
50. What at that time is straightness of body?
At that time the rightness, straightness, the absence of twistedness or crookedness or bentness in the aggregate of feeling, of the aggregate of identification and of the aggregate of formations – this, at that time, is straightness of body.
51. What at that time is straightness of mind?
At that time the rightness, straightness, the absence of twistedness or crookedness or bentness in the aggregate of consciousness – this, at that time, is straightness of mind.
52. What at that time is mindfulness?
The same as for the faculty of mindfulness (14), right mindfulness (23), the power of mindfulness (27), and mindfulness (52).
53. What at that time is clear comprehension?
The same as for the faculty of wisdom (16), right view (20 and 37), the power of wisdom (29), the absence of confusion (34), and insight (55).
54. What at that time is calm?
The same as for unification of mind (11), the faculty of concentration (15), right concentration (24), the power of concentration (28), and balance (57).
55. What at that time is insight?
The same as for the faculty of wisdom (16), right view (20 and 37), the power of wisdom (29), the absence of confusion (34), and clear comprehension (53).
56. What at that time is grasp (*paggāha*)?
The same as for the faculty of vigour (13), right effort (22), the power of vigour (26).

57. What at that time is balance?
The same as for unification of mind (11), the faculty of concentration (15), right concentration (24), the power of concentration (28), calm (54), and balance (57).

(PTS DhS 9–17)

CHAPTER FIVE

NARRATIVE AND MEDITATION

This chapter includes material from the later narrative traditions, which intersperse canonical verses with commentarial stories. In these tales, commonly told to laity and monks, meditative principles are described, evoked and embodied, through the experiences of different meditators and their sometimes long kammic histories.

JĀTAKA STORIES

Jātakas are literally 'birth-stories', about the quest of the Bodhisatta, the being bound to or attached to awakening, over the many lifetimes he prepares for Buddhahood. They are particularly popular in Asian Buddhism: according to the tradition, the historical Buddha Gotama made a vow many aeons ago, when there was another Buddha, Dipaṅkara, to defer his own awakening so that he can become a Buddha himself one day. To do this, he must cultivate ten qualities through many lifetimes: generosity, moral restraint, renunciation, wisdom, vigour, cheerful endurance, resolve, loving-kindness and equanimity, until they become 'perfections', resources enabling him to teach others in his final life. These may be cultivated by other practitioners too. Many forms of Buddhism employ *Jātaka* stories to communicate Buddhist teaching; the Pāli collection, of 547 tales, is our only complete extant one. Filled with references to *Abhidhamma* and other texts, it is throughout intertextual in its style, with some stories opening with a known 'present' situation in the lifetime of the Buddha, from another context, as he teaches his followers. Many stories refer to other stories in the collection, and verses are sometimes included from other works such as the *Dhammapada*, thus contributing to a sense of the various kinds of teaching as being connected and related to one another.

The stories are explicitly associated with the path to liberation. Described as a 'limb' of the teaching, and found in most forms of Buddhism, *Jātakas* are both descriptive of some meditative points, and are considered themselves an aid to meditation, as a means of arousing states associated with concentration and interest. At the culmination of *Jātakas*, practitioners are often described as hearing a talk on the four noble truths and then attaining enlightenment, suggesting that the other factors of the eightfold path, particularly *samādhi*, were in the early days of the tradition felt to be aroused through the act of listening with care and attentiveness to the story being told. Not a substitute for meditative practice, such listening to stories appears in some way to support it, by arousing interested attention and concentration (*samādhi*) that is sustained for some time, and so considered helpful in supporting the mindfulness practices to direct the mind towards liberation.[1] They would usually be heard in temples, probably on festive days. The collection has historically clearly been used and adapted in all sorts of ways, in art, temple murals, tableaux, sculptures, legal precedent, vernacular sayings, retellings in local vernacular languages, and in new forms such as poetry, drama and music. New Buddha images are welcomed into a temple with recountings of these stories of their past (Swearer 2004: 232). Calm and insight naturally complement each other throughout: insight, as so often in early Buddhist texts, is aroused in this case by the very structure of tales where identities, species and relationships reform and regroup for each being, enacting the fluid sense of self that has to pertain where beings are reborn in many lives in so many conditions and in different situations. Through the interest of stories of animal and human rebirths, transformed for each lifetime, the tale also introduces calm, in a sustaining of an interest unified by the Bodhisatta vow and the narrative perspective of kammic consequences and principles enacted over lifetimes. *Jātakas* provide a world-view where conscious change is taught not only as achievable, but inspiring too.

Crucially, *Jātakas* are usually set at the time when there is no Buddha or Buddhist teaching. They start with a story in the 'present', the moment when the fully awakened historical Buddha, Gotama, is teaching, and where awakening from the guidance of a teacher is possible. He decides to tell a story that reflects a situation that may be operating in his 'present' teaching career. The story itself, however, takes place 'in the past', the oceanic extents of time in *saṃsāra*, skilfully evoked by the *Jātaka* array of non-sequential births, usually when there is no fully awakened Buddha teaching. Fully awakened Buddhas come and go throughout the history of the world and world systems, but *Jātakas* are usually set at times where there is none, and a sense of the absence of a teaching figure and his path is essential for their dramatic momentum: however fortunate the circumstances of a tale, and many describe great wealth, wonders and marvels, there are limited chances for complete release from suffering. It is, however, during such periods, from the Buddhist point of view a dark background to the action, that the being destined to become a Buddha, the Bodhisatta, can emerge as the hero, who has to live and act within these worlds to develop the ten perfections.

As with most long heroic endeavours, the pursuit itself is solitary, but friends and companions are needed. *Jātakas* describe the Bodhisatta and, crucially, those who become his followers and teachers of the path too, the arahats in earlier lives, in many rebirths and settings, as animals, humans of many castes and conditions, and gods. Each rebirth is a new situation for them, and they often encounter problems, whether of serious or comic nature, or both, without the orientation of a full Buddhist teaching. So these stories resonate with our, and presumably with that of earlier meditators' unenlightened experience of their, 'present', where each situation is new and for the most part unguided and unknown. It is the test of the characters in the story that what each does, shapes his or her own kamma and destiny.

The following story describes the Bodhisatta as a peacock, reborn in that form for reasons described in the tale. Full sitting meditation is not practised by animals in *Jātakas*, and according to *Abhidhamma* teaching they cannot attain *jhāna*. This limitation is scrupulously observed in the *Jātaka* collection, but animals keep the *uposatha* and behave well, and so gain merit, whereby they can attain a higher rebirth.[2] They also talk, and this peacock can teach and debate with kings. The story also assumes an understanding that there have been many Buddhas in the past before the historical Buddha, Gotama.

Although there may not be a Buddha at the time of the story, the peacock can recollect past Buddhas, and pay homage to them, a practice that constitutes one of Buddhaghosa's forty meditation objects (see this anthology, pp. 21–2). The verses in this story are still popular, and are traditionally chanted as a protection against any form of entrapment.[3]

The Peacock Story
Mora-Jātaka (J 159)

The story from the present

'He rises, the all seeing!' The Teacher told this story while staying in the Jeta Grove about a monk who was filled with yearning. This monk was brought by some others to the Teacher, who asked him, 'Is it true, what they say, that you are filled with yearning?' 'It is true, friend.' 'What have you seen?' he asked. 'I was looking at a woman beautifully adorned,' he said. 'Monk, it is no wonder that women disturb your mind. Even ancient wise teachers of old, who had not been plagued by the defilements for seven hundred years, on hearing the voice of a woman have become assailed in one moment. Even the pure become stained. Even those of the highest honour go to disgrace – how much more the impure!'

And he told this story of long ago.

The story from the past

Once long ago, when Brahmadatta was king of Varanasi, the Bodhisatta took rebirth as a peacock. The shell of the egg that enclosed him was as yellow as the karnikara flower and when he broke the shell he emerged the colour of gold, and was beautiful and lovely, with a shining streak of red between the wings.[4] In order to preserve his life he passed over three ranges of mountains, and made his nesting place in the fourth, on a golden hilltop plateau in Daṇḍaka. When the night started to lighten, he sat on the hill, and watched the sun rising. In order to protect and defend his feeding grounds he composed a divine mantra, beginning 'He rises.. .' and chanted:

1. 'He rises, the all-seeing sole king,
Illuminating the earth with his golden light.
I pay homage to you, the one who illuminates the earth with golden light.
And today may I live protected throughout the day!'

Paying homage to the sun in this way with this verse, the Bodhisatta then paid homage with a second verse, to the wonderful qualities of the Buddhas who have attained nibbāna in times past:

2. 'Whatever wise men, those who have attained the highest knowledge, wise in all *dhammas*,
I pay homage to you, and may they protect me.
Homage to the Buddhas, and homage to awakening,
Homage to those that are free, and homage to freedom!'

Chanting this protection, the peacock went about his searchings.[5]
Flying around in this way in the daytime, he used to come back in the evening and sit on the hilltop and watch the sun setting. Then, as he reflected upon the wonderful qualities of the Buddhas, in order to protect and defend the place where he stayed at night he composed another divine mantra, beginning with the words, 'there he sets . . .' and he chanted:

3. 'And there he sets, the all-seeing sole king,
Illuminating the earth with his golden light.
I pay homage to you, the one who illuminates the earth with golden light.
And today may I live protected throughout the night!

4. 'Whatever wise men, those who have attained the highest knowledge, wise in all kinds of ways,
I pay homage to you, and may they protect me.
Homage to the Buddhas, and homage to awakening,
Homage to those that are free, and homage to freedom!'

Chanting this protection, the peacock went about his sleeping.

Now a certain hunter who lived in a village not far away was wandering in the Himalayan regions, saw the Bodhisatta sitting on the top of the golden plateau in Daṇḍaka, and told his son about him. Then one day, the king of Varanasi's queen, called Khemā, had a dream about a golden peacock teaching the *dhamma* and informed the king, 'I long to hear a golden peacock teaching the *dhamma*.' The king consulted his ministers. The ministers said, 'The priests will know about this'. The priests said, 'Yes, there are golden peacocks'. 'Where are they?' he asked. 'The hunters will know,' they said. The king asked the hunters to meet together. And one hunter said, 'Yes, great king, there is a golden hill in Daṇḍaka and there a golden coloured peacock lives'. 'Then please trap the peacock without killing him and bring him here,' he said. The hunter went and set traps around the peacock's feeding grounds. But even when the peacock stepped on it, the trap would not close. The hunter was unable to trap him even though he tried for seven years, and there he died.

And the queen Khemā, not obtaining her wish, also died. The king, thinking that his queen had died because of the peacock, was angry. He had these words inscribed on a golden plate:

> In the Himalayan regions there is a golden hill in Daṇḍaka.
> There lives a golden-coloured peacock.
> Whoever eats his flesh becomes ageless and immortal.

And he had the plate placed in a state casket. When he died, another king took over the kingdom and having read out the inscription said, 'I will be ageless and immortal!' and sent for a hunter. But he could not catch the Bodhisatta and died there. And it happened in this way for six kings in turn.

Then the seventh king took up the kingdom, and he also sent out a hunter. He went there and realised that the trap did not close when the peacock stepped on it, as he uttered a chant before going to his feeding places. So he crossed into a neighbouring territory and caught a peahen, which he trained to dance when he clapped his hands and to make her call at the snap of his fingers. Then, early in the morning, before the peacock had uttered his chant, he set the trap, and fixed the snares, and got the peahen to make her call. Hearing the sound of the female sex, the peacock became sick with the defilements and could not say his chant, and so fell into the trap.

Then the hunter took him to the king of Varanasi. The king saw his beautiful appearance and was delighted and had a seat set for him. Sitting on the seat prepared for him, the peacock asked him, 'Great king, why have you had me caught?' 'They say that those who eat your flesh will be ageless and immortal: so I, wishing to be ageless and immortal, had you caught,' he replied. 'So those that eat my flesh may become ageless and immortal – but I will die.' 'Yes, you will die.' 'But by my dying how exactly will those who eat my flesh become immortal?' 'You are golden in colour, and because of this they say that those who eat your flesh will become ageless and immortal.' 'Great king, I was not born with a golden colour without a reason. For formerly I was a universal monarch in this very city and I kept the five precepts closely, and ensured that all that lived there did so too. When I died I was born in the Heaven of the Thirty-Three Gods and lived out my span of life, and when I fell away from there, because of some unskilfulness I took rebirth as a peacock. But because of my earlier *sīla* I was born a golden colour.'

'Right – so you were a universal monarch and kept the precepts and were born golden as the result of keeping the precepts! How are we to believe this as there is no witness?' 'Oh yes there is, great king.' 'Who is that?' 'Sire, when I was a universal monarch I used to fly through the air on a jewelled carriage. This carriage is now buried in the earth under the auspicious lotus pond. Dig it up from underneath the lake, and that will be my witness.' The king agreed to this, and had the water brought up from the pond and had the carriage dug up: then he believed him.

The Bodhisatta said, 'Except for the deathless, magnificent *nibbāna*, all compounded things, without exception, are not lasting, impermanent and subject to decay.' And so he taught the king the *dhamma* and established him in the five precepts. The king was filled with faith and paid homage to the Bodhisatta, and accorded him the greatest honour by giving the kingdom to him. But the peacock gave the kingdom back to the king, and after staying a few days, gave him this advice: 'Be vigilant, great king.' And then he flew up into the air and went back to the golden hill in Daṇḍaka. The king stood firm in the Bodhisatta's advice, and did good things, like practising generosity and such like, and then passed away in accordance with his deeds.

The Teacher gave this teaching on *dhamma* and then explained the four noble truths, and identified the birth – for at the conclusion of the teaching the yearning monk attained arahatship. 'At that time Ānanda was the king, and I the golden peacock.' (Ja II 33–8)

Lucky's story
Lakkhaṇa-Jātaka (J 11).

In the following story the Bodhisatta is a deer, a rebirth often associated in these tales with his perfection of loving-kindness. His cousin, Devadatta, who opposes him in his final life, causing a schism in the monastic orders with a breakaway group, features as the careless deer; Sāriputta, his disciple, is the lucky one. The Bodhisatta's wife, Yasodharā (Rāhulamātā), who supports his quest throughout the *Jātakas*, is his spouse. The story opens at the time of the schism, and the Buddha remembers how in the past Devadatta and Sāriputta had shown their different dispositions.

Once upon a time in the kingdom of Magadha, a Magadhan king ruled in the city of Rājagaha. At that time the Bodhisatta took rebirth as a stag, and when he grew up he lived in the forest with a retinue of a thousand deer. He had two sons, called Lakkhaṇa (lucky) and Kāla (unlucky). When he grew old, he handed over authority to his sons, placing five hundred deer in the care of each. From that time the two young stags were in charge of the herd.

In Magadha, at harvest-time, it is dangerous for deer in the thick corn-fields. People hunt creatures who eat crops, and set traps and snares and stakes. Many deer are killed. So, when the Bodhisatta saw that it was harvest-time, he summoned his sons, and said: 'Sons, it's harvest-time. Many deer are killed now. We oldies will manage by staying in one spot. But you should retire with your herds to the foot-hills in the forest, and return when the crops are harvested.' The sons listened to their father and agreed, and departed with their herds.

But people on the route know the time when deer take to the hills. So they lie in wait in hiding-places here and there on the road, and shoot and kill many of them. The foolish Kāla, not knowing the times to travel and when to hold back, set off in the morning and evening, at dawn and at twilight, going close by to the villages. And people, both hidden and out in the open, destroyed many of his deer. So he, through his foolishness, brought about the destruction of all of these, and he reached the forest with only a few survivors. Lakkhaṇa, however, being wise, alert and resourceful, did know good times to travel, and when not to. He did not travel by day, at dawn or at twilight, and went nowhere near the villages. He only travelled with his half of the herd in deepest night, and so he entered the forest without losing a single deer.

They remained four months in the forest, not leaving the foothills until the crops were harvested. On the way home Kāla repeated his mistakes and so lost the rest of his herd, returning solitary, by himself, whereas Lakkhaṇa did not lose one of his herd, but brought back all five hundred deer, when he appeared before his parents. As he saw his two sons returning, the Bodhisatta, along with the herd, gave out this verse:

'The one who is good and lives and behaves with kindliness has his reward!

See Lakkhaṇa leading back his tribe and family, and see Kāla, deprived of his herd.'

In this way the Bodhisatta rejoiced in his son, and after living to a ripe old age, he went according to his *kamma.*

And then the Teacher explained: just as Sāriputta had a great retinue of relatives and sangha now, so formerly he had also shone; and just as Devadatta had lost his now, so in times past he was inferior too. He showed the connection between the two times, and identified the birth, saying, 'At that time Devadatta was Kāla, and his followers his deer. Sāriputta was Lakkhaṇa, and members of the Buddha's assembly were his deer. Rāhulamātā was the mother, and I was the father.' (Ja I 143–5)

The Bodhisatta is advised by a friend

In this story even the Bodhisatta, here a human, needs to be reminded of his goal, receiving teaching from an old friend, a *paccekabuddha*. In Pāli *Jātakas*, *paccekabuddhas*, sometimes known as silent or solitary Buddhas, feature as mysterious figures who demonstrate a kind of awakening, highly honoured in Southern Buddhist practice, for the one who spontaneously finds insight not through hearing the teaching of a Buddha, nor through finding the complete path that helps others, but through solitary practice, and, sometimes, a surprise event in the world that brings their personal path to fruition from their own knowledge. This kind of spontaneous awakening occurs in a number of *Jātakas*. Such figures do not have the resources to teach a full path of practice, though in *Jātakas* they frequently help others in various ways. Which of the three lineages or kinds of awakening, of *paccekabuddha*, arahat or Buddha, that one finally attains is considered a matter of personal choice.[6] A perhaps longstanding commitment to that path may be dependent on many lives of practice. Some from all three lineages are described as teaching others in early Buddhist texts. Arahats teach the path of the Buddha, and are often validated when they teach in front of the Buddha, by their use of creative similes that have not been used before. *Paccekabuddhas*, in many *Jātaka* stories, teach through riddles, eloquent silence, or actions that show the way for others. Sometimes, as is the case here, they simply teach from their own experience. Because *Jātakas* are set usually in the time when there is not a Buddhist path, *paccekabuddhas* then offer a genuine 'opening in the cave', to borrow the name of the one in this story, to other beings. They often get a bad press in some forms of Buddhism, where the ideal of the Bodhisatta/Bodhisattva is enjoined for everyone, but in Pāli tales they offer oblique and encouraging reminders of the possibility of freedom.

The perfection that the Bodhisatta is cultivating in this story is the third, *nekkhamma*. This is usually correctly translated as renunciation, and refers to the act of leaving the lay life for a life of meditation. It is also, however, explicitly associated with meditation itself, as in the *Paṭismabhidāmagga* passage in this anthology (p. 73).[7] As indicated earlier, only humans or higher rebirths such as gods practise 'renunciation' in *Jātakas*, reinforcing its translation as 'meditation'.

The story brings many elements in that would have contributed to an underlying appreciation of doctrine and practice amongst those that heard it. For instance, many early schools of Buddhism take the recollection of the foul as an object. It is, however, taught only under very careful conditions, to avoid unwholesome disturbance of the mind. The practice is given a different perspective as part of the narrative, introduced when the practitioner is ready. It is worth noting that here there is no criticism of kingship or the world of the senses; it just has dangers, as the pleasant grasses and reeds and water lotuses in a pool, the image used in this story's verses, can prevent one crossing the water.

The Opening in the Cave Story
Darīmukha-Jātaka (J 378)

The Teacher told this story while staying at the Jeta Grove, concerning the Great Renunciation.[8]

Once long ago in the city of Rājagaha there ruled a Magadhan king. At that time the Bodhisatta had taken rebirth in the womb of the chief queen, and they gave him the name Brahmadatta (gift of the gods). And on the very day that he was born, a son was also born to the chief priest, and his face shone with great beauty, so they made his name Darīmukha (the opening in the cave). They both grew to maturity in the kingdom, and were very dear friends to each other, and when they were sixteen years old they went to Taxila to learn all kinds of skills. 'Let's train in all kinds of skill and let's find out about the behaviour of the various directions,' they said, and they wandered through cities, villages and various regions. And when they reached Varanasi they stayed in a temple and the next day went into Varanasi for alms. There in one family, the people said, 'Let's extend an invitation to brahmins and feed them.' And they cooked rice and laid out specially arranged seats. When they saw the two boys on their alms round, they said, 'The brahmins have arrived.' And they invited them into the house and gave the Bodhisatta a white cloth on his seat, and Darīmukha a red blanket. Darīmukha saw this sign and realised, 'Today my friend is going to become king of Varanasi, and I am going to become a general.' They ate there, received the specially prepared food and, after giving a blessing, left for the royal pleasure-garden. The Great Being lay down on the auspicious slab of the city, and Darīmukha then sat massaging his feet. The king of Varanasi had been dead for seven days. The king's minister had performed the rites for the body and, as the king had had no son, sent out the wonderful state carriage, which ran of its own accord. The arrangement about the carriage will be explained in the *Mahājanaka-Jātaka*.[9] The special carriage left the city, surrounded by the four flanks of the army, and to the accompaniment of hundreds of musical instruments, and reached the gate of the pleasure-garden. Darīmukha heard the sound of musical instruments, and thought, 'This carriage is coming for my friend: today he will become king and he will give me the position of his general. But what is the householder's life for me? I will renounce and take the going forth.' Without saying anything to the Bodhisatta he went to one side and stood hidden away. The priest stopped the carriage at the gate of the pleasure garden and entered the garden, and saw the Bodhisatta lying on the auspicious stone. Observing the auspicious marks on his feet, he thought, 'This one is full of merit and is worthy of being king of four continents, with two thousand islands surrounding them. But what of his courage?' So he made all the instruments sound very loudly. The Bodhisatta woke up, and taking the cloth from his face, saw the crowd of people. Then, covering his face again, he continued to lie down for a while, and when the carriage quietened down he got up and sat cross-legged on the auspicious slab. The priest going down on his knees, said, 'Sire, the kingdom has come to you'. 'So is the kingdom without an heir?' 'Yes, sire.' 'Very well then,' agreed the Bodhisatta, and they anointed him in the pleasure-garden.

In his great splendour, he forgot all about Darīmukha. He alighted onto the carriage, and entered the city and, having made a circumambulation he stood at the royal gate and made an inspection of the ministers, arranging their places, and entered up into the palace. At that moment, Darīmukha, thinking 'And now the garden is empty', went and sat on the auspicious slab. A withered leaf dropped down in front of him. And just through this withered leaf, he apprehended decay and old age, and grasped the three signs of existence, and he gave out a great roar of joy and attained *paccekabodhi*, the awakening of the solitary Buddha. And in that moment, the clothes of the householder disappeared, and a miraculous ascetic's bowl and robe came from the sky and came onto his body, and so, right there, he was equipped with the eight requisites of an ascetic and endowed with the posture of an elder of a hundred years of age. Then, he miraculously flew into the air and sailed to the Himalayan regions, to the Nandamūla cave.

The Bodhisatta ruled his kingdom justly, but in his great splendour his mind became intoxicated with fame,[10] so that for forty years he forgot Darīmukha. In the fortieth year he did remember him, and said, 'I have a friend, who is called Darīmukha. I wonder where he is?' And he yearned to see him. And in the women's quarters and in the assembly he used to say, 'Oh where is my friend Darīmukha? I would accord great honour to anyone who could tell me where he lives.' Again and again he remembered him, and another ten years went by. Darīmukha, the *paccekabuddha*, after fifty years reflected and realized, 'My friend remembers me. Now he is old and has reached maturity with plenty of sons and daughters and the rest. I will go out to him and teach him the *dhamma*.' And through his miraculous powers he sailed through the sky and landed in the pleasure-garden and sat down on the auspicious slab, as if a golden statue. The gardener saw him and approached him. 'Sir, where did you come from?' he asked. 'From the Nandamūla cave,' he replied. 'What is your name?' 'I am the *paccekabuddha*, Darīmukha, sir,' he said. 'And you know our king, sir?' he said. 'Yes, I am a friend from the time when I was a householder.' 'Sir, the king wishes to see you. I'll let him know that you have arrived.' 'Yes, go and let him know.' So he went to the king and told him that Darīmukha was on the auspicious slab. The king said, 'My friend has arrived, they say! I'll go and see him.' And he got on his carriage, accompanied by a large retinue, and went to the pleasure garden. He paid homage to the *paccekabuddha*, made him welcome, and sat down to one side. And then the *paccekabuddha* said to him, 'And do you rule the kingdom justly, Brahmadatta? And not follow wrong paths, or oppress the people for the sake of wealth, and perform meritorious actions such as generosity?' And, making a friendly greeting to him, he said, 'Brahmadatta, you are old; the time has come for you to abandon the pleasures of the senses.' Saying this, he taught him the *dhamma*, speaking the first verse:

1. 'Pleasures of the senses are a bog of water-growing plants;[11]
Pleasures of the senses are a marsh.
A three-rooted terror they are I say![12]
Dust and smoke they're called by me.
Leave them, Brahmadatta – and take the going forth.'

Hearing this, the king explained that he was bound by sense desires, and spoke the second verse:

2. 'But I am bound,[13] stained and indulging in the senses, brahmin,
A fearful appearance. But I have a craving for life[14] and cannot give them up,
So I do actions that bring merit, ceaselessly.'

So then Darīmukha, the *paccekabuddha,* even though the Great Being had said that he could not take the going forth, gave him some more advice about giving up the burden of office.

3. 'He who does not take the advice of someone who wishes him well, full of care and compassion,
Thinking, "this world is better",
Foolish, goes again and again to rebirth.

4. 'He ends up in that hell of terrifying appearance,
Where what is foul seems good, full of filth,
Those who are greedy, who cannot get rid of bodily needs:
These are not freed from the passions of the senses.'

And so he spoke two verses, and in this way Darīmukha, the *pacceka-buddha,* showed the suffering caused by conception and the suffering caused by being conceived, and then showing the suffering caused by birth itself, spoke a verse and a half:

5. 'Bloodied and dirtied with foulness
All beings arrive covered in mucus and phlegm.
And whatever they touch with their body after that, brings all kinds of trouble.[15]

6a. 'I speak because I have seen for myself, not heard it from another:
And I remember many, many, past lives.'

Then the Perfectly Awakened teacher said, 'and so the *paccekabuddha* spoke kindly to the king, with well chosen words', and spoke a half-stanza:[16]

'With many coloured and well-chosen verses, Darīmukha won over Sumedha.'[17]

The *paccekabuddha,* having shown him the fault of sense-pleasures, making his words easy to grasp for him, said, 'Great King, take the going forth, or do not. But, since I have told you about the danger of the sense-pleasures and in praise of the going forth, then – be vigilant.'

Then he flew through the air, like a regal golden goose, and, stepping over tufts of clouds, he arrived right back at the Nandamūla cave. The Great Being brought his hands together and, making a resplendent ten-fingered *añjali* over his head, he bowed down deeply and stood still, right until the time that his friend had passed out of sight. Then he summoned his eldest son, and gave him the kingdom. And, despite the weeping and lamentation of the people, he did abandon the pleasures of the sense and went to the Himalayan regions. Building a leaf hut, he took the going forth as an ascetic, and developed the higher knowledges and the meditations. At the end of his life he went to Brahmā's heaven.

The Teacher, after finishing his talk, revealed the four noble truths, and made the connections for the story. At the conclusion of the truths, many there attained stream entry. 'At that time indeed it was I who was the king,' he said. (Ja III 238–46)

DHAMMAPADA STORIES: MEDITATORS AND THEIR STRUGGLES

The most well-known Buddhist text is the *Dhammapada*, now translated into many languages. The verses, often simple homilies and formulae, encapsulate the essence of the Buddhist path with a succinct and simple saying or image. Few outside Southeast Asia and Sri Lanka, however, know the sometimes intricate stories accompanying these verses. Alongside *Jātakas*, they are the principal means by which Southern Buddhists have learnt Buddhist doctrine and they are recounted at festivals, family events, blessings and at schools.[18] Often complex, and in some cases involving tragic and comic life-stories that encompass successions of lives, the stories introduce almost tangentially all kinds of information about the far-reaching consequences of *kamma*, and meditation in practice. They also show the Buddha's attitudes to those he taught, differing approaches to the practice and ways of dealing with various problems and crises in the practitioners' lives.

The atmosphere is of leisurely storytelling rather than didacticism; teachings are geared to individuals. *Suttas* describe 'one time' or 'one occasion', with a single set of circumstances and a formal interchange between the Buddha or one of his followers and others. But these less overtly doctrinal stories describe a far longer time span, following details of people's meditative history in a more discursive and idiosyncratic way. There is also a narrative interest, largely peculiar to this collection, in the moments leading up to a change of state or enlightenment. People become enlightened through an interplay of life events, meditative experience, based on objects, given or perceived in the world, and sometimes the teaching of riddles, often carefully selected for that person on the basis of past-life experience or predisposition.[19] These triggers to awakening defy conventional classification. Meditators, working on a particular object, or 'place of work', are described chancing upon a bubble, dissolving in water, a flickering flame, or a withered leaf, that prompts insight, perceived through a fusion of *samatha* and *vipassanā*. These subtle stories become a means of describing what it feels like to undertake a personal meditative journey, over a long time, which can yet find surprise fruition. Set in the lifetime of the Buddha, as well as 'in the past', they show the Buddha reacting, guiding and appearing to meditators. They can be read as an extended meditative path, peculiar to individuals, yet governed by multiple conditions, with the Buddha or teacher as a creative guide, coming to help from outside or from the mind itself when there is a problem to hand.

In *Dhammapada* stories the whole process of meditation is described as a lengthy collaboration between teacher and meditator. The Buddha surveys the world with the 'net' of his divine vision, employs psychic powers to help others, and is always on the lookout for people whose meditation he can assist and take to another level. He delivers his teaching in verse, often re-articulating the insight made by his follower, thus providing the prompt that brings about enlightenment or validating it. Sometimes he visits a meditator on several occasions, at different times, when different teachings are needed, demonstrating a graduated path. Multiple causes are needed to bring the work of meditation to fruition, a radically different emphasis from the way meditation is described in the *suttas (Nikāyas)*, where the teaching of the Buddha is articulated in a more formal way.

Meditators also actively use their own initiative and resources. This interpenetration of factors makes these tales like psychodramas, where the necessary balance of insight and calm is achieved through a culmination of personal effort and events, often based on deeply entrenched kammic patterns, that support, complement or introduce a necessary shock within the practice itself. The stories, formed in a pre-literate culture where they would have provided lengthy diversion, give boxes within boxes of incidents and surprise reversals; deeply entrenched kammic patterns are balanced by the power of a single moment of choice to effect dramatic change. The mythical language and the idea of 'past lives' communicate the character of a person through, and as the product of, their earlier experience, demonstrating that meditative suitability for certain objects and types of practice varies according to this. The tales are clearly designed to be heard over a long time. Complicatedness is a fact of all our lives; the multiple causality and the intricacy of the narrative can be seen as a way of including a great deal of information about Buddhist principles in action, in a complex setting that evokes a sense of a graduated path.

1. The weapon of loving-kindness

This story has been chosen for the pre-eminence it gives to the *Mettā-Sutta*, the great early Buddhist text on loving-kindness, both for its magical efficacious properties when chanted aloud, which it frequently is today in both private and public contexts, but primarily for its link to the meditation practice. The story is highly intertextual, because, as a later text, it includes material from three quite different collections, all used as meditative and practice-based aids: by this stage, in a world without books, many and even most monks and laity would understand references to other texts, genres, leading characters and situations.

So what are the principal layers of the text? The first is the story itself. This is likely to be a later composition: although it could date back centuries, it was not written down until the sixth century CE, and so is regarded as commentarial material, accretions to the original first layers. As such stories have evolved over a long period of time, they acquired various layers in the centuries after the Buddha's death. But they should not be dismissed as 'late': they serve a particular purpose in communicating to us a sense of how the early Buddhists felt meditation teaching worked in practice, and the kinds of narratives they felt were useful for those wishing to hear about meditation, its effects and its goal. The second kind of text is the verse that caps the story, the *Dhammapada* verse. The *Dhammapada* verses communicate the spirit and principles of the eightfold path like small medicinal capsules of teaching, biting, sweet and even shocking, as folk wisdom sometimes is.

In this story, a third kind of text, perhaps more closely aligned to the *Dhammapada* verses, is used. This is the greatly loved and ancient text on loving-kindness, which is taken from the *Sutta Nipāta*, considered the oldest stratum of the canon. To this day it is chanted at all occasions, and felt to be particularly helpful, if there is a new enterprise, like the opening of a new hotel, or an unhappy atmosphere to dispel, as at a funeral, or just as a general way of introducing confidence and goodwill. It can also act as a preliminary to a more formal, sitting practice on loving-kindness, which takes the mind to the meditation (see this anthology, pp. 42ff.). It would have been well known and revered at the time of the probable evolution of this story: it is a chanted, ceremonial text, with an unusual and 'old' metrical arrangement, as well as a teaching device, and is introduced here as a magical 'weapon'. Accompanied by the practice of loving-kindness, it is supposed, as it does in this story, to have a mildly and happily contagious effect, as it does on the spirits, who though virtuous, are mischievous too.

The story in many ways captures the spirit of Buddhist meditation in one narrative. The humour of scary but basically benign spirits, mildly annoyed, like many humans, with guests that do not leave, the practical way suggested by the Buddha of coping with danger and the fact that the five hundred work collectively together to dispel bad feelings, and then obtain insight soon afterwards, all make this multilevelled discourse an exercise in dealing with apparently external problems. As so often in Buddhist story collections, insight practices seem to be seamlessly delivered by means of diverting and lively adventures.

In Buddhist countries, the idea of spirits that may need propitiation or help from humans would be familiar, not unlike European ideas of beings who hide things or cause loud noises. Tree spirits, spirits of lakes, rivers and even dwellings and families, may be on the level of the Realm of the Four Kings, a lower heaven realm, but can be troublesome: hence the need for transferred merit and sensitivity to the well-being and needs of local spirits of an unhappier nature that may be around (see this anthology, p. 132). Whether the story can be taken as referring to difficulties in the mind, as well as in the world around, and both are probably intended, the psychology is clear, shown in the advice given. This is not a superstitious text, but rather a clever one, in its injunction that the monks take responsibility for their mental state, chant together rather than moan, and use collective confidence to clear their own miasmatic mental state and the inhospitable environs. This all provides preparation for the practice of insight meditation.

At the end, the Buddha, the compassionate Teacher who appears in visual form, articulates the perception the monks have already developed for themselves.

Just like a jar

The Teacher gave this teaching about the *dhamma* while staying at Sāvatthī regarding some monks who had obtained insight.

Now it is said that five hundred monks at Sāvatthī had learnt a meditation object leading to arahantship from the Teacher and, saying, 'Let's practise the meditative life', went so far as a hundred yojanas and arrived at a large town. When people saw them they arranged seating, served them with plenty of rice-gruel and other foods, and asked them, 'Where are you going, sirs?' They replied, 'Where there is a pleasant place'. The people asked, 'Sirs, stay right here for these three months. We will establish ourselves in the refuges with you and guard the precepts.' Finding their agreeableness to this, they said, 'Not far from here there is a large jungle thicket: stay there, sirs.' They sent them there, and the monks entered the jungle thicket.

Now some virtuous gods (*devatās*) who lived in that jungle thicket, thought, 'Some venerable sirs have reached the jungle thicket. But while these venerable people are staying here it would be improper for us to take sons and wives, and climb the trees and live there.' So they came to the ground, sat down and had a think. 'The venerable sirs are staying today for one night in this spot. Surely they'll be on their way tomorrow.' But the next day the monks again went on the almsround to the edge of the town and then returned right back to the jungle thicket. The gods thought, 'The group of monks must have been invited to someone's house tomorrow, so they have come back here today and will not go away: it looks like they'll be off tomorrow.' Working things out in this way, they stayed put on the ground for a fortnight. Then they thought, 'Looks like these revered people are going to stay right here for three months. But if they do stay here for three months, it would be improper for us to take sons and wives, climb trees and live here too. But these seats on the ground are painful. What can we do to drive these monks away?' So in all the places the monks stayed at night, and in the places they stayed during the day, and at the ends of the places they did walking practice, they caused bodies without heads to appear, and heads that had been chopped off bodies. And they got them to hear the wailing of demons. And they got diseases to turn up in the monks, who started sneezing and coughing and having other ailments. The monks asked one another, 'What's wrong with you, sir?' 'I have got the sneezes', 'I've got a cough', they said. 'I, sir, went to the edge of where we do our walking practice and saw a head without a body!' 'I went to where we go at night and saw a body without a head!' 'I went to where we spend our day and heard the wailing of demons!' 'This place is not suitable and should be avoided. This is not a pleasant place for us. Let's go to see the teacher.' So by and by they left and went to the presence of the Teacher, paid their respects and sat to one side.

And the Teacher said to them, 'So, monks, you will not be able to stay in this place?' 'Exactly, sir: while we were staying in that place such terrifying objects appeared! It was just awful. So we thought it was not suitable and should be avoided. So we have abandoned it and come here to you.' 'Monks, to that very place you should return.' It's not possible, sir!' they said. 'You went there without taking a weapon. Now, go back, and this time take a weapon.'[20] 'What kind of weapon, sir?' they asked. The Teacher said, 'I'll give you a weapon. Go back, and take with you the weapon I'm going to give you,' he said:

LOVING-KINDNESS (*METTĀ- SUTTA*)

143. He who is skilled in welfare, who wishes to attain that calm state (*nibbāna*), should act in this way: he should be able, upright, perfectly upright, of noble speech, gentle and humble.

144. Contented, easily supported, with few duties, of simple livelihood, with senses calmed, discreet, not impudent, he should not be greedily attached to families.

145. He should not pursue the slightest thing for which other wise men might blame him. May all beings be happy and secure, may their hearts be wholesome!

146–7. Whatever living beings there be: feeble or strong, tall, stout or medium, short, small or large, without exception; seen or unseen, those dwelling far or near, those who are born or those who are yet to be born, may all beings be happy!

148. Let one not deceive another, nor despise any person, whatsoever, in any place. Let him not wish any harm to another out of anger or ill-will.

149. Just as a mother would protect her only child at the risk of her own life, even so, let him cultivate a boundless heart towards all beings.

150. Let his thoughts of boundless love pervade the whole world: above, below and across without any obstruction, without any hatred, without any enmity.

151. Whether he stands, walks, sits or lies down, as long as he is awake, he should develop this mindfulness. This they say is a heaven realm, here in this world.[21]

152. Not falling into wrong views, being virtuous and endowed with insight, by discarding attachment to sense desires, he never again knows rebirth. (Sn 143–52)[22]

And he recited the entire *Mettā-sutta* (on loving-kindness) to them.

'Monks: chant[23] this *sutta* starting out from the jungle thicket, to outside the place you are staying and then you may enter where you are staying.' And he sent them on their way.

They paid respects to the Teacher, and by and by left, and reaching that place, they did a group chant,[24] and chanting, entered the jungle thicket. The *devatās* in the entire jungle thicket received the mind of loving-kindness,[25] and gave a welcome to them; they asked to take their robes and bowls, offered to massage their limbs, put up a good guard here and there, and met together with them.

And there was no more wailing of demons anywhere. The monks' minds became unified. Sitting in the places they used at night and the places they used in the day, they sat and brought the mind down for the sake of insight,[26] and establishing in their minds the principle of decay and ageing, increased insight with the thought, 'what we call self is only the same as a potter's jar, of an easily broken nature and unstable form'.

The Fully Awakened Buddha sat in his perfumed hut, and, recognizing their growing achievement in insight, addressed these monks: 'What we call self is only the same as a potter's jar, of an easily broken nature and unstable form.' Saying this, he stood suffusing radiance for a hundred leagues, and, by means of a form appearing to be seated in front of them, diffused six-coloured rays[27]. And he said this verse:

'He knows the body for what it is
Making his mind firm like a citadel:
Fight Māra with the weapon of wisdom
And guard your territory without resting!'[28]

(DhpA I 313–16/Dhp 40)

2. Different approaches to teaching meditation

Much of the Buddha's teaching is enacted through his disciples and followers, who embody various abilities, approaches to meditation and practice, and different kinds of temperament. Sāriputta is the Buddha's chief disciple, literally his right-hand man in artistic depictions, and the arahant principally renowned for his skill in insight and wisdom. In this story even he is at a loss with one meditator. The story does not indicate any great failure on Sāriputta's part; he importantly knows well the time to ask advice, a quality constantly extolled in both canonical and commentarial passages. Rather the story provides a vindication of the powers of the Buddha, the experienced teacher of meditation, who has developed the perfections and the psychic powers, is alert to those whom he is teaching, and able to see not only the problem, but an effective way of addressing it in any given individual. So the right object for the person is chosen, at the right time, to produce the four *jhānas* and mastery of calm meditation. The same object is used, again only at the right time, for insight. When the Buddha causes the flower, the basis of the boy's meditative attainments, to wither and blacken, the boy sees the three signs, of impermanence (*anicca*), unsatisfactoriness (*dukkha*), and the lack of a solid and enduring self (*anattā*), understood through the decomposition of this visual object.

The story also demonstrates 'past-life' narrative as an indicator of present-day disposition. Past-life analysis in its new age usage is not encouraged in Southern Buddhism; it is said that one should develop the fourth meditation, and equanimity, before trying to explore this area of the mind. However, the assumption that longstanding kammic patterns, for good or ill, have an internal, perhaps even metaphoric application, gives complex colour to a sense of the resources and tendencies of each being, adding a new dimension to the Buddhist emphasis on teaching according to disposition. The 'past' narrative expresses the hidden potential and propensities of each meditator. The importance of frequent consultation, and for one teacher to consult another when in doubt, are also important incidental details here.

The story of the goldsmith's son

The teacher gave this *dhamma* talk while staying in the Jetavana Grove about a monk who was a co-resident of the elder Sāriputta. Now it is said that a certain young son of a goldsmith, of handsome appearance, took the going forth under the auspices of the elder Sāriputta. The elder reflected to himself that, 'Passion (*rāga*) is abundant[29] in the young'. So he gave him the meditation object of the impure[30] for the warding away (*paṭighāta*) of passion. But this was not a suitable practice for the boy, so when he entered the forest, he made an effort for a month, but did not obtain any measure of unification.[31] He went to the elder again and when asked, 'Is your meditation object in hand, brother?' he informed him about what had been happening. The elder said, 'You should never give up, saying, "My meditation object does not work"'. So he taught him the meditation object thoroughly, yet again. For a second time he could not develop any distinction and he went back and told the elder. But the elder [426] taught him the same subject as before, explaining to him its ins and outs and illustrating the subject with similes. But the young monk came back, with the news that he had failed in his meditations yet again.

Now the elder thought to himself: 'An active monk knows when the sense-desires are active in him, "the sense-desires are active"; he knows when they are not, that they are not. This monk is active, and is not inactive; he is on the path, and is not away from the path. It is just that I do not understand his disposition. He should be capable of being trained by the Buddha.' So he took the young man with him and approached the teacher in the evening, and said, 'This young man, sir, is a co-resident with me, and I gave him this particular meditation object, for this reason'. And he explained everything that had happened to him.

Then the Teacher said to him: 'As regards knowledge of thoughts and dispositions: this is for those who have fulfilled the perfections,[32] who have caused the ten-thousand world systems to shout for joy and who have obtained omniscience.' He pondered to himself, 'From what family has this man taken the going forth?' Realising that it was a goldsmith's, he looked over the man's earlier existences in the past and saw that for five hundred earlier existences in succession he had been reborn only in this very goldsmith clan. 'For a very long time this boy has done the work of a goldsmith. For a long time he has said, "I will make karnikara flowers and lotus flowers", turning over only gold in his hands. A meditation object on the impure and the repulsive just is not suitable for him.' Then he reflected, 'A pleasant object of meditation is the only one suitable for him'.

So he said, dismissing the elder: 'Sāriputta, this monk that you gave a meditation object that did not suit him, who was tired out for four months: you are going to see him attain arahantship this very day, after breakfast. And now you can go.'

The Teacher, with his supernatural power, created a golden lotus the size of a wheel, and made the leaves and the stalks as if to drip water-drops, and gave this lotus to the monk, saying, 'Sir, take this lotus and go to the boundary of your monastery and place it on a heap of sand, and sitting cross-legged in front of it, do the preparatory practice (*parikamma*) repeating the words "golden red, golden red"'.[33] Just by taking the lotus from the hand of the Teacher, the monk's mind became clear (*cittam pasīdi*).

He went to the boundary of his monastery, made a heap of sand and pressed the stalk of the lotus into it, and, sitting down cross-legged in front of it, began the preparatory practice, saying 'red, red'. At this the hindrances vanished and the access stage for *jhāna* arose.[34] Immediately afterwards he developed the first *jhāna*. Keeping it under control by means of the five skills,[35] even as he sat right there he attained the second meditation, and the third. When he had brought the fourth meditation under control he sat playing in the play of the meditations.[36]

The Teacher, recognising that he had attained the meditations, wondered, 'And will he now be able to come to the utmost distinction of the teaching for himself?' Seeing that he would not, the Buddha made a resolve: 'Let this lotus flower wither!' The flower became black, just as if it were a withered lotus flower crushed in the hands. The boy emerged from his meditation (*vuṭṭhāya*)[37] and surveyed the flower: 'How is it that this lotus is discerned (*paññāyati*) attacked by old age? If those things with no clinging to the world are assailed by old age, how much the more will old age come to those that do have clinging?' In this way he saw the mark of impermanence. [428] And as soon as he had seen this, he also saw the mark of dis-ease and the mark of non-self. And these three characteristics of existence were as if on fire, or like carrion tied around the neck.

At that moment some young boys went down to a certain pool not far from him, breaking off the lotus flowers and making a pile on the bank. The young man surveyed first the lotuses that were in the water and then those on the bank. The lotuses in the water, raising their heads and dripping with water, appeared to him exceedingly beautiful. Those that lay on the bank were withered at the tips.

He thought: 'Old age assails even the one without clinging: how much the more will it afflict the one who does have clinging!' And he saw more even more clearly the marks of impermanence, dis-ease and non-self.

The Teacher realized: 'Now the meditation object has become completely clear in this monk.' And, sitting in his perfumed hut, he released a luminous image of himself and touched the young man's face. 'What was that?' thought the young boy. Looking around, he saw the Teacher approaching as if he were standing right in front of him. Rising, he made an *añjali*, and the Teacher, wishing to give what was the right remedy for him, spoke the following verse:

'Cut off partiality towards yourself
As you would pick an autumn lily with your hand.
Develop the path to peace,
Nibbāna has been taught by the one who lives in happiness.'

(Dhp 285)

At the conclusion of the teaching, the monk was established in arahatship.

(DhpA III 424–9)

3. Quick and slow progress

Throughout these Buddhist stories all kinds of meditators are found and meditation is not always successful at first. The following story is an example of an extended *Dhammapada* narrative, with a full familial and personal history of two brothers: one finds meditation easy, while the other does not; both, however, find success. The story culminates in *Jātakas*, paralleling the failure but eventual success of an earlier life with the student's present failure and eventual success in the path. Beset by problems, in several lives, showing the repetitive nature of *kamma*, the 'slow' meditator, unlike his brother, has to face repeated failure. Encouragingly, however, he is rewarded in each life, through persistent effort. The 'wealth' that the hero wins in his earlier existence is used as a metaphor for the riches found in his final life, potentially undermined by such bandits and thieves as attack houses and property. As seen in the *sutta* on the city, 'thieves' are often a metaphor for unskilful states (this anthology, pp. 51–7). The means by which the slow practitioner attains success, in the stories here, is unusual in each case. As so often in stories, practitioners create their own path. Indeed, the paradoxical means by which he also eventually finds awakening is through a device that aligns the tale with stories involving *gongans/koans* in the Chan/Zen/Seon traditions, where surprise or contradiction forms an essential part of bypassing usual mental patterns (Luk 1999).

This story uses some interesting vocabulary, replete with associations in early Buddhist literature. The word translated here as 'very existence as an individual' (*attabhāva*) means 'self' and the state known as '-ness'. In this way, as Steven Collins points out, it is that used for individuality. He writes:

Many passages which speak of houses or 'huts' (*kuṭī* – a term both for a monk's cell within a monastery, and a hermitage retreat) are explained by the commentaries as referring to the *attabhāva*, which may be closed or open to the rain of the 'defilements'. The *attabhāva*, as we have seen, is the sense of individuality which appears to the unenlightened man, through the physical fact of the body, and the psychological fact of *asmi-māna* [the conceit, 'I am']; what it 'really' (in 'ultimate' terms) refers to is the group of the five *khandhā* in existence at any given moment of time.[38]

The word *kiliṭṭha* that features in this passage, which can be translated as dirty, defiled, troubled, or stained, is associated with the word used for the defilements (*kilesa*) of the mind too (PED 216–17 and DP I 693-4). Dust or dirt is often linked in early Buddhism with the householder's life, metaphorically and literally (PED 562).[39] The first kind of 'dust' here is greed or passion (*raga*), a word associated with *raj*, to 'dye', the first of the three types or orientations of the mind (PED 567). The pun on dye or colouring, with greed and the defilements, runs throughout this passage, as it does through discussion on the subject generally in early Buddhism, as we have seen in 'The Simile of the Cloth' (this anthology, pp. 76–81). As seen earlier, desire, hatred and ignorance often feature as fundamental orientations in the mind.[40]

Two brothers

This is the teaching known as 'By rousing himself with diligence (*appamāda*)'. The Teacher recounted it while staying at Veḷuvana with reference to Little Tracker (Cūḷapanthaka).

Now it is said that the daughter of a rich businessman in Rājagāha, upon reaching maturity, was provided by her mother and her father with the top floor of a seven-storeyed palace and guarded with excessive care. But in spite of this, intoxicated with the folly of youth and full of desire, [240] she had relations with her servant. Frightened, she thought, 'Other people might find out what I have done!' So she said to him, 'We cannot stay here any longer; if my mother and father find out my fault they'll tear me apart, limb from limb. Let's live somewhere else.'

Taking what they could in their hands, they went out by the front door, and left together: 'We'll go and live anywhere where people do not know about this.' They settled in a certain spot and as a result of this she conceived a child. When her unborn child had reached the time to be born, she said, 'My child is now ready to be born. If I give birth in a place where we are far removed from my family and relatives, it will bring us great suffering. So let's go back to my home.' He was terrified: 'But if I go back there, they will not spare my life.' So he kept putting off the departure day, saying, 'We'll go today; we'll go tomorrow'.

She thought, 'This fool realizes the gravity of his wrongdoing, and so does not have the guts to go. But mothers and fathers are so sympathetic – he does not have to go, but I will.'

So while her husband was away from home she put the household things away, and told her near neighbours that she was going, and then set off on the road. When her husband came back home and could not see her, he asked the neighbours, who said, 'She has gone back to her family.' When he heard this he followed her as quickly as possible and caught up with her on the track. And right there she gave birth to her baby. 'What is it?' asked her husband. [241] 'It is a boy, my husband.' 'So what do we do now?' 'The event for which we were going to go home to my parents has happened. So why do we need to go there? Let's go back to our own home.'

Being of the same mind about this, they went back. And since their son was born when they were on the road, they gave him the name 'Tracker'. Not long passed before she conceived another child. And everything is to be related in detail just as it was explained before.[41] Since the baby was born by the side of the tracks, they gave him the name Little Tracker (Cūḷapanthaka), and called the older son Big Tracker (Mahāpanthaka). Taking their own sons, they returned to their home.

When they were living there, Big Tracker heard other children talking about their 'uncles' and 'grandfathers', and 'Granny and Grandpa', and he asked his mother, 'Other children talk about "Granny and Grandpa", but we do not have any relatives, do we?' 'We do. There are none here, but you have a grandfather, who is a rich businessman, living in Rājagaha, and there are many other relatives there too.' 'Why don't we go there?' he asked, but she avoided answering the question and the children kept on asking her about it, again and again. [242] Finally, she said to her husband, 'These children are exhausting me! Will my parents really eat us for breakfast?[42] Come, why don't we just show them their grandparents' family.' 'I just cannot remain with them face to face. But I will take you there.' 'Very good: and some strategem needs to be done to get them to meet their grandparents' family.'

So they both took the children and when in time they arrived at Rājagaha, they went to lodge in a hall belonging to a certain woman near the gate to the city. Then the children's mother had her parents informed that she and her children had arrived. When her parents heard the message, they said, 'We have wandered through *saṃsāra*, but never before did we have a son, or a daughter. But these two have committed a terrible offence. It is just not possible for them to come and stand even in our line of vision. Let the two of them take as much money as they want and go and live somewhere where they will be comfortable. But let them send the children here.' The two accepted the money that was sent to them, and putting the children in the hands of the messengers who had come there, sent them to their grandparents.

Of the two, Little Tracker was still very young. Big Tracker, however, used to go with his grandfather to hear the Ten-Powered One teach the dhamma. And as he constantly went into the presence of the Teacher, his heart inclined towards taking the going forth. He told his grandfather, 'If you were to give me permission, [243] I would take the going forth.' 'What are you saying! There is no one in the entire world whose going forth would be more dear to me. So if you feel you can – then do it!' So he took him to the Teacher who said, 'So, householder, you have now got a boy!' 'Yes, sir, this is my grandson and he would like to take the going forth with you.' The Teacher had a certain monk who was on his almsround admit him to the order, and said, 'Give this boy the going forth.' The elder admitted him to the order, and explained to him the five parts of the body meditation object.[43] The boy soon grasped the Buddha's teaching and stayed a full rains season, after which he took full ordination, and by practising his meditation with wise attention, attained arahatship.[44]

As Big Tracker spent his time in the happiness of meditation, and in the happiness of the fruit of meditation,[45] he reflected to himself: 'It is possible to impart this happiness to Little Tracker!' So he went to his grandfather, the businessman, and said, 'Great merchant, if you would give your permission, I would give Little Tracker the going forth.' 'Certainly, sir, receive him into the order.' For, they say, the businessman was full of faith (*suppasanno*) and when he was asked 'From which daughter are these boys?' was very ashamed to say, 'From the one who ran away', and because of these factors gave his permission for them to take the going forth with some contentment. The elder gave the going forth to Little Tracker [244] and established him in the precepts. But having taken the going forth, he was very slow.[46]

Just as the lotus, the red lotus in flower, sweet in perfume,
Might, early in the morning, be in full blossom, undiminished in scent,
See the Buddha, the shining one, how brilliant he is,
Like the sun, blazing in the sky.

In four months he was unable to learn even this verse. For he, the story goes, had taken the going forth in the time of the fully awakened Buddha Kassapa, and had been wise and accomplished, but at the time for learning recitations, he had made a joke about another, slow bhikkhu, and this monk, shamed by the teasing, had not been able to learn the recitation and had not chanted it. As a result of this *kamma,* Little Tracker was born slow: learning one verse made the one he had learned before just disappear. Even though he tried to learn this *gātha* for over four months, he could not grasp it. Then Big Tracker said, 'Little Tracker, you are hopeless! You have been on that seat for four months and cannot learn just one verse. How much more are you incapable of fulfilling the work involved with taking going forth! Leave this monastery.' And he expelled him. But Little Tracker, in his great affection for the teaching of the Buddha, had no wish for the householder's existence.

Now at that time Big Tracker was the elder who supervised the distribution of food. And Jīvaka Komārabhacca brought a large quantity of flowers, garlands and ointments and came to his own mango grove, paid homage to the Teacher, listened to the *dhamma,* and then, rising from his seat, paid respects to the Ten-Powered One, approached

Big Tracker and asked, 'Sir, how many monks are living with the Teacher?' Big Tracker replied, 'Five hundred'. 'Then, tomorrow, bring the five hundred monks, who have the Buddha at their head, and take your meal at my house.' 'But the layman Little Tracker is slow: and he has made no growth in the *dhamma*. I accept the invitation for everyone except for him,' the elder replied.

When Little Tracker heard this he thought, 'The elder has accepted an invitation for so many monks, but he has left me out. There's no doubt about it, my brother's heart has been divided from me. What is there for me in this teaching now? I'll live as a householder and make merit through acts of generosity and things like that.' On the next morning he left the order and started out. Very early, at dawn, the Teacher surveyed the world and seeing this event crossed ahead first, and going ahead of Little Tracker at the gateway he walked backwards and forwards. Little Tracker came by and, seeing the Teacher, approached him and paid respects. And then the Teacher asked, 'But Little Tracker, where are going to at this time?'

'My brother has expelled me, sir, and I am leaving the order.'

'Little Tracker, you received your ordination from me; when your brother expelled you, why did you not come to me? Come: what have you to do with the householder's life; you will stay with me.' He touched his head with his hand, whose palm was adorned with a wheel,[47] and took him and went before the perfumed hut, where he got him to sit down. He said, 'Little Tracker, looking eastwards, rub this piece of cloth and say, "removing the dirt, removing the dirt", and stay right here.'[48] And he gave him a completely clean cloth, created by his psychic power. As the time for the meal was being announced, he went to Jīvaka's house with a retinue of the order of monks and sat down on the seat that had been arranged.

Meanwhile, Little Tracker, turning to the sun, sat down and rubbed the cloth, saying, 'removing the dirt, removing the dirt'. But as he was rubbing this cloth rag, it became dirty. So then he thought: 'This cloth rag was completely clean before, but because of my very existence as an individual has lost its former, original nature; it has become dirty:

Impermanent are conditioned things!' Establishing understanding of decay and death, he increased insight (*vipassanā*).

The Teacher, recognizing this, said: 'Little Tracker has embarked upon insight.'[49]

'Little Tracker, do you not think that it is just this cloth rag that has become soiled and dyed with dirt with impurity; the dirt of desire, and other defilements are within you: remove them.'

And he emitted a luminous image of himself, appearing in bodily form, as if sitting down in front of him, and uttered these verses:[50]

'Passion, not dirt, is properly called "dust";[51]
This name "dust" is for passion.

'Abandoning this dust bhikkus live in this teaching, with dust departed.
Hatred, not dirt, is properly called "dust";
This name "dust" is for hatred.
Abandoning this dust, bhikkus live in this teaching, with dust departed.

'Delusion, not dirt, is properly called "dust";
This name "dust" is for delusion.
Abandoning this dust, monks live in this teaching, with dust departed.'

[247] At the conclusion of these verses, Little Tracker attained arahatship, with the discriminatory knowledges (*paṭisambhidā*)[52] and, along with the discriminatory knowledges, there even came to him the three baskets.[53]

Now, the story goes that in past times he had been a king. While making a ceremonial circuit of the city with sweat pouring down his brow, he had wiped it, and the cloth became dirty. He had thought, 'Depending (*nissaya*) upon this body as a basis, such a nice clean cloth has become dirty, and lost its former nature.' And he apprehended the perception of impermanence (*anicca*). Because of this occurrence, 'removal of dirt' became a condition (*paccaya*) for him.[54]

Meanwhile, Jīvaka Komārabhacca was offering water as an auspicious offering to the Ten-Powered One. The teacher, covering his bowl with his hand, said, 'Jīvaka, are there really no monks in the monastery?' Big Tracker said, 'No sir, there are no monks in the monastery.' The teacher said, 'But there are!' So Jīvaka gave an order to a man, saying, 'Go to the monastery and find out whether there is or is not any monk there. At that very moment Little Tracker thought, 'My brother has said there are no monks in the monastery; I'll show him monks in the monastery!' And he filled the whole of the mango grove with monks: some making robes, some dyeing robes, others chanting. In this way, he caused there to be a thousand monks, each one different from the others.

When the messenger had seen so many monks in the monastery, he went back and informed Jīvaka, 'Sir, the whole mango grove is filled with monks!'

So, right there, the elder[55] Tracker multiplied himself a thousand-fold and sat in the delightful mango grove, until the time when he was summoned.

And then the Teacher said this to the man: 'Go to the vihāra and say that the teacher wants to speak to Little Tracker.' The man went and did what he was told, and a cry went up from a thousand mouths. The man returned and said, 'Well, it seems that everyone is called Little Tracker!' 'Then go and take the hands of the first person that says "I am Little Tracker" – and the rest will disappear.' So the man did this, and sure enough, immediately the thousand monks disappeared. The elder Little Tracker came back with the man who had come to collect him. At the end of the ceremony for the meal he said to Jīvaka, 'Jīvaka, take Little Tracker's bowl, and he will do the transference of merit for you (*anumodana*)'. The elder, like a young lion roaring the lion's roar, gave the transference of merit, moving through the whole of the three baskets.

The Teacher got up from his seat and surrounded by the retinue of monks, went to the monastery. After the monks had paid their respects, the Teacher, standing in front of the perfumed hut, gave a discourse to the community of monks, a teaching from the Fortunate One. He explained a meditation subject and asked the order of monks to leave, and then, entering the perfumed hut, the fragrant and highly perfumed place where he stayed, lay down like a lion, on his right side.

Then, in the evening the monks gathered together from here and there and, as if drawing close crimson woollen curtains, [249] sat down and discussed the wonderful qualities of the Teacher: 'Friends, Big Tracker, not understanding the disposition of Little Tracker, thought, "In four months this fool has not been able to understand a single verse." And he expelled him from the monastery. But the Fully Awakened Buddha, because he is the monarch of the unsurpassable teaching, during the time of just one meal, established him in arahatship, with the discriminatory knowledges, together with knowledge of the Three Baskets: ah, great is the power of Buddhas.'

Now the Blessed One, realizing that they were discussing the event in the Dhamma Hall, thought to himself, 'Now is the moment to go to them'. So he arose from his Buddha seat, put on his well-dyed robes, and over his shoulders threw the great robe of the Fortunate One, like a crimson woollen cloth; he stirred as if lightning were quickening. He came out of his deeply perfumed meditation hut, and walking with the gait of an elephant in rut, with the incomparable grace of Buddha, he went to the Dhamma Hall. He mounted the gloriously arrayed and excellent seat of the Buddha, and diffusing the six-coloured rays of a Buddha, just as the powerful sun, newly dawning on the top of Mount Yugandhara, stirs the deepest depths of the waters, he sat down in the middle of the seat.

And at the moment that the Fully Awakened Buddha arrived, the order of monks put aside their talk, and became silent. The Teacher looked over [250] the assembly with a heart softened by loving-kindness. 'This assembly is radiant: there is no fidgeting of the hands or the feet, and there is no sound of coughing or sneezing. All these monks, out of respect for the Buddha, moved to respect by the majesty of the Buddha, even if I sat for an aeon without speaking, would not speak first, or as much as open their lips. It is for me to decide when it is the right time to begin speaking.' And he addressed the assembly with the soft voice of Brahmā.[56] 'Monks, what was the subject of your conversation, as you were gathered here? What were you talking about that you left unfinished?' When they told him, he said, 'This is not the first time that Little Tracker has been slow. In earlier lives he was also slow. And this is not the first time I have been his support. In another life I was also his support. But in that earlier life I established him as lord of a great worldly household. Just now I have established him as lord of a transcendent household.' The monks all wanted to hear about it, so responding to their request, he told this story about long ago.

Once upon a time a certain young man who lived in Varanasi went to Taxila to learn all kinds of skills, and became the pupil of a teacher of great renown in the world. The young man was the most well behaved of all the five hundred students who were his pupils. All of his duties, such as bathing and perfuming his teacher's feet, he performed with diligence. But he was so slow he could not learn a single thing. The teacher thought to himself, 'This man is so attentive to me, I will train him.' But although he tried as hard as he could, he could not teach him anything. [251] After the youth had stayed for a long time, but still could not grasp one verse, he decided to leave, and asked his teacher. The teacher thought: 'This young man is so attentive to me, I would like to make him a learned wise man, but I cannot do this. So I'll compose a spell[57] for him and give him that.' So he took him to the forest and composed for him the chant: 'You are rubbing, you are rubbing! Why are you rubbing? That I know!' And he taught him this spell, and got him to repeat it over and over again, many hundreds of times. 'Do you know it now?' 'Yes, I know it.' The teacher thought to himself: 'If someone who is slow makes a good effort and learns a skill thoroughly, it will not leave him.' And he sent him on his way, giving him expenses for the journey. 'Go and make a living from this spell. But do keep repeating it again and again so you always remember it!' When he arrived back at Varanasi, his mother said, 'My son has come back, well-trained!' And she gave a festive meal in his honour.

At that time the king of Varanasi reviewed his own behaviour: 'Have I committed any misdemeanour?' He could not see any fault, but he thought some more: 'The person involved cannot see any fault in himself, but others can. I'll make a tour of the city and ask around.' So in the evening he put on a disguise. 'When people have eaten their meal in the evening, they sit around and have all kinds of conversations and gossip. If I am ruling unjustly, they will say, "We are being ruined by wrongful punishments and unfair taxes". And if I am ruling justly, they will say, "Long live our king!" [251] And they will talk all about my good points.' And he went about the city, walking close to the walls of houses.

At that moment, some tunnel-burglars were making a tunnel between two houses, in order to break into two houses by one tunnel. The king stood there watching in the shadow of the house. Now in this house lived the young man who had just come back from Taxila with the spell. When the burglars had dug the tunnel, they entered the house and started to go over all the goods in it. The young man woke up and chanted his spell: 'You are rubbing, you are rubbing! Why are you rubbing? That I know, that I know!' When the burglars heard this, they said: 'It looks like this man knows what we are up to! Now he'll kill us.' And immediately dropping even the clothes they were wearing, they fled, terrified, by the first route they could see. The king, seeing them run away, and hearing the words of the young man as he repeated his spell, carried on walking around the city and then went home.

When the night started to lighten, and the dawn to come, the king summoned a certain man. 'Go, my good man, to such and such street, and in a certain house, where a tunnel has been dug, you will find a young man who has returned from Taxila, learning various skills. Bring him here.' The man went to get him, and saying that he was summoned by the king, brought him back to him. The king said, 'My friend, are you the youth who has just come back from Taxila after learning various skills?' 'Yes, sire.' 'Give us this particular craft.' 'Very well, sire, sit down on the same seat as me and learn it.' The king learned the spell there and then, and said to him, [253] 'This is your teaching fee'. And he gave him a thousand coins.

Now at this time, the general of the army said to the king's barber, 'When will you be shaving the king's beard?' 'Either tomorrow or the next day.' He gave him a thousand coins, and said, 'I have a job for you to do.' 'What is it, sir?' 'Act just as if you are shaving the king's beard, and then cut his windpipe. Then I will be king and you will be general of the army.' The barber said, 'Very well' and agreed. On the day for the king's beard shaving, he moistened the beard with perfumed water, sharpened his razor, and applied it to the king's cheek. But he thought, 'This razor is a bit blunt, and his windpipe should be cut with a single stroke.' So he stood at one side and sharpened the razor. At that moment the king remembered the spell he had been given, and chanted it: 'You are rubbing, you are rubbing! Why are you rubbing? That I know, that I know!' Sweat poured out of the barber's forehead. 'The king knows all about this plot.' Terrified, he threw his razor to the ground and prostrated himself, flat on his chest, before the feet of the king.

Kings are pretty worldly wise. The king of Varanasi said: 'You dastardly barber! That you could think, "The king does not know about this!"' 'Please grant me freedom from fear, sire.' 'Very well: you will be spared. Now tell me about it.' 'The general of the army gave me a thousand coins, sire. And he said to me, "Act as if you are shaving the king's beard, and then cut his windpipe."' The king thought, 'It is because of my teacher that my life was spared'. [254] He summoned the general and said to him, 'So, great general of the army. What is there that you have not received from me? Now I cannot bear to look at you. Get out of this kingdom.' And he banished him from the kingdom. Then he sent for the teacher. 'It is because of you, my teacher, that my life was spared.' He bestowed great honour upon him, and made him general of the army instead.

At that time, Little Tracker was the young man, and the world-renowned teacher was the Teacher himself. Therefore, when he had finished recounting the tale from the past, he said, 'In this way, monks, in earlier lives, Little Tracker was also dull, and I was his support, and set him up with a worldly household.'

[The Buddha, the commentary continues, then tells the *Cullakaseṭṭhi-Jātaka* (J 4), about Little Tracker in an earlier life, who is guided by the Bodhisatta, the Buddha's previous self, into selling a dead mouse to a household that needs to feed a cat. Through a series of escalating enterprises the young man becomes a wealthy shipowner. Making a parallel with progress in meditation, he concludes his storytelling about Little Tracker with another verse, summing up the journey of the slow struggler in meditation, who eventually finds success, in life and in the path:]

A man of even little means can, with understanding and training, raise himself up:
Just by blowing on a little flame one can start a great fire

(Ja I 121).

[The Buddha then announces Little Tracker's arahatship, and reassures his followers that the monk who follows his precepts wholeheartedly cannot fail to find transcendent wealth too:]

By rousing himself, and by diligence, and by self-control, the one who is wise makes an island no flood can overcome.

(DhpA I 239–55/ Dhp 25)[58]

CHAPTER SIX

BUDDHAGHOSA: SOME PRACTICAL TIPS ON MEDITATION

From the outset of the tradition, teachers gave guidance and commentary on the texts formally recited as part of the canon. But it is to Buddhaghosa, the fifth-century commentator whose magisterial writings have provided the Southern Buddhist tradition with meditational advice, anecdote and instruction on points of *dhamma* for centuries, that we owe the fact that so many of these oral traditions have survived in written form to the present day. Throughout the many commentaries attributed to him, and from their sheer quantity many other authors were involved, Buddhaghosa provides glosses on the texts, helpful lists of 'check points' to the practice, injunctions and 'how to' details to aid the meditator, based largely on canonical instructions, but developed and elaborated more for practical guidance. The meditation manual ascribed to him, *The Path of Purification* (*Visuddhimagga*), is filled with notes, stories, advice, tips, anecdotes, exempla, warnings and admonitions, ancient precedents and straightforwardly practical physical tips as to what to do when ill or when there is too much building work going on where you are trying to meditate. The great popularity of this volume, which has continued to the present day, is not surprising. Unlike the canonical texts, it was composed as a written text.

Buddhaghosa was born to a high-caste brahmin family in India, and we do not know much about his life except that at some point he travelled to, and remained in, Sri Lanka. Stationed at the great centre of the Mahāvihāra monastery in Anuradhapura, when asked, he set about recording oral traditions that had accreted around the practice of Buddhism over what was by now the many hundreds of years since the founder of the tradition had died. The rest of his life seems to have been spent writing about Buddhism, its practices, and its meditations, making commentaries on the *suttas*, and composing *The Path of Purification (Visuddhimagga)*. He did not see himself, nor wanted to be, innovative: he cites other sources frequently, such as canonical and *Abhidhamma* texts, and recounts many stories, often taken from earlier centuries of a now established meditative tradition. In the case of instructions, say, as to how to make *kasiṇa* devices, the constructions devised by the meditator for some forms of calm practice, or different ways of conducting loving-kindness meditation, there is no reason to suppose that he is not recording instructions around at the time of the Buddha that were perhaps so frequently observed, or so often taught in person, that they would not have been thought necessary to be included in the more formal composition of early Buddhist texts.

His guidance, stories and practical advice have provided the basis of the Southern Buddhist meditative traditions. While these modern schools are still inventive and richly diverse, most in some way relate to the way he codified meditation practice – in his list of forty meditation objects, for instance, or the recommendations to adjust the practice where necessary or when it is unbalanced. Given the various vicissitudes that have come to Buddhist practice over the centuries, in Sri Lanka, for example, where the fortunes of the sangha of monks have sometimes faltered and declined, *The Path of Purification* must have ensured that the meditative traditions were not completely lost. At some point in the twelfth century, the temple with which he was associated, the Mahāvihāra, seems to have been accepted as a general authority on Buddhist practice throughout Southeast Asia and Sri Lanka, and given rise to the form of Buddhism that has been called in the twentieth century Theravāda, the teaching of the elders. Whether or not it really is the oldest lineage of Buddhist practice we do not know, but the Southern Buddhist Pāli tradition maintains one strand of early Buddhism that has, uniquely, been preserved in its entirety, and has continued to be the main practice tradition of nearly all of the Buddhists in Southeast Asia and Sri Lanka.

The following passage is typical of the kind of lists of advice and practical help in meditation. The first list gives seven areas to consider when practising *samatha* meditation, in order to 'guard' the sign or mental image.

The mental image (*nimitta*), a visual sign of some *samatha* meditation, sometimes arises in the mind at different stages of development, when pursuing practices such as *kasiṇa* meditation and some forms of breathing mindfulness. This initial advice is aimed at those pursuing meditation when it has already been developed, with the help of the teacher. This care is compared to that of a mother, who knows she is carrying a universal monarch in her womb, and wants to protect it. It is noteworthy that he repeatedly recommends asking the teacher and 'mixing with concentrated people', or those experienced in *samatha* practice, for most problems: such an emphasis on skilled guidance was and remains a central feature in meditation practice. For progress in calm meditation a healthy attitude and non-attached friendliness to any objects that arise in the mind are helped by the teacher.

This extract has been chosen, however, not only for this specialized application, but as a guide to care and practicality in the *kinds* of factors that can affect many forms of meditation practice. So some adjustments for modern and lay life need to be made. A practitioner might not be able to move to a better climate or nicer flat, for instance, but it is important to see that the physical base where one lives gives a welcoming space for practice, and that, if possible, it is best to avoid living in a situation of conflict or difficulty. Posture may need varying, as diet may, according to what suits. Suitability to person and meditation is key. One new term here is that of access concentration (*upacāra-samādhi*). Not used in the canon, it describes entering the 'neighbourhood' of *jhāna*, without the mind yet having the strength of the balance of the five faculties of meditation, faith, vigour, mindfulness, concentration and wisdom, to enter it fully.

Next is the 'The Ten Kinds of Skills in Absorption' (Vism IV 42–73). The extract works through its use of carefully compiled lists, overlaid with canonical categories; oral features such as repetition and reiteration can still be seen in this written text. One list it exploits heavily is that of the factors of awakening (*bojjhaṅga*) featuring earlier in this anthology. Buddhaghosa, acting on canonical suggestions, shows how one *bojjhaṅga* may be used when the mind is unbalanced in some way. The first part of the sequence is associated more with wisdom and vigour, and problems can involve too much effort or excitement. The second part of the list is associated with concentration and stilling the mind: potential problems are that the mind may become sleepy or sluggish. Here, we can see his painstaking, commentarial style of systematization and exhaustive explanation of canonical statements: the freshness and lucidity of canonical material is sometimes lost, but all contingencies are carefully investigated. All these texts would be known by those who read or heard the commentarial material. His advice organizes centuries of an accumulative hyper-text created by generations of teachers and practitioners; commentaries are the product of the way practices were taught over all this time. It is possible the manuals were still learnt by heart as teaching supports, with the tradition continuing to be heavily reliant on interaction and exchange.

Again, the list has been chosen for its consideration of so many aspects of life and their implications for meditation. Its wide-ranging advice, indicating factors that may help any meditator at certain times, ends with the five similes, useful for understanding 'right effort' in any meditative system.

Concentration
Guarding the mental image

[127] 1. Lodging place

In this case, a lodging place is unsuitable if the mental image does not arise for one living there, or, if it does arise, it disappears; and it is unsuitable where mindfulness that has not been aroused does not arise and the unconcentrated mind does not go to calm. A lodging place is a suitable one if the mental image does arise for one staying there, becomes steady (*thāvaraṅ*), and if mindfulness is aroused and the mind goes to calm, as was the case for the elder Tissa, resident at the Nāga mountain. So, if a monastery has many places to stay in, then he can live in them one by one, staying in each for three days, and staying put at the place where his mind becomes one-pointed. For it was due to suitability of lodging place that five hundred monks attained arahantship while still staying at the Lesser Nāga Cave in

Tambapaṇṇi after apprehending their object of meditation there. Yet there is no counting the stream-enterers who have attained arahantship there after attaining the noble plane elsewhere.[1]

2. Daily round (*gocara*)[2]
An almsround village lying to the north or the south of the lodging, not too far away, within one and a half *kosas*,[3] where it is easy to obtain almsfood, is suitable; the opposite is not.

3. Speech
Talk under the category of the thirty-two kinds of aimless talk is unsuitable, for it leads to the disappearance of the mental image. However, talk that has its basis in the ten kinds of suitable talk is suitable, though even that should be discussed in moderation.[4]

4. Person
Someone who does not indulge in aimless chatter and who has excellent moral restraint (*sīla*), from whose guidance the unconcentrated mind becomes calm, the calmed mind becomes more stable: such is the suitable person. One who is obsessed with bodily exercise, or who is addicted to aimless talk, is unsuitable; he just creates disturbance, like muddy water added to clear water. It was because of someone like this that the attainments of the young monk who lived at the Peak Mountain disappeared, not to mention the mental image.[5]

5. Food
Sweet food suits one person; sour suits another.

6. Season
A cool climate is suitable for one person; a hot for another. So, when he finds that by eating certain food, or by living in a certain climate, he is comfortable, the unconcentrated mind becomes calm, and the concentrated mind becomes more stable, then that food and climate are suitable. Any other food or climate is unsuitable.

7. Postures

Walking is suitable for one person; standing or sitting or lying down suits another. So he should try them out, like the dwelling place, for three days each, and the posture is suitable in which his unconcentrated mind becomes concentrated or his concentrated mind becomes more stable. Any other is to be understood as unsuitable.

So, he should avoid the seven unsuitable kinds and cultivate the suitable. For when he practises in this way, diligently cultivating the sign, it will not be long before he attains concentration.

In addition, for someone who does attain concentration, then the ten skills in skilful absorption are desirable to accomplish his aim. The method is as follows:

Ten skills needed for skilful absorption[6]

1. Making the base clean
2. Bringing the faculties into balance
3. Skill in the mental image
4. At the time when the mind should be exerted, at that time he exerts the mind
5. At the time when the mind should be restrained, at that time he restrains the mind
6. At the time when the mind should be encouraged, at that time he encourages the mind
7. At the time when the mind should be looked upon with equanimity, at that time he looks upon the mind with equanimity
8. Keeping away from unconcentrated people
9. Keeping company with concentrated people
10. Releasing onto that[7]

1. Making the base clean

This is making sure the personal and the outer bases are clean. For if the head hair, nails and bodily hair are long, or the body soaked in sweat, then the personal base is not clean and is dirty.[8] And if the robe is old, dirty, stained and foul smelling, then the outer base is not clean and is dirty. [129] Where the personal and the outer base are not clean, knowledge, with the mental state and the accompanying factors that have arisen with it, is unpurified, as if a flame has arisen depending on a butter-lamp bowl that has not been cleaned out.[9] With unpurified knowledge, the formations (*saṅkhārā*) are not clear to the one trying to understand them, and when he devotes himself to his meditation object, the meditation object does not go to maturity, growth and full development. But with the personal and the outer base clean, knowledge, with the mental state and the accompanying factors that have arisen with it, is purified, as if a flame has arisen depending on [oil in] a butter-lamp bowl that has been cleaned up. And with purified knowledge, the formations are clear to the one trying to understand them and when he devotes himself to his meditation object, the meditation object does go to maturity, growth and full development.

2. Bringing the faculties into balance

Is making the faculties evenly balanced, starting with faith.[10] For if the faculty of faith is strong, but the others weak, then the faculty of vigour cannot do its job of exerting, mindfulness cannot do its job of attending, the faculty of concentration cannot do its job of not distracting, and the faculty of wisdom cannot do its job of seeing. So the faculty of faith should be modified, through reviewing the essential nature of phenomena,[11] or by not paying attention to it in a way that faculty of faith becomes too strong. This is illustrated by the case of the elder Vakkali.[12]

If the faculty of vigour is strong and the others weak, then the faculty of faith cannot do its job of releasing, and the other faculties cannot do their jobs either. Therefore, the faculty of vigour should be allayed by the cultivation of tranquillity and such factors. This should be seen in the case of the elder Soṇa.[13] So too with the rest of them: for it is to be understood that if any one of them becomes unbalanced, the others cannot perform their separate functions. But what they particularly recommend is the balancing of faith with wisdom and concentration with vigour. The one strong in faith and weak in wisdom is intoxicated in his confidence (*muddhappasanna*) and has devotion without basis. The one who is strong in wisdom and weak in faith errs on the side of cunning deceit, and is as hard to cure as the one who is sick through too much medicine. With the balance of the two faculties, the man is confident with grounds to be so.

But indolence overcomes the one who is strong in concentration and weak in vigour, because concentration can err on the side of indolence. [130] Restlessness overcomes the one who is strong in vigour and weak in concentration, because vigour can err on the side of restlessness. But concentration coupled with vigour does not lapse into indolence; vigour coupled with concentration does not lapse into restlessness. Therefore, both are to be cultivated evenly: for absorption (*appanā*) comes with the balance of the two.

Again, for the one working on concentration, strong faith is required. For through having such faith he has trust when he reaches absorption. Then there is the relationship between concentration and wisdom. For the one working on concentration (*samādhi*) strong unification (*ekaggatā*) is needed, since that is how he reaches absorption. For the one working on insight (*vipassanā*) wisdom needs to be strong, as this is how he reaches penetration of the three marks (*lakkhaṇa paṭivedha*).[14] Yet with both in balance, he reaches absorption too.

Strong mindfulness, however, is needed in all instances. For mindfulness protects the mind from lapsing into restlessness, through faith, vigour and wisdom, which can tend towards restlessness; and from lapsing into indolence, through concentration, which can tend towards indolence. So it is desirable in all circumstances, just as seasoning with salt is in all kinds of dishes, or just as a minister in overall command is in all of the king's business. Because of this, it is said that mindfulness has been termed universally applicable by the Blessed One. And what is the reason for this? Mindfulness is the true refuge of the mind, mindfulness is manifested as protection, and there is no exerting or restraining of the mind without mindfulness.[15]

3. Skill in the mental image
This is skill in developing the mental image of unification of the mind, through the earth *kasiṇa* and the rest, when it has not arisen. And it is skill in developing the sign when it has arisen; and it is skill in guarding the mental image when it has been obtained through cultivation. This last is what is meant here.

4. And in what way, *at the time when the mind should be exerted, at that time he exerts the mind*? When the mind is sluggish through slackened vigour and the rest, then instead of developing the three factors of awakening starting with tranquillity [tranquillity, concentration and equanimity], he should develop those beginning with investigation of states [investigation of states, vigour and joy].[16] For this is said by the Blessed One:

'Monks, suppose a man wanted to make a little fire burn up, and he laid wet grasses on it, put wet cow dung on it, put wet sticks on it, left rainy winds to go on it, and scattered it with dust: now would that man be able to make a little fire blaze up?'

'Surely not, venerable Sir.'

'Just so, monks, when the mind is sluggish, that is the wrong time to cultivate the factor of awakening that is tranquillity, the factor of awakening that is concentration and the factor of awakening that is equanimity. Why so? Because the sluggish mind cannot be aroused well by these states. When the mind is sluggish, that is the time to develop the factor of awakening that is investigation of states, the factor of awakening that is vigour and the factor of awakening that is joy. Why is that? Because a sluggish mind can be aroused well by these states.'

'Monks, suppose a man wanted to make a little fire burn up, and he put dry grasses on it, put dry cow dung on it, put dry sticks on it, blew it with his mouth, and did not scatter dust on it, would that man be able to make the little fire burn up?'

'Yes, venerable Sir.'

(S V 112)

And here, the development of the factor of awakening that is investigation of states and the rest [and the other two, vigour and joy] are to be understood as the nutriment for each. As it is said:

'There are, monks, skilful and unskilful states, blameworthy and unblameworthy states, inferior and superior states, dark and bright states, the opposites to one another. Wise attention (*yoniso-manasikāra*), practised frequently there: this is the food for the arising of the unarisen factor of awakening that is investigation of states, or for the getting greater, full development, cultivation and perfection of the factor of awakening that is investigation of states.' (S V 104)[17]

In the same way, 'There is, monks, the element of making a start, the element of exerting (*nikkamadhātu*) and the element of heroic striving (*parakkamadhātu*). Wise attention, practised frequently there: this is the food for the arising of the unarisen factor of awakening that is vigour, or for the getting greater, full development, cultivation and perfection of the factor of awakening that is vigour.'

In the same way, 'There are, monks, states that are founded on the factor of awakening that is joy. Wise attention, practised frequently there: this is the food for the arising of the unarisen factor of awakening that is joy, or for the getting greater, full development, cultivation and perfection of the factor of awakening that is joy.' [132]

Here, 'wise attention', given to skilful states and the rest, means the turning of attention towards the penetration of the essential nature of things (*sabhāva*) and of the three marks of existence. 'Wise attention given to the element of making a start' and the rest is the turning of attention involved in the arousing of the element of making a start, and so on. Here, 'making a start' refers to the vigour used at the beginning. The 'element of being strong in' is the stronger than that because it makes an exertion, getting out of idleness (*kosajjato nikkhantattā*). The element of heroic striving is even stronger than that, because it goes on striving in successive later stages. And here 'states that are founded on the factor of awakening that is joy' just means joy itself; attention that arouses that is 'wise attention'.

There are, in addition, seven things that lead to the arising of the factor of awakening that is **investigation of states**:

1. Asking questions
2. Making the base clean
3. Balancing the faculties
4. Avoiding the company of those without wisdom
5. Keeping company with wise people
6. Reviewing the field of profound knowledge
7. Releasing onto that[18]

Eleven factors lead to the arising of the factor of awakening that is **vigour**:

1. Reviewing the fearfulness of states of loss, such as the hell realms
2. Seeing the benefit of attaining the worldly and the supramundane distinction based on vigour
3. Reviewing the way ahead that is to be taken, in the following way: 'The path taken by the Buddha, *paccekabuddhas* and arahats is to be undertaken by me, and it is not be entered upon by a lazy person'
4. Being a credit to the almsround by producing great fruit for donors
5. Reviewing the greatness of the teacher in the following way: 'My teacher praises the getting going of vigour; and this unsurpassable teaching that is so helpful to us is honoured by practising it, not by anything else'
6. Reviewing the greatness of the inheritance in the following way: 'The teaching that is good and has been called the great inheritance is for me to take hold of; it is not possible for a lazy person to grasp it'
7. Removing sloth and torpor by paying attention to the perception of light, by change in posture, and by spending time in the open air, and the rest[19]

8. Avoiding the company of lazy people
9. Keeping company with those who have aroused vigour
10. Reviewing the four right efforts[20]
11. Releasing on to that

Eleven things lead to the factor of awakening that is **joy**:

1. The recollection of the Buddha
2. The recollection of *dhamma*
3. The recollection of the sangha
4. The recollection of good conduct (*sīla*)
5. The recollection of generosity
6. The recollection of the *devas*[21]
7. The recollection of peace[22]
8. Avoiding the company of unpleasant people
9. Keeping company with friendly people
10. Reviewing *suttas* that bring happy confidence (*pasādanīyasuttantā*)
11. Releasing on to that

Through these skills (*ākārā*) he develops the factor of awakening that is investigation of states, and the rest [vigour and joy]. This is how he exerts his mind at the time when it needs to be exerted.

5. How is it that *at the time when the mind should be restrained, at that time he restrains the mind*?

When his mind is restless through the excessive use of vigour and the rest, then, instead of developing the three factors of awakening beginning with investigation of states, he should develop those beginning with tranquillity. For the Blessed One said this:

'Suppose, monks, a man should wish to quench a great fire, and he put dry grasses on it, put dry cow dung on it, put dry sticks on it, blew it with his mouth, and did not scatter dust on it, would that man be able to quench a great fire?'

'No, Venerable sir.'

'So it is, monks, at such time as the mind is restless, that is not the time to develop the factor of awakening that is investigation of states, the factor of awakening that is vigour and the factor of awakening that is joy. What is the reason for this? Because a restless mind cannot be brought to peacefulness with these factors. When the mind is restless, that is the time to develop the factor of awakening that is tranquillity, the factor of awakening that is concentration and the factor of awakening that is equanimity. What is the reason for this? Because the restless mind can be brought to peacefulness with these factors.

Monks, suppose a man would wish to quench a great fire, and he put wet grasses on it, put wet cow dung on it, put wet sticks on it and left rainy winds to go on it, and scattered ashes on it, would that man be able to quench a great fire?'

'Certainly, sir.' (S V 114)

'Just so, monks, at the time the mind is restless, that is the time to cultivate the factor of awakening that is tranquillity, the factor of awakening that is concentration and the factor of awakening that is equanimity. What is the reason for this? Because, monks, the restless mind can be brought to peacefulness with these factors.'

And here the development of the factor of awakening that is tranquillity should be understood as the food for each one in turn, for it is said:

'Monks, there is tranquillity of mind and there is tranquillity of body.[23] Wise attention, practised frequently, is the food for the unarisen factor of awakening that is tranquillity, or for the getting greater, full development, cultivation and perfection of the factor of awakening that is tranquillity.' Likewise, 'Monks, there is the sign of calm (*samathanimitta*) and the sign of non-distraction (*avyagganimitta*). Here wise attention, practised frequently: this is the food for the arousing of the unarisen factor of awakening that is concentration, or for the getting greater, full development, cultivation and perfection of the factor of awakening that is concentration.'

Likewise: 'There are states, monks, that are founded in the factor of awakening that is equanimity. Wise attention, practised frequently: this is the food for the arising of the unarisen factor of awakening that is equanimity; or for the getting greater, full development, cultivation and perfection of the factor of awakening that is equanimity.' (S V 104)

Here, 'wise attention' in three situations refers to the attention that occurs in the skill that had been exercised in causing their arising, where the factors have arisen earlier. 'The sign of calm' is this denoter (*adhiva-cana*) of calm. 'The sign of non-distraction' is the non-scattering of this.

Seven things cause the appearance of the factor of awakening that is **tranquillity**:

1. Having contact with superior food
2. Living in a pleasant climate
3. Adopting comfortable postures
4. Keeping to middleness
5. Avoiding people who are angry
6. Keeping company with people who are tranquil
7. Releasing on to that

Eleven things cause the arousal of the factor of awakening that is **concentration**:

1. Making the base clean
2. Skill in the mental image
3. Balancing the faculties
4. Restraining the mind at the time for that
5. Exerting the mind at the time for that
6. Encouraging the mind with faith and a sense of urgency
7. Looking on with equanimity at what is occurring that is right
8. Avoiding unconcentrated people
9. Keeping company with concentrated people

10. Reviewing of the *jhānas* and liberation
11. Releasing on to that

Five things cause the arousal of the factor of awakening that is **equanimity**:

1. Staying in the middle with regard to beings
2. Staying in the middle with regard to formations
3. Avoiding people who show partiality towards beings and formations
4. Keeping company with people who stay in the middle with regard to beings and formations
5. Releasing on to that

By means of these skills aroused in these ways, he develops the factor of awakening that is tranquillity, and the rest. This is how at the time when the mind should be restrained, at that time he restrains the mind.

6. How is it that *at the time when the mind should be encouraged, at that time he encourages the mind*?
When his mind is 'without taste' because of dullness in the exercise of wisdom or failure to attain the happiness of peace, at that time he urges his mind by means of reviewing the eight grounds for a sense of urgency. The eight grounds for a sense of urgency are: the four of birth, ageing, sickness and death; the fifth, the suffering of loss; past suffering that has its roots in the cycle of births; future suffering that has its roots in the cycle of rebirths; and the suffering of the present that has its roots in the search for food. And he produces confidence (*pasāda*) through recollecting the qualities of the Buddha, the *dhamma* and the sangha. In this way, at the time when the mind should be encouraged, at that time he encourages the mind.

7. How is it that *at the time when the mind should be looked upon with equanimity, at that time he looks upon the mind with equanimity*?

When he is practising in this way and his mind is following the path of calm (*samatha*), progressing evenly with regard to the object, and is not sluggish, restless, or without taste: that is the time he does not enter into the business of exerting or restraining or encouraging, like a charioteer with evenly progressing horses. In this way, at the time when the mind should be looked upon with equanimity, at that time he looks upon the mind with equanimity.

8) *Keeping away from unconcentrated people* means keeping far away from those who have never followed the path of meditation (*nekkhamapaṭipadaṃ*), who are preoccupied with all kinds of business and who are distracted in their hearts.

9) *Keeping company with concentrated people* means approaching from time to time those who have followed the path of meditation and who have obtained concentration.

10. *Releasing onto that* means the state of releasing onto concentration: the meaning of this is the according of value to concentration, inclining towards concentration, leaning towards concentration, tending towards concentration.

In this way, the tenfold skill in absorption is to undertaken by someone who has obtained the sign, and turns to absorption.

The Five Similes

For the one who undertakes this, this is skill in absorption.
With the obtaining of the mental image, absorption follows.

And if in spite of his following this practice, no mental image turns up –
still the sensible person just keeps on making an effort.

A young man cannot attain to distinction if he does not make right effort;

Even if what he attains is slight, still he holds his ground.

The one who is awake therefore notices the state of his mind as it presents itself.[24]
And repeatedly brings vigour into balance with calm.

So he stirs up the slack mind, stretching a loose string,
And restrains the overexerted mind, and so he guides the mind to evenness.

Just as with the examples of a bee to pollen, the lotus leaf, the thread, the boat, and the oil tubes, so there is an apt way of doing things.

So he releases completely both the sluggish and overexerted mind.
And in this manner he steers his mind on its way in the presence of the mental image.

(Vism 125–37 (Pāli)/IV 125–35)

The way of progress in the presence of the mental image

The bee

Here is the explanation of the meaning. When an overhasty bee, finding out that a flower on a tree is in bloom, dashes there with great haste, it overshoots the mark, turns back and finds the pollen has been finished. And another, not eager enough, goes too slowly and arrives when the pollen is finished too. But a skilled bee sets off with an evenly balanced speed, easily finds the cluster of flowers, and taking as much pollen as it pleases, it enjoys the honey.

The lotus leaf

And when a surgeon's pupils are being trained in using a scalpel on a lotus leaf floating in a dish of water, one who is too eager applies the scalpel hastily and either cuts the lotus leaf in half or pushes it under the water. Another, not eager enough, does not even dare to touch it with the scalpel for fear of cutting it in half or pushing it under the water. But another, who is skilled, applies the scalpel onto it with an evenly balanced effort and showing himself highly trained in such matters, receives the prize.

The thread

And again, when the king announces, 'Anyone who can draw out a spider's thread four measures long shall receive four thousand coins'. The one who is too eager fills it in haste and breaks it in various places. Another who is not eager enough does not dare to touch it with his hand for fear of breaking it. But a skilled man pulls it out, starting from the end, with an evenly balanced effort, and winds it on a stick and so wins the reward.

The boat

And again, when a too eager skipper hoists full sails in a high wind, he sends his ship off course, when one who is not eager enough lowers his sails in a light wind and just remains where he is. A skilled skipper hoists full sails in a light wind, takes in half the sails in a high wind and so arrives safely at his desired destination.

The oil tubes

And again, a teacher says, 'Anyone who can fill the oil tube without spilling any oil will win a prize'. One who is too eager, out of greed for the reward, fills it in haste, and spills the oil. Another, not eager enough, does not dare to pour the oil at all out of fear of spilling it. But the one who is skilled fills it and wins the prize.

In this way a practitioner, when the mental image has arisen, applies excessive vigour, thinking, 'I am going to get to absorption quickly!'

Then his mind falls into restlessness through overexertion, and he cannot reach absorption. Another, seeing the fault in overexertion, slacks off the effort and his mind falls into indolence through sluggishness and he too cannot reach absorption. Yet another, who frees his mind from slackness even when it is just a little slack and from restlessness even when it is just a little restless, comes into the presence of the mental image with an evenly balanced effort, and so reaches absorption. This last example is the one to follow.

Just as with the examples of a bee to pollen, the lotus leaf, the thread, the boat, and the oil tubes, so there is an apt way of doing things. So he releases completely both the sluggish and overexerted mind. In this manner he steers his mind on its way in the presence of the mental image. (Vism 127–37/IV 35–73)

CHAPTER SEVEN

MILINDA'S QUESTIONS

In the second century BCE a Greek-born king, Menander (Milinda), who probably ruled from around 160–150 BCE to 135 BCE, appears to have converted to Buddhism and taken up the practice of meditation. An extended dialogue, *Milinda's Questions*, between him and a sage and teacher, Nāgasena, of whom we know nothing from other sources, describes his conversion. Historical accounts, alongside extensive numismatic, inscriptional and other archaeological evidence, attest for a strong Greek presence in the North and Northwestern regions of the subcontinent by this period. Relationships between the cultures seem to have been cordial, with literary accounts indicating both cultures were sympathetic to the ideas and mores of the other.[1] Tolerance, so strongly promulgated by the Buddhist Indian king Aśoka, who instructed fairness to different religious groups as part of his doctrine of *dharma*, seems to have survived, resurfaced or perhaps been taken for granted in the region, for a short period at any rate. We cannot ascertain whether he really did renounce his kingdom for meditation, as the *Milinda's Questions* maintains, but coins of his reign show the eight-spoked wheel, with inscriptions in Greek and Bactrian in Kharoṣṭhi script.

Menander's kingdom appears to have been greatly prosperous. According to the *Milinda's Questions* his city, Sāgalā, now Sāgkot in Pakistan, from which he ruled with considerable success a large region of Northwest India, was hilly, well watered, populous, and rich. It seems he was regarded, and considered himself to be, a Buddhist monarch in the Aśokan style, with aspirations to the ideals of a universal monarch, cited in the extract below. Plutarch notes that Menander's relics were distributed after his death, a practice associated with the universal monarch.[2] Whether or not Milinda did become a Buddhist, the presence of this dialogue testifies to a flowering of Buddhist culture, theory and meditative practice in a period and place where the tradition encountered radically different peoples and mores, and flourished within that context: it is a 'dialogue' that has grown out of and gives expression to real interactions and human interchanges.

The original date of *Milinda's Questions* is unclear, or indeed the language in which it was first composed. It has been suggested that the first version of the work may have been composed in Sanskrit or another Indo-Aryan language, but no other evidence of such a text has survived. The *Questions* appears to have been compiled over a period of time, apparently accreting new material, a hypothesis supported by the fact that translations of the text in China, where the work might have travelled at an early date, are so much shorter.[3] In some regards the pattern of questioning seems to resemble the style of Platonic dialogues. Its most obvious counterpart is the *sutta* style of the *nikāyas*: the Burmese include it in their list of canonical texts. Whatever its date and origins, in its question and answer method, extensive use of simile, metaphor and word plays, there is a pattern familiar from early Buddhist discourse, found, for instance, in the *Katthavatthu*. In South and Southeast Asia its popularity continues to the present day: an animated television series of King Milinda and some of his questions is very successful in Thailand. From the perspective of Buddhist meditation, this extract is helpful to show how various features like the five faculties of meditative practice are understood.

The five faculties of meditation

As a preliminary to an explanation of 'skilful mental states' (*kusalā dhammā*), Nāgasena speaks first of *sīla* and the thirty-seven factors leading to awakening, and then the five faculties needed for the skilful mind and for meditation: faith, vigour, mindfulness, concentration and wisdom. This is a canonical list, but this extended passage gives explanations of each of the five faculties describing their distinguishing marks and giving similes for how they work in the meditation practice. The five working together provide the meditator with all the resources needed to develop the meditations: they are described as needing 'balancing' for, and through, meditation by Buddhaghosa in the passage in the previous chapter of this anthology. Throughout the interchange, the practitioner is referred to as *yogāvacara*, a term usually found in *Abhidhamma* texts, referring to the follower of practices leading to awakening. This is suitable, of course, here rather than the generic 'monk' used in early Buddhist texts, which seems to be used there even where the practitioner is a lay-person.[4] Another notable feature is the way that the images extend or add to canonical precedents: many of these will be recognized from other texts in the anthology.

The king said: 'Nāgasena, sir, what is the distinguishing mark of faith?'

'Great king, making tranquil (*sampasādana*) is a distinguishing mark (*lakkhaṇa*) of faith and leaping out is a distinguishing mark of faith.'[5]

'How, venerable sir, is making tranquil a distinguishing mark of faith?'

'When faith has arisen the hindrances disappear, great king, and the mind is clear, pure, and serene: in this way, great king, making tranquil is the distinguishing mark of faith.'

'Make a simile!'

'Just as, great king, a universal monarch with a four-limbed army, proceeding along a road, might cross over a small amount of water, and that water, disturbed by elephants, horses, chariots, and foot-soldiers, would become foul, brackish and muddy. The king, who has just crossed over, might give a command to his men: "Sir, bring water; let us drink." And the king might have a water-purifying jewel, and so the people, when they had assented to the king, saying, "Certainly, sire", might throw the jewel into the water, and as soon as it had been thrown into the water the various water-weeds would disappear and the mud subside and the water become clear, pure and serene. Then they would offer drinking water to that king, a wheel-turning monarch, saying: 'May his majesty drink this water.' In this way, great king, the water is to be seen as the mind, the men are to be understood as like the practitioner, the various water weeds are understood to be like the defilements, the water-purifying gem is understood to be like faith, and just as the water weeds would disappear and the mud subside as soon as the water-purifying jewel had been cast in the water and the water would become clear, pure and serene, in just this way, great king, faith, as it arises, makes the hindrances subside, and the unobstructed mind is clear, pure and serene. In this way, great king, making tranquil is a distinguishing mark of faith.'

'And how, great king, is leaping out a distinguishing mark of faith?'

'Great king, just as a practitioner sees the mind of others freed, and so leaps out to the fruits of stream-entry, once-return, never-return and arahatship and practises meditation for the sake of the unattained, for the mastery of the unmastered, for the realization of the unrealized, even so, great king, leaping out is a distinguishing mark of faith.'

'Make a simile.'

'Just as, great king, a great rain-cloud might pour down rain on a high mountain so that the water, coursing along down the side of the mountain, after filling up the gullies, clefts and tributaries on the mountain-slope, would fill up a river so that it would run along overflowing both its banks. And then, if a crowd of people were to come, but, not knowing the width or the depth or the river, they might stand terrified and hesitant on the bank. But if a man were to come along who recognized his own power and strength, and if he were to tie on his loin-cloth and leap out, he would cross the river.[6] The crowd of people, seeing that he had crossed over, would cross over too. Even so, just as a practitioner, having seen that the minds of others are freed, and so leaps out to the fruits of stream-entry, once-return, never-return and arahatship, in turn, and practises meditation for the attainment of the unattained, for the mastery of the unmastered, for the realizing of the unrealized. And this is how, great king, leaping out is a distinguishing mark of faith. Indeed, the Blessed One made this statement in the *Saṃyuttanikāya*,

With faith he crosses the flood, with awareness the waters.
Through vigour he passes over suffering; with wisdom he purifies the mind.'

'Good, Nāgasena!'

The king said, 'Nāgasena, sir, what is a distinguishing mark of vigour?' 'Supporting is a distinguishing mark of vigour, great king. All those good qualities (*kusalā dhammā*) it supports do not cave in.'

'Make a simile.'

'Just as a man, if a house was falling down, would make a support for it with a post, and the house would not then cave in, as it was supported, just so, great king, giving support is the distinguishing mark of vigour, and all those good qualities it supports do not cave in.'

'Make a simile.'

'Just as, great king, when a large army has broken up a small one, then the king might bring to mind another ally and send out for him[7] and with this ally the small army would break up the large army. In this way, great king, the giving of support is the characteristic mark of vigour, and all of the good and skilful qualities it supports do not cave in. For it has been said by the Blessed One, great king, "The noble disciple with vigour abandons the unskilful and cultivates the skilful, abandons what is blameworthy and cultivates what is irreproachable; thus he keeps himself pure."'

'Good, Nāgasena!'

The king asked, 'Venerable Nāgasena, what is the distinguishing mark of mindfulness?' 'Not drifting away (*apilāpana*) is a distinguishing mark of mindfulness,[8] and taking up (*upagaṇhanā*) is a distinguishing mark of mindfulness.'[9]

'And how, Venerable sir, is not drifting away a distinguishing mark of mindfulness?' 'Mindfulness, great king, when it arises,[10] keeps the measure of skilful and unskilful states, blameworthy and irreproachable states, inferior and superior states, dark, bright and evenly mixed states: "These are the four foundations of mindfulness, these are the four bases of success, these are the five faculties, these are the five powers, these are the seven factors of awakening, this the noble eightfold path.[11] This is calm, this is insight, this is knowledge, this is release." The practitioner then practises the things that should be practised, and does not practise the things that should not be practised. He follows things that should be followed and does not follow things that should not be followed. In this way, great king, not drifting away is a distinguishing mark of mindfulness.'

'Make a simile.'

'Just as, great king, the treasurer[12] of the universal monarch reminds the universal monarch of his glory in the evening and in the morning, saying, "Sire, you have so many elephants, so many horses, so many chariots, so many foot-soldiers, so much gold, so much money, so much property", and keeps the measure of the king's property, in this way, great king, mindfulness keeps the measure of skilful and unskilful states, blameworthy and irreproachable states, inferior and superior states, dark, bright and evenly mixed states: "These are the four foundations of mindfulness, these are the four bases of success, these are the five faculties, these are the five powers, these are the seven factors of awakening, this the noble eightfold path. This is calm, this is insight, this is knowledge, this is release." The practitioner then practises the things that should be practised, and does not practise the things that should not be practised. He follows things that should be followed and does not follow things that should not be followed. In this way, great king, not drifting away is a distinguishing mark of mindfulness.'

'How, Venerable sir, is taking up a distinguishing mark of mindfulness?' 'Mindfulness, great king, when it arises, examines the course of mental states that are of benefit and not of benefit, thinking: "These mental states are of benefit, these are not of benefit, these mental states are helpful (*upakāra*), these mental states are not helpful". And then the practitioner removes mental states that are not of benefit and takes up mental states that are of benefit, and removes mental states that are not helpful and takes up mental states that are helpful. In this way, great king, taking up is a distinguishing mark of mindfulness.'

'Make a simile.'

'Just as, great king, the adviser treasure of a universal monarch knows what is of benefit and what is not of benefit to the king, and knows what is helpful and what is not helpful to him, in this way, great king, mindfulness, when it arises, examines the course (*gati*) of mental states that are of benefit and not of benefit, thinking: "These mental states are of benefit, these are not of benefit, these mental states are helpful, these mental states are not helpful", and then the practitioner removes mental states that are not of benefit and takes up mental states that are of benefit, and removes mental states that are not helpful and takes up mental states that are not helpful. In this way, great king, taking up is a distinguishing mark of mindfulness. And indeed the Blessed One said this, "Mindfulness, I say, is applicable on all occasions".'

'Good, Nāgasena!'

The king said, 'Venerable Nāgasena, what is the distinguishing mark of concentration?'

'The distinguishing mark of concentration, great king, is being the chief.[13] All skilful states, of whatever kind, all have concentration as the chief, incline towards concentration, converge towards concentration, tend towards concentration.'

'Make a simile.'

'Just as, great king, in a house with a ridge-pole, all the rafters go towards the ridge-pole, incline towards it, come together towards it, and the ridge-pole is called the chief, all skilful states, of whatever kind, all have concentration as chief, incline towards concentration, converge towards concentration, tend towards concentration.'

'Make a further simile.'

'Just as, great king, a certain king might enter into battle with his fourfold army, and all of the army, having elephants, horses, chariots and foot soldiers, inclines, converges and tends towards him: he would be the chief and they would order themselves around him. So all skilful states, of whatever kind, all have concentration as chief, incline towards concentration, converge towards concentration, tend towards concentration. In this way, great king, the distinguishing mark of concentration is being the chief. And indeed the Blessed One said this: "Monks, cultivate concentration, as he who is concentrated knows things as they really are."'[14]

'Good, Nāgasena!'

The king said, 'Venerable Nāgasena, what is the distinguishing mark of wisdom?'

'Earlier, great king, I said that cutting off is a distinguishing mark of wisdom; but illuminating is also a distinguishing mark of wisdom.'

'How, Venerable sir, is illuminating a distinguishing mark of wisdom?'

'Wisdom, great king, when it arises, dispels the darkness of ignorance, produces the brilliance of clear knowledge, makes the light of understanding (*ñāṇaloka*) appear, and makes the noble truths easy to discern. And the practitioner then knows impermanence, suffering and non-self with right wisdom.'

'Make a simile.'

'Just as, great king, a man might set a lamp in a house, and when he has set the lamp down, the lamp dispels darkness, produces brilliance, makes light appear, and makes material shapes easy to discern. In this way, great king, wisdom, when it arises, dispels the darkness of ignorance, produces the brilliance of clear knowledge, makes the light of understanding appear, and makes the noble truths easy to discern. And the practitioner then knows impermanence, suffering and non-self with right wisdom. In this way, great king, illumination is a distinguishing mark of wisdom.'

'Good, Nāgasena!'

The king said, 'Venerable Nāgasena, although these mental states are diverse, do they produce one goal?'

'Yes, great king. Although these mental states are diverse, they do produce one goal. They slay the defilements (*kilesa*).'

'How, Venerable sir, do these diverse mental states produce one goal: they slay the defilements?'

'Just as, great king, an army, being diverse, having elephants, horses, chariots and foot soldiers, produces one goal: it conquers the opposing army in battle, in this way, great king, these mental states, being diverse, produce one goal: they slay the defilements.'

'Good, Nāgasena!' (MP 34–9)

CHAPTER EIGHT

SANSKRIT TEXTS

As Buddhism developed and evolved, a number of new texts, styles and movements emerged, with important doctrinal and practical implications. This chapter includes short extracts from just a few texts, showing some ways different techniques or attitudes emerged. There is simply not space to include a sense of all variations and developments. For instance, a key text for the Chan/Seon/Zen traditions of China, Korea and Japan is the *Lankāvatāra-Sūtra* (probably fourth century CE). Although it is too complex to explore here, these lines communicate something of the *sūtra* that has been so influential in Eastern Buddhism.[1]

Mind only is all this: Dually the mind goes along;
In the absence of subject and object, a self, and what belongs to it cannot exist.

Up to the realm of Brahmā, I declare, all is mind only.
Outside mind only, Brahmā and so on cannot be understood. (*Lankāvatāra-Sutra* 208–9)

The growth of Tantric movements, so important in India, China, Japan and Tibet, should also be mentioned; with some exceptions, many key texts are in Chinese or Tibetan. So the Sanskrit texts here therefore represent just some of the styles that developed as Buddhism evolved at different times, in varied regions of India, and influenced the waves of Buddhist dissemination occurring during the time of the their composition. Some vocabulary has slightly different spelling in Sanskrit: *śamatha/vipaśyanā*; *dhyāna*; *dharma*.

1. Aśvaghoṣa

The poet Aśvaghoṣa shows a new direction in Buddhist composition, as a high-caste figure, writing in the highly ornate and formal verse of the top levels of ancient Indian society. His dates are unknown, but it is thought that he was born towards the end of the first century and composed his poetry in the early part of the second century. Unlike previous writers on Buddhist themes, he wrote in Classical Sanskrit, instead of vernacular 'hybrids' previously employed. Buddhism seems to have found its place within Indian society, as the tenor and confidence of the argument presented in the extract below attest. Aśvaghoṣa's association with a particular tradition of practice is uncertain, but his work bears the hallmark of meditators of the school that subsequently became known as Yogācāra, and perhaps was also aligned with some elements of early schools known as the Dāraṣṭāntika and Sautrāntika, who appear to have been more meditation-based than others, such as the theoretical Sārvasatavādins.[2] At any rate, the poet seems to have had contact with those active in the meditative traditions, whose techniques and practices may have transcended boundaries of particular schools, and who may have been working with very varied approaches amongst themselves too.[3]

This poem is in *kāvya*, a courtly verse form used for a genre of poetic drama that became particularly popular in the first centuries CE. The use of this sophisticated form is itself suggestive of a highly educated, upper-class and even court poet. The work demonstrates the gracefully expressed epithets and carefully crafted debate that is found both in *Saundarananda* and in his other extant Buddhist work, a poetic life of the Buddha (*Buddhacarita*). These works demonstrate an entirely new approach for Buddhist expression, in their dramatization of principle, their highly expressive style and polished composition, distilling teaching into succinct epigrammatic verse. Traditional Buddhist oppositions and imagery, many of which have been encountered already in this book, are here refined and placed in a measured metrical arrangement in opposition to one another, with powerful poetic effect.

The exposition of meditation described here is sustained by such measured confidence: its innately balanced rhythms support antithesis and a sometimes surprisingly shocking juxtaposition of images. Aśvaghoṣa is a master of this form: his dramatic skill lies in part through the crafting of images traditional to Buddhism in succinct and new formulations, and making them sit seamlessly with his own often deeply atmospheric and even wistful analogies, such as the groupings and regroupings of birds flocking together in the evening, or the chance meeting together of strangers in a guesthouse, both compared to the shifting alignments and fallings away that characterize progress through *saṃsāra*. Indeed, the tenor of the imagery is often stark and alarming, leavened perhaps by some sense of the middle way through the resolution of apparent contradictions within the traditional *pada* framework. Despite his courtly style, Linda Covill notes, Aśvaghoṣa writes 'as a truly Buddhist poet who is urgently concerned with the dissemination of his message' and his 'metaphors are always explanatory rather than decorative in function' (Covill 2007: 24).[4]

The chapters on meditation from this poem were influential for centuries through their adaptation in a meditation manual in Chinese compiled by Kumarajīva (344–413 CE), one of the great figures of Buddhism in the first millennium.[5] A foreign teacher to the Chinese emperor and court, he involved himself with the various translation bureaux working on Sanskrit Buddhist texts: his works were particularly favoured there, and his meditation manual was instrumental in establishing Buddhist practice in Chinese regions. Aśvaghoṣa's advice is so well expressed that one can understand why Kumarajīva felt this and other chapters on meditation from this poem to be so suited to being transported to a new setting. The passage is written in a friendly if sometimes admonitory imperative, addressing the 'friend', presumably a layman, to whom advice is being given.

Beautiful Nanda (Saundarananda)

In whatever secluded place you are, sitting with legs crossed, holding your body straight, bring mindfulness up in front of you, such as at the tip of the nose, or the forehead, or the space between the eyebrows. If your mind is feverish with distracting thoughts about the senses, do not make the unsteady heart (*citta*) a support for them, but brush them away, like dust that has settled on your clothes.

Even though you have let go of sense-desires as the result of careful investigation, destroy them by their opposite quality, just as darkness is overcome by its opposite quality, light. The tendency (*anuśaya*) towards them persists, as with a fire covered by ashes. Extinguish them with meditation (*bhāvanā*), dear friend, as fire is put out with water. It is because of this tendency that sense-desires re-emerge, like shoots from a seed; they would not exist if it were destroyed, just as shoots would not if the seed were destroyed.

Observe the sufferings that arise for those desiring sense-pleasures, from desire for the senses, beginning with wealth, and cut them at the root, as though they were enemies that have been mistaken as friends. For sense pleasures are impermanent, emptily worthless, the cause of (*hetu*) trouble. They are held in common by many others, and by their very nature can be stolen. Avoid them like poisonous snakes! Those that are hunted come with suffering; those guarded, however, do not bring peace. Indeed, losing them brings great grief; their acquisition, however, brings no satisfaction.

Whoever sees contentment in great prosperity, heaven in great wealth or the source of happiness in sense pleasures, destroys himself. These things are unstable, not real, without essence, shifting. The happiness associated with them is a fabrication: you should not bring them to mind now.

If malevolent or cruel thoughts agitate your mind, again make them tranquil with their opposite, as turbulent waters are with a wish-granting jewel.[6] It is known that loving-kindness and compassion are their opposites, for they are always contrary to one another, just as light is to dark. When malevolence emerges in someone who has turned away from bad behaviour, like an elephant throwing dirt on himself after bathing, he heaps dirt upon himself. A noble man forms a sympathetic measure of other beings; how should he be able to pile yet more suffering on those already suffering from sickness, death, ageing and suchlike?

The other person may or may not be harmed in this world by a malicious mind; the mind of the malicious person is, however, burned up immediately. Therefore you should cultivate loving-kindness and compassion towards all living beings, as an alternative to malevolence and cruelty.

Whatever it is that a man thinks about continually, the mind becomes inclined there, through force of habit. Therefore, you should abandon the unskilful and bring to mind the skilful, which will be for your own benefit in this world, and for the attainment of the highest benefit too. When unskilful thoughts gather together in the heart, they become strong, bringing failure equally to oneself and to the other. Because they obstruct the excellent, they cause things to go badly for oneself. And because of the harm done to one's worthiness as a recipient, they cause things to go badly in friendships with others.

You should practise being collected in activities of the mind and do not, my friend, think unskilful thoughts. Whatever thought there is in a mind revolving around three passions, of greed, hatred and delusion, does not obtain virtue, but produces bondage. Foulness leads to the harming of sentient beings, defilement to oneself and delusion. It leads to hell. So you should not harm the self with unskilful thoughts, like a man digging earth who throws it on himself when he is well-armed and decked with jewels.

Just as an ignorant man might burn the best aloe-wood as if it were ordinary wood, so the state of being human is destroyed through the absence of this method. Just as a man might take clods of earth from a jewel island but leave the jewels behind, so is the man who leaves behind the unsurpassed teaching, through thinking evil.

Just as a man who goes to the Himalayas might feed on poisonous, and not medicinal, herbs, so is one who has obtained the state of being human, who follows the bad rather than the wholesome. Understanding this, you should throw away distracted thought by means of its opposite, just as a wedge is dislodged from a piece of wood by means of a finer, contrary wedge.

Perhaps you are thinking about whether your family and people are flourishing or not. So you should consider the true nature of the world of the living, and these thoughts will disappear again.

Among beings who are dragged by their deeds in the cycle of *saṃsāra*, who is a stranger? Who is a member of one's own family? Through delusion people cling to one another. For in the past, someone who is now a member of one's family was then a stranger on the road; in the future, the one who is now a stranger on the road will become one of one's own family.

Just as birds flock together in the evening, sometimes here and sometimes there, so stranger and relative embrace each other, some in one birth, some in another. Just as travellers lodge together in various kinds of guesthouse, and when they go, take leave, so it is with the gathering together of those in family groupings.

In this world, separate by nature, nobody is really dear to anyone. Cause and effect bind things together, like sand held together in the fist. For a mother loves her son, thinking, 'He'll look after me', and the son his mother with the thought, 'She carried me in her womb'. Whenever relatives treat each other well, they show affection, but in disagreements, they show discord.

A member of the family might see you with hostile eyes; someone unrelated might view you with friendliness. A man breaks or makes affection according to his needs. Just as a painter of pictures might become attached to a woman he has painted himself, so a man goes for attachment to people when he has created the affection himself. The person who was a relative in another life, what does he do for your benefit now, or you for his? You should not let distracting thoughts about your family preoccupy your mind, since in *saṃsāra* there is no difference between family and stranger.

'That country is safe; in that one they are hospitable; that one is happy.' If any thought like that arises in you, just abandon it in this way, dear friend. Do not dwell on it in any way, knowing that the whole world is burning, with the various fires of defilement. Suffering is inevitable, everywhere, whether from the revolving cycle of the seasons, or from hunger, thirst and tiredness. Nowhere is happiness found. Somewhere, there is cold; somewhere, heat, somewhere illness, somewhere fear: therefore the world holds no refuge. Old age, sickness and death are the great fear of the world: there is no region where that fear does not arise.

Wherever this body goes, there suffering follows it. What state is there in the world where there is no affliction? Even a safe and delightful region, where there is generous hospitality, should be perceived as burned with the defilements, if burnt with defilements. What safe place is there to go and feel at ease, in a world stricken with sufferings of the mind and of the body?

Suffering turns up everywhere, in each person, at all times, dear friend, do not let your wish or your passion go to the many-coloured things of the world. When your wish and your passion have turned away from them, you will see clearly all the world of living beings as on fire.

And then, whatever plan that might occur to you that is not based on death should be strenuously fought away, as if it were an illness. You should trust in life not even for a moment, for time slays the trusting man like a tiger lying in wait. You should not think that you are strong or young: death kills in all situations, not paying attention to age.

You should not think that you are too warrior-like and young to die, for death strikes down people whatever their situation, and does not care about youth. The body we drag along with us is fertile soil for misfortunes, and no wise person would expect well-being or a long life. Who could be free from care, carrying around the body, the dwelling place of the great elements, as though carrying a jar full of snakes fighting each other?

Just think how strange and wonderful it is that this person, on breathing in, can immediately breathe out again. So little is life to be trusted. Another wonder is that the one who is asleep wakes up, or that having got up, one goes later to sleep; for those in bodies have many enemies to them.

Who would feel safe against death, the one who, with murderous intent, pursues those in the world from the womb onwards, like an enemy with a raised sword?

What man born in the world, although he may be learned and strong, can defeat the endmaker, or has ever defeated him, or ever will?

For when impetuous death arrives, he cannot be opposed, with bargaining, gifts, hostility, punishment, or restraint.

Therefore you should not place trust in unstable life, for time perpetually seizes people and does not wait for you to become old. What man would make plans that did not take into account death, when he sees the world so insubstantial and fragile, like a bubble of water? So, in order to eliminate such distracting thoughts, you should make yourself distinguished in mindfulness of breathing. With this method, you will be in time to practise the opposite of distracting thoughts, just as a medicine against sickness.

In order to obtain gold, the one who washes the dirt gets rid of first the gross bits of grit, and then he refines it more and gets rid of the finer particles. After this purification, he retains particles of gold.

In order to attain liberation, a man of trained (*yukta*) mind abandons first gross faults and, to purify his mind more, he then abandons subtle ones. After this purification, he retains particles of the *dhamma*.

Just as the goldsmith takes gold that has been washed with water and separated from dirt in gradual stages, and heats it in the fire, and turns it frequently, in this way the practitioner (*yogācāra*) separates his mind from faults by cleansing the defilements, and then makes his mind calm and composed.[7]

And just as the goldsmith brings gold to a good state for working into various kinds of ornaments, according to his wishes, so the monk whose mind is purified calms his mind so that it is under his control, and directs it as he wishes, wherever he wishes, with the higher knowledges. (*Saundarananda* Canto XV)

II. ŚĀNTIDEVA

By the seventh century the ideal of the Bodhisattva had evolved in Indic regions, in what is known as the *Mahāyāna*, an ideal whereby the Bodhisattva vow is encouraged for everyone. Śāntideva (c 685–763) is one of its most eloquent exponents, writing his great work, the *Bodhicaryāvatāra*, as a response to charges that he was lazy, if stories about his studies at the famous Buddhist university of Nālandā are accepted. He famously refuted Chinese Buddhists at the great debate in Samye (792–794). This work describes the work on the six perfections needed to cultivate the Bodhisattva 'way of life', an ideal now encouraged for everyone: 'As long as space abides and as long as the world abides, so long may I abide, destroying the sufferings of the world' (10.55).

The famous passage that follows occurs in the chapter on meditation that follows the sequence of six perfections: it occurs after discussion of vigour.[8] It introduces the doctrine of the equalization of self and others, whereby the suffering of other beings is seen as equal to one's own. It provides an interesting counterbalance to Buddhaghosa's chapter on the *brahmavihāras* (Vism IX). Crosby and Skilton suggest that these meditations derive from *Cittamātra* (*Yogācāra*) metaphysical views on the ultimate equivalence of self and other (1995: 84–5).

The question has been raised as to why metaphysical arguments are present in a chapter on meditation. One possibility is that encouraging such deliberations could be an expression of 'skill in means' and considered helpful for certain stages of meditation, where the suffering of 'self' and that perceived as 'other' both need to be transcended through the practice of *jhāna*, the subject of this chapter: the emphasis on seclusion (*viveka*), associated with this practice from the earliest texts, supports this possibility, as does the practice of *jhāna* where the *brahmavihāras*, which involve extending loving-kindness, compassion, sympathetic joy or equanimity to all beings, are encouraged.

Chapter 8.

1. Having developed vigour in this way, one should settle the mind in meditative concentration, because a person with an agitated mind is a person stuck between the fangs of the defilements.
2. Through the seclusion[9] (*viveka*) of mind and body no distraction can occur. Therefore, after giving up worldly attachments, one should give up distracting thoughts.

3. One is unable to forsake worldly relationships due to attachment and gain. Therefore in renouncing these things, the wise person should reflect:
4. By means of *śamatha*, possessing *vipaśyanā*, and realising that the removal of the defilements (*kileśa*) is essential, the practitioner seeks first tranquillity, renouncing attachment to the world. . . .
80. In this way, those with desires get very little comfort, owing to their manifold miseries. They are like animals pulling a cart and getting only odd bits of grass.
81. For the sake of that meagre joy which is easily available even to animals, this ill-fated person destroys the wealth that is hard to come by in life.
82. These little desires are truly transient and they hurl a person into hells and suchlike. The immense labour done at all times to procure them goes to waste.
83. On the other hand, even with a billionth part of that labour, one attains Buddhahood. This awakening does not arise for the lustful and therefore their suffering is greater than that for achieving the path to awakening.
84. Remembering the torments of hells, there is nothing, in the context of the sufferings of a person of lustful desire, comparable: neither weapons nor fire nor poison nor a fall from a cliff nor even enemies.
85. Having thus developed fear about desires, one should generate delight in seclusion, and in quiet forest places free from commotion and dispute.
86. Contemplating the welfare of others, these fortunate ones roam about in vast places, like beautiful palaces for them, under rocks cooled by moon beams, fanned by pleasing and quiet forest breezes.
87. Staying as long as he wishes in empty places, under trees and in caves, free from the sorrow of clinging to and protecting possessions he, the wise one, stays free from care.

88. Living as he pleases, homeless and unfettered by anything, he enjoys the pleasure and contentment even Indra would find difficult to obtain.
89. Having in these ways cultivated the qualities of seclusion, having calmed distracted thoughts, one should cultivate the awakened mind.
90. In this way, one should first make an effort to cultivate the sense of the equality between oneself and other beings, through the identical experience of joy and sorrow.
91. Just as the body should be nurtured, despite its great variety of parts, such as hands, and suchlike, so this entire world of wide variety, which is also undivided by nature, should be too, owing to joy and suffering being common to all sentient beings.
92. Although the suffering that I endure does not cause a hindrance or harm to other beings, their suffering should become unbearable for me because of the partiality I have for myself.
93. Similarly, even though the suffering of another is not endured by me, still that suffering too becomes unbearable for me, when others are conceived as my own self.
94. Hence the suffering of others should be destroyed by me, because it is the same as my own suffering. Other beings should also be helped by me as they are sentient beings too, like myself.
95. When happiness is as dear to me as to others, in equal manner, then what is so special about me that I am always striving just for my own happiness?
96. If for me, and for others, fear and suffering are not welcome, what is so special about me that I protect only myself and not others from fear and suffering?
97. Just because his suffering does not oppress me, is he not to be protected too? And why do I protect myself from sufferings that have not even come yet?
98. It is delusional to think 'I shall be the same person in a next birth', for it is a different person who dies and a different person who is born again.

99. If it is to be believed that the suffering of another person is to be guarded against by oneself alone, how is it then that the hand protects the foot in pain when the suffering is not the hand's?
100. Even if this approach cannot be justified because it proceeds from the sense of self, it is equally unjustifiable in the case of guarding against one's own suffering. This approach must be discarded as far as possible in both cases.
101. The continuity of consciousness, like a row, and the assemblage of constituents, like an army, are in fact false entities.[10] The one who experiences suffering does not exist. Then whose suffering will you own?
102. All sufferings are without an overlord; so they must be removed without any distinction between one's own or those of others. Why is any limitation put on this?
103. Why should, indisputably enough, the misery of everyone be removed? Because all things are like one's own self: if misery is to be removed, it is not only in one's own case, but in everyone's case.
104. It may be said that compassion may bring much suffering; so why practise it? However, looking at the world's suffering, is the suffering arising from compassion that great?
105. If by virtue of one suffering the suffering of many can be removed, that suffering should be produced with sympathetic kindness, for the sake of others and oneself.
106. In this way the Bodhisatta Supuṣpacandra, even though he was aware of the disposition of the king, did not ward off his own suffering to exhaust the sufferings of others.[11]
107. Those who have developed the continuity of their consciousness in this way, to whom the suffering of others is as important as the things they hold dear themselves, gladly enter the lowest hell like a swan plunging into a lotus pool.
108. With all beings released, the resultant ocean of joy will be sufficient for all beings to be happy: what use then is the longing for liberation?

109. Therefore, even while working for the welfare of others, there should be neither conceit nor dismay. With the sole thirst for the good of others, there should also be no desire for the fruit of the action.
110. Just as I shall guard myself restlessly from unpleasant things, so shall I make my mind full of compassion and generosity for others.
111. Through constantly thinking of things there is the understanding that they are 'mine', born from the drops of others' blood and sperm as if they are one's own.
112. So why is another's body not accepted as my own? It is not difficult to regard my own body as that of others.
113. Realising the mistake of cherishing one's own self and thinking of the means of merit in cherishing others, one should abjure the sense of self and practice the acceptance of others.
114. Just as hands and limbs are cherished as being limbs of the same body, why are all beings not then regarded as limbs of the same world?
115. Just as a sense of ownership towards body, that is non-self, is born through constant practice, so also how can a sense of identical ownership not be born for other beings?
116. Working like this for others, there should be neither conceit nor dismay. When one feeds oneself there is no desire for any fruit; then why desire the fruit of action done for the sake of others?
117. Therefore, just as you want to protect yourself against pain and grief and suchlike, so should you practise with a caring and compassionate mind for the whole world.
118. The lord Avalokiteśvara prescribed even his own name as most mighty and efficacious in rescuing people from the fear of working in the midst of others.
119. One should not shy away from difficulty, because, with the power of practice, one can so change that one may not at all feel happy in the absence of something, whose very name was once so frightening for one.

120. He who wants to save himself and others soon should practise the highest mystery (*guyham*): the exchanging of his own self for others.

(*Bodhicaryāvatāra* 8:1–4, 80–120)

III. Shorter *Sukhāvativuyha-Sūtra*[12]

This text introduces imagery familiar from the city of the universal monarch, with the lotus ponds, railings, stairs, seven types of jewels and even the tinkling bells and other features of his mandala-like palace and a city ruled with justice and generosity by a benevolent king, dedicated to the service of his subjects (D II 169–99). Here, these features are deployed to describe a heaven realm promised to those who call wholeheartedly on the Buddha Amitāyus. There are some differences from the Pāli texts: from a doctrinal point of the view, the inclusion of Buddha-fields, throughout a universe filled with Bodhisattvas, becomes a key element of Mahāyāna. There are also important shifts in perspective: lotus-blossom showers fall on a now deeply devout populace, and the variegated singing birds enrich the aural element. This feature is emphasized further by the chanting together of the people, whose attention to the Triple Gem is first roused in the area of sound, of a thousand different kinds, which they then feel throughout their body. The text, a meditation in itself, has formed part of the basis of Pure Land schools, where chanting constitutes the core daily practice.

Then the Blessed One addressed the Venerable Śāriputra, saying, 'There is, Śariputra, to the west, a hundred thousand million Buddhafields from here, a world called the Land of Bliss.[13] And at this very moment, a Tathāgata, an arahat, a fully awakened Buddha, called Amitayus, lives in that Buddha field, and here he remains and passes the time, and here too he teaches the dharma. So what do you think, Śāriputra, for what reason is this world called the Land of Bliss? Here, in the world called the Land of Bliss, Śāriputra, there is no physical pain or mental pain for living beings. Beings there only experience immeasurable happiness, and so it is called the Land of Bliss.

'In addition, Śāriputra, the world called the Land of Bliss is adorned and surrounded on every side by seven railings and seven rows of palm trees, all festooned with nets of tinkling bells. It is surrounded and made brightly coloured and beautiful by four precious jewels, that is gold, silver, beryl and crystal: That is how Buddha fields are adorned, Śāriputra, with such arrays of wonderful qualities peculiar to Buddha fields.

'In addition, Śāriputra, in the world called the Land of Bliss there are lotus ponds, all made of seven jewels, that is, gold, silver, beryl, crystal, ruby, sapphire and mother-of-pearl is the seventh jewel.

'In addition, Śāriputra, the ponds are filled to the brim, up to the beautiful banks and bathing places, with waters that possess the eight qualities[14] so that even the crows can drink there. They are strewn with golden sands. And in these lotus ponds, there are, all around the four sides, four sets of steps, brightly coloured and beautiful with the seven jewels, gold, silver, beryl, crystal, ruby, sapphire and mother-of-pearl. And in these lotus ponds jewel trees are growing: they are blue, of blue colouring, or shining blue, or with a tinge of blue, some are yellow, of yellow colouring, or shining yellow, or with a tinge of yellow, some are red, of red colouring, or shining red, or with a tinge of red, or white, of white colouring, or shining white, or with a tinge of white, and in circumference they are as wide as the carriage wheel.

'And in addition, Śāriputra, in that Buddha field divine musical instruments are playing continuously, and the earth is lovely and golden-coloured. And in that Buddha field a shower of divine coral-tree blossoms pours down three times a day and three times a night. And the beings who are born there pay homage to a hundred thousand million Buddhas, going before their morning meal to other worlds. And after showering a hundred thousand million blossoms on each Tathāgata, they return to their own world in time for their afternoon rest. That is how Buddha fields are adorned, Śāriputra, with such arrays of wonderful qualities peculiar to Buddha fields.

'And in addition, Śāriputra, there are in that Buddha field wild geese, curlews and peacocks. Three times a day, and three times a night, they flock together and perform a great chanting together, each singing with a different voice. And they sing a sound extolling the five faculties, the five powers and the seven factors of awakening. And when human beings in that world hear this sound, attention (*manisakāra*) to the Buddha arises, and attention to *dharma*, and attention to the sangha.

'Now what do you think, Śāriputra, that these birds are born from other birds? You could not consider this possible! Why? Because even the names of the hells, the names of animal rebirths, and the name of the realm of Yama, the king of death, are not known in that Buddha field – let alone birth in any of these forms. Instead, these birds flock together to chant the voice of *dharma*, only because they have been created by the Buddha Amitayus, and they chant the sound of *dharma*.

'That is how Buddha fields are adorned, Śariputra, with such arrays of wonderful qualities peculiar to Buddha fields.

'And in addition, Śāriputra, when the rows of palm trees and the nets of tinkling bells in that Buddha field are moved by the wind, a sweet and enrapturing sound emanates from them. This chanting and singing together of sounds is, Śāriputra, like musical instruments with a hundred thousand million parts; when these instruments are played by noble players, a sweet and enrapturing sound emanates from them. In the same way a sweet and enrapturing sound emanates from the rows of palm trees and the nets of tinkling bells when they are moved by the wind. When human beings hear these sounds, recollection of the Buddha, recollection of the Dharma, and the recollection of the Sangha remain in their entire body (*kāya*).

'That is how Buddha fields are adorned, Śāriputra, with such arrays of wonderful qualities peculiar to Buddha fields.' (Müller and Nanjio 1883: 92–5)

IV. KAMĀLAŚĪLA

Kamālaśīla (c 713–763?) was an Indian practitioner, from the great temple and centre of learning at Nālandā, who accompanied his teacher Śāntarakṣita to Tibet. Apparently influenced by Madhyamaka teachings, he taught a detailed path dependent on the six perfections, ten moral guidelines and Mahāyāna texts. The three books of the *Bhāvanākrama*, though animated by his Indic background, were composed in Tibet, and became highly influential in Northern Buddhist meditation. Their teachings received their most complete expression in the *Lam-rim chenmo*, or *Graduated Path to Enlightenment* of Tsong-kha-pa, founder the the Gelug school.[15] Here is an extract from the third book, which distils some of the teaching on *śamatha* and *vipaśyanā*.[16] Kamālaśīla's *Bhāvanākrama* follows closely the classical pattern of spiritual progression as envisaged in the Yogācāra system, but with some distinctive features, fusing other strands of contemporary practice and doctrine.[17] The way the Buddha image is seen externally, visualized internally, and then allowed to dissolve, anticipates the methods of Tibetan visual practices. The marks and signs on the Buddha include the thirty-two marks of the Great Man, destined to become a Buddha or a universal monarch, an iconography found in most forms of Buddhism (*Lakkhaṇa-Sutta:* D III 142–78).[18]

[1] For those who have entered upon the path in accordance with the *Mahāyāna Sūtras, bhāvanākrama,* or the stages of meditative practice, are recounted in brief. In that connection, although the Blessed One has taught the different concentrations of the bodhisattvas as without limit and immeasurable, still *śamatha* and *vipaśyanā* cover all concentrations. That is why the path is called the yoked together path of *śamatha* and *vipaśyanā*. So the Blessed One said: 'By cultivating *vipaśyanā* and *śamatha* in this way the meditator is freed from bondage to mental images and bondage to bad behaviour.'

Therefore those who wish to remove all the coverings of illusion should practise *śamatha* and *vipaśyana*. Through the power of *śamatha,* the mind becomes motionless like a lamp in a place where there is no wind. Through *vipaśyanā,* because of 'such *dharma*' the light of true understanding is produced. After that, the entire covering of illusion is eradicated, like the disappearance of darkness with the dawn. . . .

[3] Here, the practitioner (*yogi*), through purifying moral conduct and suchlike, and remaining steady in the accumulation of calm and insight, arouses the Great Compassion for all sentient beings. He should practise listening to the *dharma*, reflecting upon the *dharma*, and meditating upon it, by means of the awakening mind (*bodhicitta*). Then, at the time for his meditation,[19] the practitioner should first of all deal with all the things that need doing beforehand. Then he should consider, 'May all beings be established in awakening through me', bearing in mind the Great Compassion which aims at the welfare of the entire world, and then bow with all five limbs[20] to all Buddhas and Bodhisattvas in the ten directions. He should place images of the Buddha on a [4] stool, or wherever he likes, and he should pay homage to them, as he wishes. He should acknowledge his own faults, and he should transfer merit to the entire world.[21] He should sit on a soft and comfortable seat,[22] in the cross-legged posture of Bhattaraka Vairocana, or in the half cross-legged posture, with eyes neither closed nor open,[23] and his gaze on the tip of the nose. His body should be straight but relaxed, not too stooping nor too stiff. He should make his mindfulness inward-looking. He should make his shoulders evenly balanced, and his head neither raised up nor bent forward, but remaining steady. The nose is to be made in line with the navel, and the tongue should be placed at the roots of the upper teeth. The inbreaths and outbreaths should not be loud, strenuous or quick, entering in and going out in a natural pace.

Then, the practitioner should first practice calm by settling his mind (*citta*) on the image of the Tathāgata that he has either seen or heard about. He should constantly bring to mind this image of the Tathāgata, that shines like heated or smelted gold, endowed with the marks and signs, sitting in the midst of the circle of the retinue of the Buddha, ministering through all kinds of means to the benefit of living beings, and he should generate the aspiration to cultivate the wonderful qualities of the Tathāgata. After calming down states that have arisen with restlessness, he sees, in *jhāna*, the image of the Tathāgata as vividly as if it were in front of him.

[5] Then, he should cultivate insight by seeing the reflection of the image as it comes, goes and comes again, repeatedly. Then he should reflect in this way: 'Just as the reflection of the image of the Tathāgata did not come from anywhere and did not go anywhere, and the seated image is by nature empty, and without self, in this way all *dharmas* are empty by nature and come and go, just like the reflection of the image, and are without existence.' So, exploring and considering this suchness of reality (*tattva*) with a stainless mind, he should remain as long as he wishes.

This concentration has been termed the Being in the Presence of the Buddha seated in front concentration. The detailed praise of its merits should be considered in the *sūtra* of that name.[24]

Through such means acquisitions of *dharmas* come about. By directing the mind onto these, one should practise *śamatha* for the calming down of states that have arisen with restlessness and suchlike. The acquisition of all *dharmas* is arranged through the distinction of 'with form' or 'without form'.[25] Here, those based on the aggregate (*skandha*) of form are called 'with form'; those based on the aggregates of feeling and the rest are 'without form'.[26] And foolish people, because of their fixation on the acquiring of becoming, wander around in *saṃsāra* with their minds deluded. In order to remove their delusion, the practitioner should direct his Great Compassion towards them, and, after perfecting *śamatha*, develop *vipaśyanā* in order to reach the suchness of reality (*tattva*) (extracts from *Bhāvanākrama* III 1–5).

Conclusion

The Buddha is said to give eighty-four thousand teachings, suitable for all different temperaments and practices. An anthology cannot even begin to address this! It attempts, though, to show something of the range of types of text in early Buddhism, how they were apparently used in the early days, and how they are now used, particularly in South and Southeast Asia. Just as there are so many varieties of ways of expressing Buddhist teaching and various approaches, for different temperaments, so there are many types of practitioners too: through often many lives, meditators create their own *kamma* and follow paths of different kinds. For each person these various methods may take time, but as the Buddha taught, this courageous and liberating wish is described as possible for anyone:

Whatever living beings there be: feeble or strong, tall, stout or medium, short, small or large, without exception; seen or unseen, those dwelling far or near, those who are born or those who are yet to be born, may all beings be happy. (Sn 146–7)

GLOSSARY

This includes some commonly used terms, in English alphabetical order.

Abhidhamma 'Higher teaching'. The third 'basket' of the Buddha's teaching.

Anattā Non-self, or the lack of an abiding, permanent self. Third of three marks of existence.

Anicca Impermanence; first mark of existence.

Añjali Gesture of respect made by placing palms together at the chest.

Anussati Recollection (objects 21–30).

Arahat One who has obtained awakening when there is the teaching of the Buddha. They have destroyed all ten 'fetters' (*saṃyojana*).

Arūpa Formless.

Āsava Corruption, taint; eliminated at awakening.

Bhava Becoming, existence, state.

Bhāvanā Bringing into being, development, cultivation, meditation.

Bojjhaṅga Factor of awakening.

Brahmā A being inhabiting the heaven realms where those are reborn who practise calm (*samatha*) meditation.

Buddha Literally, 'one who is awake'. The fully awakened being who rediscovers and teaches the full eightfold path. Epithets include: *Tathāgata* (Thus-gone), Happy One (*Sugato*), Blessed One (*Bhagavā*). The first aspect of the Triple Gem.

Bodhisatta (Sanskrit: Bodhisattva) The one who has made a long-term vow, that varies slightly in different traditions, to teach and serve others; in Pāli texts the Buddha is described as Bodhisatta in earlier lives.

Brahmavihāra Divine Abiding: loving-kindness, compassion, sympathetic joy and equanimity.

Citta Mind, consciousness, heart. In traditional Buddhism the centre of consciousness is considered to be the heart not the head.

Dagoba A structure that offers a focus for devotional practice, often housing relics and sacred objects.

Deva Literally 'one who shines': a sense-sphere god.

Dhamma 1. Buddhist teaching and the second aspect of the Triple Gem; 2. State, event; 3. Law.

Dhammavicaya Investigation of *dhamma*.

Dukkha Dis-ease, suffering, tension: the first noble truth, 'to be understood'; the second mark for insight.

Ekagattā Unification, one-pointedness.

Heaven of the Thirty-Three Gods (*Tāvatiṃsa*) A sense-sphere heaven, where beings are reborn as gods (*devas*) on the basis of generosity, morality, faith and investigation.

Hetu Root. According to the *Abhidhamma*, the human mind partakes of the three roots of greed, hatred and delusion, but also the three roots of generosity, loving-kindness and, usually, wisdom.

Hiri Self-respect.

Iddhi Power of the mind, success.

Jhāna Meditation state characterised by five factors: thinking of (*vitakka*), examining (*vicāra*), joy (*pīti*), happiness (*sukha*) and onepointedness (*ekaggatā*).

Kamma Action, of mind, and of body.

Karunā Compassion, second *brahmavihāra*.

Kasiṇa One of the aids to meditation used to obtain *jhāna*. Often a disc, sometimes constructed by the practitioner.

Khandha (Skt *skandha*) One of five 'heaps': bodily form (*rūpa*), feeling (*vedanā*), perception (*saññā*), formations (*saṅkhārā*) and consciousness (*viññāṇa*).

Kusala Skilful, healthy, good opposite to *akusala*.

Jhāna Meditation state.

Lokuttara Transcendent.

Manasikāra Attention; *yoniso-manasikāra*, wise attention.

Māra A being/demon who tries to undermine practices leading to salvation.

Magga Path: the fourth noble truth, the eightfold path of the Buddha, to be 'brought into being'.

Mettā Loving-kindness, second *brahmavihāra*.

Mudita Sympathetic joy, third *brahmavihāra*.

Nāga Mythical underwater snake-like being.

Nibbāna Goal of the Buddhist path (nirvana); the release from the cycle of existence.

Nekkhamma Renunciation, meditation; third perfection of the Bodhisatta.

Nimitta Mental image, sign.

Nirodha Cessation.

Nirvana, *nibbāna* Literally 'quenching', the end of suffering, the third noble truth, 'to be realised'.

Nissaraṇa Escape.

Ottappa Scrupulousness.

Pabbajā 'The going forth': becoming a monk or nun.

Paccavekkha Recollection, reviewing.

Paccekkabuddha One who obtains awakening on his own, who does not teach a full path.

Paññā Wisdom.

Passaddhi Tranquillity; fifth factor of awakening.

Paticcusamapāda Dependent origination or arising.

Perfections (*pāramis*): The ten qualities the Bodhisatta made a vow to cultivate in order to attain Buddhahood.

Pīti Joy, third jhāna factor and fourth factor of awakening.

Rūpa 1. Body, as in *nāma-rūpa*, name-and-form or mind-and-body; 2. Subtle form, as in the *jhāna* meditations and realms.

Saṃyojana Fetter of becoming: the first five, eradicated at stages of path, are belief in self, doubt, attachment to precepts and vows, sense-desire, ill-will. The remaining are: desire for existence in a form realm, desire for existence in a formless realm, conceit, restlessness and ignorance, all eradicated at arahatship.

Saññā Identification, perception.

Saddhā Faith.

Samādhi Concentration: fourth faculty; fourth power; sixth factor of awakening; last factor of eightfold path.

Samatha (Sanskrit *śamatha*) Calm.

Saṃsāra Literally 'wandering', the cycle of rebirths.

Sangha (Pāli *saṅgha*) The community of those that have achieved one of the four stages of awakening; the third aspect of the 'Triple Gem'. This community is represented by the order of monks.

Sati Mindfulness, awareness, balanced attentiveness to the present. The four foundations of mindfulness are body, feelings, mind and *dhamma*. Third faculty, third power, first factor of awakening, and seventh path factor.

Stūpa A structure that provides a focus for devotional practice, often in a dome-like shape with a base and peak. See *dagoba*.

Sukha Happiness: fourth *jhāna* factor.

Sutta Discourses for specific situations, the second 'basket' of the Buddha's teaching.

Taṇhā Thirst, craving: the second noble truth, 'to be abandoned'. Eighth of the twelve links of dependent origination.

Triple Gem The three aspects of the Buddha, the teaching and the community, revered by Southern Buddhists in the *Iti pi so* chant.

Upakāra Aid.

Upekkhā Equanimity: seventh factor of awakening; fourth *brahmavihāra*.

Vicāra Sustained thought, examination; second *jhāna* factor.

Vimokkha Release of the mind, usually in set of eight.

Vimutti Release, liberation.

Vipassanā (Sanskrit *vipaśyanā*) Insight.

Virāga Dispassion.

Viriya Vigour, effort; second faculty, second power, second basis for success, third factor of awakening; associated with sixth path factor.

Vitakka Initial thought, intention. Rightly placed, it is the second factor of the eightfold path, right intention (*Abhidhamma*); first *jhāna* factor.

Vinaya The monastic code, the first 'basket'.

NOTES

Chapter 1. Introduction

1. See Bronkhorst 1993: 1–30.
2. For his own words, see M I 160–75 and M I 237–51.
3. The Buddha uses this image in the advice to Soṇa (see this anthology, p. 248). For the story of the three strings, see Appleton, Shaw and Unebe 2013: 72.
4. For the best brief historical account, see Cousins 1985, and the more extended work of Harvey 2013.
5. This image also occurs at M I 161. Bodhi discusses the commentary (NDB 1690 n 725).

Chapter 2. Meditation and the eightfold path

1. Rahula 1967: 74 and see Gombrich 2009: 171–2.
2. See e.g. A IV 84–8/Shaw 2006a 56–8.
3. (PED 433). PTS 184: *pariyāyadassāvī* (variants Ph. *Pariyāyakathaṃ* M6: *pariyādassāmi kathaṃ*).
4. See Shaw 2006 24–9 and Ud 34–7.
5. See Cousins 1973; Swearer 1973.
6. Some meditations taught by the Buddha fit no later list: see A V 336/Shaw 2006a: 132, or the teaching on internal space in M I 423/Shaw 2006a: 192.
7. See Shaw 2006a: 6–8; Vajirañāṇa 1975: 75.
8. See three *vandanas*, Buddhanet internet resource.
9. The *sutta* recurs at Vin I 179–85.
10. Literally 'make merit'.
11. See for instance the NICE website (2013) https://www.evidence.nhs.uk/search?q—editation and (2010) 'Oxford Mindfulness Centre': http://www.oxford-mindfulness.org/index.php?option=com_content&task=view&id=14&Itemid=9
12. See Soma Thera 1981 and Shaw 2006a: 150–3.
13. See Soma Thera 1981, Dhammasāmi 1999, Ñāṇamoli 1998, Nyanaponika 1969, Shaw 2006a: 76–85.
14. Ajahn Amaro, at Sambuddha Jayanthi celebration, Hammersmith, May 2011.
15. A good recent study is Brown 2007.
16. See, for instance, Guneratana 1985.
17. Snyder and Rasmussen 2009: vii.
18. See Shaw 2006a: 59–75.

19. See also Vism XXII 20, where recollection, or reviewing, is said to occur at the fruit of the second stage of the path moment of path, as the meditator recollects the path, its fruit, the defilements that have been abandoned, the defilements that still remain, and recollects *nibbāna*. See also UdA 336, where reviewing is said to be the result of the Bodhisatta vow. On this image in Chinese recensions see Shaw 2006a: 98, and 213, n.65. The sequence *suggahitaṃ hoti sumanasikataṃ sūpadhāritaṃ suppaṭividdhaṃ paññāya* is the same as in the five things that help breathing mindfulness (this anthology, p. 74).
20. See NDB, 1669, n 562.
21. See M III 96.
22. See the story of Little Tracker, this anthology, Chapter Five.
23. In the *Sāmaññaphala-sutta* this eightfold *iddhi* is compared to a skilled potter or goldsmith, capable of fashioning any shape he wishes (D I 78–85). The Buddha uses these skills to teach others (pp. 25–7).
24. This is compared to hearing varied drums (D I 79).
25. This is compared to looking into a clear pool or mirror (D I 80).
26. This is compared to revisiting a village or town where one used to live (D I 81).
27. This is compared to watching people around a busy crossroads from a high building (D I 81). The Buddha frequently employs this skill in *Dhammapada* stories, in order to be able to help those he teaches (this anthology, Chapter Five).
28. This last refers to awakening insight. It is compared to a man looking into a clear pool and seeing all the pebbles at the bottom (D I 85).
29. Boonman Poonyathiro, Samatha Centre, Greenstreete, Llangunllo, Powys, Wales, August 2013.
30. On this subject, see Wynne 2009.
31. Dhammadhāro 2010 (unpaginated internet resource).
32. See Shaw 2006a: 94–5 and MLDB 1284–5, n. 2, quoted in Shaw, 2006a: 212, n. 38.
33. I am grateful to Stefano Zacchetti for discussion about this. The *Aṭṭhakanāgara-Sutta* (M I 349–53), describing eleven gates to liberation, the four *jhānas*, four divine abidings and three of the formless spheres, anticipates this system. In Pāli the *Haliddavasana-Sutta* also links the divine abidings and the formless attainments (see S V 115–21, this anthology, pp. 81–6).
34. Migāramātā was a distinguished laywoman who supported the Buddha, and was given the name 'mother of Migāra' after converting her father-in-law.
35. The wording of this may also be found in the third part of the *Iti pi so* chant, the daily homage of Southern Buddhists, to the Triple Gem of Buddha, *dhamma* and sangha.
36. See *Rohitassa-Sutta*, this anthology, pp. 9–11.
37. This insight into phenomena (*dhamma*) is that which comprehends formations and conditioned phenomena (*saṇkhārapariggāhakavipassanā*). See NDB 1696, n 787.
38. According to *Abhidhamma* there are four kinds of food (*āhāra*): physical nutriment, contact (*phassa*), volition (*cetanā*) and mind (*citta*).
39. The pillar is a frequent symbol of stability (to D II 171, S III 200). Descriptive epithets are usually those used here: *acalā* and *asampavedhi* (variant T *asampadhi*).
40. The same word is used for the guarding of the senses (*indriyānam gutti*) at Dh 375, DhS 1348.

41. The image of the gate-keeper is common for mindfulness. See for instance this anthology, p. 55.
42. 'Living comfortably' (*phāsuvihāra*) is significantly distinguished from 'living happily' (*sukhavihāra*), or following the *dhamma*. See later in text: *ratiyā paritassāya phāsuvihārāya okkamanāya nibbānassa.*
43. *Abhicetasikānaṃ diṭṭhadhammasukhavihārānaṃ*. Cone gives *a/ābhicetasika*, as 'concerned with higher consciousness' (DP I 313).
44. Māra personifies the forces militating against meditation and the practice of the path.
45. *Saddho*, the adjective derived from *saddhā*, sometimes translated as faith, the first of the five faculties, is not the same as belief: purification of mental associates (*sampasādana*) is its subside chief characteristic; as in the comparison with the water-purifying gem that dispels mud and weeds (see this anthology, pp. 218–19).
46. *Sāvajja/anāvajja* (DP I 245).
47. The word translated as 'to keep', *pariharati*, has associations of safeguarding. This whole sentence is found repeatedly in Buddhist texts.
48. The key word is *hiri*, governing the verb *hiriyati*, to feel shame or dread, translated in this anthology in the *Abhidhamma* section as 'self-respect'. It is usually placed in a pair with scrupulousness (*ottappa*), and is in this capacity one of the pair of the 'guardians of the world'.
49. The word for stored up (*sutasannicayo*) is the same used for store of weapons.
50. See *vacasā paricita* (PED 424).

Chapter 3. The practice of meditation

1. The commentary discusses a threefold escape for each hindrance in turn: when temporarily suppressed, through calm, in *jhāna*; when eliminated, with regard to a particular respect, through insight practice; and finally, when eradicated through the path (see CDB II 1912–13, n 113).
2. See D I 71–85, and Shaw 2006a: 59–75.
3. For a helpfully clear explanation of the four kinds of clear comprehension, with commentarial description and advice for daily practice, see Nyanaponika 1962: 45–55.
4. This sequence is frequent in association with *samatha* practice. See, for instance, 'The Simile of the Cloth', this anthology, pp. 76–81.
5. See Vism VIII 145–244; Buddhadasa 1989; Ñānamoli, 1998; Shaw 2006a 146–58.
6. Ehara 1998: 165–6.
7. But see, for instance, Buddhadasa 1989.
8. See Bizot 1993. An important new study by Kate Crosby explores the presence of esoteric practices in Burma/Myanmar (Crosby 2013).
9. See Dennison, 1996, 1997.
10. This is associated with *akuppā cetovimutti*, unshakeable release of mind, identified with arahatship (NDB 1734, n. 1099).
11. This is the same wording used for the sign of recollection in the text on five-limbed concentration (*suggahitaṃ hoti sumanasikataṃ sūpadhāritaṃ suppaṭividdhaṃ paññāya*; see this anthology, pp. 37ff.).
12. See Vajiriñāṇa's excellent chapter 21 (1975) and Aronson 1980.
13. This is the first section of the *iti pi so* chant: the chants to the *dhamma* and the sangha, the other aspects of the Triple Gem, follow.

14. This sequence is very common.
15. See for extensive discussion of this, Gombrich 2009: 71–91.
16. These last three correspond to the three last stages of the sixteen stages of breathing mindfulness. *Vossagga* means 'relinquishing, relaxation; handing over, donation, gift' (PED 652), with associations of letting go.
17. The commentary says this is for one who cannot attain liberation through examining formations on the basis of the *jhāna* based in loving-kindness (CDB II 1911, n 111).
18. For some variations, see Harvey 2013: 103ff.
19. The four bases of success (*iddhipada*) are willingness (*chanda*), vigour, mind (*citta*) and investigation.
20. See *Samatha Chanting Book* (internet resource), p. 30.
21. U Pandita Sayadaw 1992: 164ff. describes some of the anecdotes about people cured physically and mentally. See also Rahula 1967: 74ff.
22. See this anthology, pp. 27ff., Gethin 1998: 192–7, Saddhatissa 1971: 54ff.
23. DhS 11 (this anthology, p. 151) and Gethin 1992a: 147–54.
24. Derived from *aj* to go+ *īr* (*vi* is substituted for *aj*). It is cognate, through Latin *vir* and old English *vertu,* with words like virility, virtue and virtuosity.
25. Derived from *pi* to delight (see Gethin 1992a: 181–4).
26. See Dennison 2013 for recent EEG studies on *samatha* meditators experiencing various types of joy.
27. *Passaddhi* is derived from *pa+sambh* to calm (PED 447).
28. Woodward (1930: 55 n.2) notes the commentary's observation that this refers to hearing about rather than listening to, a reading I have followed as the list seems to involve greater proximity at each stage, though Bhikkhu Bodhi's decision to take the verb here as 'listening to' is also justified (see CDB II 1571).
29. Literally, to apply the mind to the object (*anuvitakketi*), derived from the same roots as the first *jhāna* factor, initial thought, or bringing the mind to the object (*vitakka*). The prefix *anu* suggests 'along towards'. The translation 'put his mind to' is suggestive of another meaning in English, when someone decides upon something, but this also seems appropriate for a word based on *vitakka,* a quality which, when in skilful consciousness, is equated with the second path factor of right intention (DhS 7, 21). While the first *jhāna* factor is sometimes used with a negative sense, as describing obstructive thoughts (see M I 118–22), when it is associated with the meditation object, or, as here, reflection about the teaching, it has a positive connotation.
30. Bodhi notes (CDB II 1901–2, n. 63) that the three stages, applied to each factor of awakening, can be seen as a process of maturation.
31. I am taking *paññāya* as a gerund, not a noun.
32. As so often in such lists, a succession of broadly synonymous terms is suggestive of both intensification and sequence. The first, *vicinati,* translated as 'put his mind to', comes from the root *vi,* suggesting a number of directions, and *cināti,* to heap up or accumulate. The next factor, investigation of states, the teaching or *dhammas (dhammavicaya),* derives from this word. This factor is broadly inclusive of the next two verbs in the series here: *pavicarati,* a word associated with the second *jhāna* factor of examining, or exploring the object (*vicāra*), and *parivimaṃsam āpajjati,* literally, to 'get into' or 'meet up with' examination of the object.
33. See CDB II 1902, n 64 on alternative readings.

34. Reading *paṭikacca* with Woodward (1930: 57 n3); see also PED 392.
35. See CDB II 1902–3, n 65.

Chapter 4. Various kinds of texts and meditation

1. See MLDB 1214–15, nn 285–92.
2. This can be found on the *Bhāvanā* Society's site (2007). Another meditative commentary on the text, relating the stages to various features of insight practice, is provided by Mahasi Sayadaw (1904–1982) (internet resource: 1994–2011).
3. An 'ordinary person' is one who has not attained any of the four stages of the path, or their fruits.
4. See Gombrich 1996: 43–8; 120ff.
5. Mind and body.
6. On this see Bodhi 1995: 11–18.
7. See Gombrich 1996: 46 for important comment on this.
8. See Gombrich 1967: 120–3.
9. Dependent Origination retreat, Oxford Buddha Vihāra, November 2013.
10. The word *uttāna* (*uttānakuttānaka*) also has connotations of being shallow or easy to see, as in a flat clear stream of water. See DP I 413, Bodhi 1995: 6.
11. These last two are heavenly minstrels and ogres.
12. See Bodhi 1995: 77–9.
13. The word *ākāra* is that also used to denote 'skill' in the ten skills in absorption: here it means an attribute or characteristic (DP 1 276–7).
14. *Paṭighasamphassa.*
15. The experience of any of the *jhānas* can be mistaken for a 'true' self: see Patis I 143–4 and M II 229–33.
16. For details of these realms, see Harvey 2013: 32–6.
17. These are the first three of the higher spheres (*abhibhāyatanas*), which occur before *appanā-samādhi*, the steadying and attainment of meditation. Buddhaghosa explains that this is through not finding, or not wishing to find, the preliminary object for meditation (*parikamma*) in his own body (Asl 188).
18. The word used is *adhimutto*, akin to the 'releasing onto' (*adhimuttito*) described by Buddhaghosa, this anthology, Chapter Six. The 'beautiful' is the object of the *kasiṇa* practice (see MA III 256).
19. See Gombrich 1997: 121 and DA II 514–15.
20. See Gombrich 2009: 111–22.
21. See *Aditta-Sutta*, internet resources.
22. For an excellent discussion of the date, background and language of the verses, see Norman 1997: vii–xxii.
23. See Pruitt 1998: 204–6.
24. The term is *vivaṭṭūpanissaya? kusalam*: strong support (*upanissaya*) is one of the twenty-four conditions (*paccaya*), and is associated with the conditions that enable the practitioner to obtain *jhāna*, or liberating insight; *vivaṭṭa* means literally 'pulling away', here the veil of ignorance (for *vivaṭṭa* and *vivatta* see PED 637).
25. This refers to the three skilful roots of generosity (non-greed), loving-kindness (non-hatred) and wisdom (absence of delusion). See this anthology, pp. 147–8.
26. The Buddha said that Khemā is foremost amongst the nuns for her wisdom (A I 25).
27. See Cousins 1983.

28. See Rhys Davids 1959/1977: 282–3.
29. Nanasampanno, 316 (undated; internet resource).
30. I am grateful to Ajahn Maha Laow and Anne Schilizzi for discussion about this (2006).
31. See Collins 1998:297–309; Gethin 1998: 112–32; see also Shaw 2006b: xxxvii–xliv.
32. *Ātappa*: ascetic energy, exertion. On visualization and the *Mahāsamaya-Sutta*, see Gombrich 1997.
33. 'Visitor' (*āgantu*), is sometimes translated as 'adventitious corruption' (Exp I 185) or 'adventitious defilement' (NDB 97), but can also mean guest or stranger, an importantly simple meaning retained here (CPD II 22–3).
34. For this story, see BL 3: 47–52 (DhpA III 216ff.).
35. See Rowlands 1982, internet resource. As we go to press I have just seen Kate Crosby's useful introduction to modern *Abhidhamma* in practice (Crosby 2014: 174–93).
36. Bodhi says elsewhere of these: 'the word "body" was intended quite literally as meaning the physical body, considered as actively contributing to the qualitative tone of the experience' (CDB II 1901 n. 61).
37. A helpful account of the relationship between the six pairs is given by Nyanaponika 1998: 71–81. See also Shaw 2006a: 33–4; for discussion of the pairs in practice, see van Gorkem 1975: 180–91 and Rowlands 1982: 21–6.
38. For full discussion of this, see Asl 128–3.
38. The absence of scatteredness (*avikkhepa*).
40. CPD 2 682 *okappanā*: firm assurance.
41. The verb *nikkamati* (associated with *nekkhamma)* is 'to go out, to go forth; in figurative meaning: to leave behind lust, evil and the world, to get rid of *kāma* (craving), to show right exertion and strength' (PED 189).
42. The translation for these terms is based on the verb from which they are derived, *ussahati* (to be able, to be fit for, to dare, venture: PED 158, and see *ussāha*). As PED notes, there is an air both of goodwill and adventurousness about the verb and hence the nouns.
43. *Thāma* (PED 143); the same root as stamina: *sthā.*
44. This word is also used for the recollections of the Triple Gem, the Buddha, *dhamma* and sangha, often chanted before meditation practice. The prefix *anu* intensifies: so the recollection is practised repeatedly and frequently. The prefix *paṭi* tends to denote the opposite to *anu*: so here it is a bringing back to mind as well.
45. BPE 14 n 3 says this refers to not floating away on the surface, like pumpkins and pots at sea.
46. An excellent account of this and subsequent passages in other Buddhist *Abhidharma* schools is given by Collett Cox (1992).

Chapter 5. Narrative and meditation

1. I am grateful to Sanjukta Gupta for this useful observation about the function of extended narrative and concentration in a non-literate society.
2. See Shaw 2006b: xxxvii–xliv.
3. See Piyadassi Thera (1999–2013: internet resource) and *Samatha Chanting Book*, Samatha Trust, Llangungllo, Wales, 25. The *Mora Paritta* chant is on YouTube: Ven. Jandure Pagngnananda Thero: http://www.youtube.com/watch?v=kSj0KKIUfe4

4. The flower is *pterospermum acerifolium.*
5. This line is in metre, as is the line following the next two verses, and both are included in the *Mora Paritta* chant used today.
6. See, for more on these figures, Norman 1991.
7. See DP II 638–9 and, for instance, D III 215.
8. The story from the present also says that the incident that led to its telling has been told before: but we get no more details than that.
9. *Jātakas* frequently refer to others, reinforcing a sense of their interconnectedness. In the *Mahājanaka-Jātaka* the Bodhisatta (J 539) is asleep on the auspicious slab of the city and is chosen as king by a *Jātaka* device: a special carriage is set loose when the kingdom is without a monarch, which eventually stops before the true king.
10. The word *yaso* is also used for 'glory' here (PED 551).
11. The commentary associates *paṃko* (PED 378–9, *paṃsu* = mud, soil) with the slithery plants, reeds and lotuses, etc., which make a stretch of water attractive, but mean that you cannot cross, just as sense-pleasures prevent the practitioner from crossing over the ocean of *saṃsāra.*
12. The play on 'roots' describes those common to all humans: greed, hatred and delusion.
13. Emending *gatito* to *ganthito* (DP II 19).
14. Reading with commentary *jīvikaya atthiko* for *jīvikattho.*
15. For *asāta* see PED 88: 'disagreeable'.
16. The story introduces here the comments of the Buddha 'in the present'.
17. The word Sumedha is curious, as that is not given as the Bodhisatta's name. It is possible that it is the adjective 'wise', used to describe the Bodhisatta.
18. I am grateful to Ven. Dr Mahinda Degalle for discussion about this.
19. Within *Jātaka* stories *paccekabuddhas* become enlightened, as they find a path for themselves. Only at the end of the tale, in the 'present' and the presence of the Buddha teaching the four noble truths, do others attain stages of arahatship.
20. The word weapon (*āvudha*) is used mainly for martial purposes, but in J 55 it is used in a comparable way as the diamond weapon of wisdom (Ja I 274/Shaw *Jātakas* 2006b: 51–9).
21. Concerning *brahmam etam vihāram idha-m-ahu* Norman writes, 'it would be possible to translate as "They say this realm is Brahmā"' (Norman 1995: 177).
22. The *Mettā-Sutta* is in a less common metre, the old āryā (see Norman 1995: 176, n.143–52 and Norman 2005). This would probably sound very poetic, and unlike usual spoken interchange.
23. The word *sajjhāya* refers specifically to the chanting of texts.
24. *Gaṇasajjhāya.* The word *gaṇa* is related to our word 'gang' and denotes a collection or a group.
25. The idea that loving-kindness is contagious is a feature of Buddhist stories. See Shaw 2006b: 285 and 308, n.19.
26. The text says this literally – *vipassanāya cittaṃ otāretvā attanī khāyavayaṃ apaṭṭheptvā.* One reading, Ca, has *suvipassanāya,* 'for the sake of good insight'.
27. Reading *chabbaṇṇarasmiyo* with Ca.
28. See Roebuck 2010: 10, and note 127.
29. The word is *ussanno* from *ussīdati* (see DP I 519)
30. The ten stages of decomposition of a corpse are described as suitable for the person with great desire. It is taught only under supervision with considerable care in a modern and ancient context (see Shaw 2006a: 101–8).

31. *Ekaggatā*, the word here for 'unification', is often translated as 'one-pointedness' or 'gone to oneness', the fifth *jhāna* factor.
32. See this anthology, pp. 157ff.
33. The word *parikamma* refers to the preparations for *jhāna* (J I 141). The colour chosen is a little odd. The karnikara (*kaṇṇikāra*) flower (*pterospermum acerifolium*) is usually associated with the yellow *kasiṇa* in the canon (see Shaw 2006a: 95) and one might expect him to say, 'yellow, yellow', like gold. Burlingame sensibly suggests by implication that the 'red, red' is appropriate by translating (BL III 162) the 'gold' that the boy had worked on as 'ruddy gold'.
34. Reading *nikkhamiṃsu* with B rather than *vikkhambiṃsu*. Access (*upacāra*) concentration refers to a state where the hindrances are suppressed, but the *jhāna* factors not yet established with sufficient power to direct the mind to *jhāna* (see this anthology, p. 199).
35. The word *ākāra*, or skill, is used in the commentaries to describe the ten skills in absorption (see this anthology, p. 202). It perhaps refers here to the five 'masteries' of meditation: adverting, entering, sustaining, emerging and recollecting.
36. The words *jhānakīḷaṃ kīlanto* – playing with the play of meditation – here, and in other contexts, are found in later works, referring to the lightness of touch needed to move flexibly from one meditation (*jhāna*) to another with ease (see Shaw 2006b: 26–36).
37. The word 'emerging' is very important in Buddhist meditation (see Shaw 2006a: 96–9).
38. Collins 1990: 167 and 156ff.
39. The word for 'removing the dirt' is *rajoharaṇa*, literally meaning the removal of dirt, but also a duster. Another word (*reṇu*) used in this passage for dust is Vedic (SED 887).
40. And see D I 79, 156, S I 184.
41. The reader is being instructed to give to his audience the same story here as applied to the birth of the first son, an indicator that the commentaries probably functioned as manuals for those teaching.
42. Literally 'Will they really eat our flesh?'
43. This refers to the parts of the body, given as the first meditation object to a new monk. In their fivefold aspect, hairs of the head, hairs on the body, nails, teeth and skin, are the first elements described under mindfulness of body in the *Satipaṭṭhāna-Sutta* (PED 293). These are all the obviously visible parts of the body; others are mostly internal.
44. Wise attention (*yoniso manasikāra*) steers the mind towards skilful objects.
45. The word 'fruit' is usually associated with the fruit of path, and so means here the resultant *citta* from his attainment of arahatship.
46. According to early texts, there are four modes of progress in the teaching, varying from person to person (PED 314 and D III 106): painful progress and slow insight, painful progress with swift insight, pleasant progress with slow insight, and pleasant progress with swift insight. Big Tracker seems to have been the last type. Little Tracker, for reasons that are explained later in the story, the first.
47. This is the second of the thirty-two marks that distinguish a universal monarch or Buddha (D III 143).
48. See introduction to this story.
49. The word *abhirūḷha* means literally ascended, or stepped up on to: the same word is used for embarking on a boat (DP I 213).

50. The image of the mind-made form is one of the fruits of the recluse in the *Sāmaññaphala-sutta*, the first of the higher knowledges (*abhiññā*) possible after the fourth *jhāna*. The mind-made body looks identical to the practitioner's original body, and has form (*rūpa*): it is 'created *by* the power of the mind' (Hamilton 1996: 156–7). It is matter of a subtle kind, as the *rūpa* of the *rūpa jhānas*, the first four *jhānas*, is subtle.
51. See the introduction to this story.
52. *Paṭisambhidā* (PED 400): the four branches of discriminatory knowledge are of meaning, conditions, definitions and analysis (*paṭibhāna*). The formula that someone attains arahatship with the discriminations, as here, is frequent in later literature.
53. Knowledge of the three 'baskets' of *Vinaya, Sutta* and *Abhidhamma*.
54. According to the *Abhidhamma* all events in the mind and body are related to those that have arisen before, arise at the same time and will arise in the future by means of twenty-four conditions (*paccaya*), described in the seventh book of the *Abhidhamma*. The condition here is 'strong support' (*upanissaya*), associated with prompting a change of state.
55. The meditator is now called an 'elder' (*thera*).
56. This indicates a talk about meditation. Brahmā is the lord of the heaven associated with the first *jhāna*, and 'Brahmā' abiding. The voice of Brahmā, and the power to speak to an assembly so that each person feels they are being addressed as an individual, is the twenty-eighth of the thirty-two marks of a Buddha (D II 211; D III 144,173).
57. *Manta*: spell, chant.
58. The story can also be found translated in BL 30: 161–3 (DhpA 3: 425-431/ Dhp 285).

Chapter 6. Buddhaghosa: some practical tips on meditation

1. The first stage of path; arahatship is the last. 'The noble plane' is any stage of path.
2. This is literally the 'grazing-place' of a monk: where he goes each day for his customary alms round.
3. *Kosa*: 500 bow-lengths (DP I 739). North and south is to avoid the sun coming on one's face.
4. See e.g. M I 145 and *Rathavinīta-Sutta* (this anthology, pp. 103–9)
5. The manual is full of such unknown anecdotal references.
6. The word translated as absorption (*appanā*) denotes the mind's release into a meditative state. It differs from concentration, though requires it, in that it only applies to the skilful *citta* and right *jhāna* (DP I 180, DhSA 55, 142).
7. The word is *adhimuttito*: literally a 'releasing onto', a relaxed commitment or resolve (PED 29).
8. The word is *ajjhatikaṃ*: with regard to the self, internal.
9. 'The associated mental state and accompanying factors that have arisen with it' (*uppanesu cittacetasikesu*).
10. The five faculties in meditation are faith, vigour, mindfulness, concentration and wisdom (see this anthology, Chapter Seven).
11. '*Dhammasabhāva*' the *sabhāva* is the condition proper to something, its essence.

12. Vakkali had excessive faith, unbalanced with the other faculties. He 'clung to the Buddha's robe' and neglected his own practice (It 902). He has to be sent away by the Buddha to develop his own meditation, and after a struggle, finds success (Th 350–4; Shaw 2006a: 120–1).
13. See this anthology, pp. 25ff.
14. The three marks of existence: impermanence (*anicca*), dis-ease (*dukkha*) and non-self (*anattā*).
15. It is not clear where exactly this is said. See PTS Vism: 130, n. 3.
16. See the section in this anthology on the factors of awakening (*bojjhaṅgas*). This advice is also given in S V 112.
17. The text of the PTS edition of the *sutta* quoted here (S V 104) leaves out the words 'for the getting greater, for the full development of (*bhiyyo bhāvāya vepullāya*)'.
18. *Adhimutti*: DP I 92 gives 'conviction, intent, inclination, will, freedom'.
19. These are some of the recommendations for the eradication of sloth and torpor, as for instance given to Moggallāna, a great practitioner of concentration, liable before enlightenment to sleepiness (see also A I 257). The Buddha suggests that he should reflect on the teaching, massage his limbs, splash the eyes with cold water, pay attention to the perception of light, take walks and finally, if that does not work, have a rest. He does not suggest going into the open air, perhaps because Moggallāna, meditating in a deer park, would have been there anyway (A IV 84–8; Shaw 2006a: 56–8).
20. See this anthology, pp. 24ff.
21. All of these meditation objects, the recollections (*anussatis*), objects 21–7 in Buddhaghosa's system, are designed, he says, to bring happiness, freedom from fear, and contentment. See Vism VII and Shaw 2006a: 109–34.
22. Object 30 in Buddhaghosa's system.
23. *Cittapassaddhi* and *kāyapassadhi*. For a description of these *cetasikas*, present, from the point of view of the *Abhidhamma*, in all skilful consciousness, see DhS 14–15 (this anthology, pp. 146 and 154).
24. The one who is awake is *buddho*.

Chapter 7. Milinda's questions

1. See Horner 1964; Masefield 2004; Halkias 2013.
2. Halkias 2013: 500–1.
3. Chinese versions date from the fourth and fifth century CE. Oskar von Hinüber has noted that whereas King Milinda is a known historical figure, Nāgasena, his mentor, is not, and argues that the text includes some anachronistic features, as well as betraying the influence of the *Upaniṣads* rather than Greek elements (von Hinüber 2000: 83–6).
4. PED 559. 'Monk' in Pāli is sometimes used to describe any meditator. See Shaw 2006a: 14–15.
5. See Horner 1964: 47 n. 3.
6. There are rich associations with the word 'crossing over' (*tiṇṇo/uttiṇṇo*), often used as a metaphor for liberation (PED 302).
7. See Rhys Davids 1890/1925: 57, n. 3 on *aññamaññam anusāreyya anupeseyya*.
8. See DhS 11 and this anthology, p. 151. It is not allowing things to float away when at sea, or be forgotten. Horner's excellent choice is 'not wobbling'. See also Rhys Davids 1890/1925: 58, n. 2.

9. For *upagaṇhanā*, see DP I 441: 'seizing, drawing to oneself, becoming master of' or 'taking up' (CPD II 436). See also Horner 1964: 50, n. 6 and MA I 82–3. Rhys Davids gives 'keeping up' 1890/1925: 58 n. 2.
10. The verb *apilāpati*, to remind, enumerate, here in the causative, is of a different root from 'not floating away', so a pun is intended.
11. The thirty-seven factors contributing to awakening (*bodhipakkhiyādhammā*).
12. See this anthology, pp. 100–1.
13. *Pamukha* literally means 'in front of the face' (PED 417).
14. See S III 13.

Chapter 8. Sanskrit texts

1. See Williams 1989: 97–109 for discussion of the *Tathāgatagarbha* notion and Eastern Buddhism.
2. I am grateful to Professor Florin Deleanu for discussion in his seminar in Oxford on this and related subjects.
3. For examination of this and some tentative hypotheses as to Aśvaghoṣa's allegiance and basis for his meditative advice, see Yamabe 2003.
4. I am grateful to Linda Covill for discussion and her extensive work on this poem.
5. See Yamabe and Sueki 2009; for sections influenced by Aśvaghoṣa's poem, see xv–xvii.
6. The 'wish-granting jewel' supposedly clears muddy waters (see this anthology, pp. 218–19).
7. See for instance S V 92 for this image, frequent in early Buddhist texts.
8. The Southern Buddhist tradition does not include *jhāna* (*dhyāna*) here, as a perfection, though the perfection of renunciation (*nekkhamma*) encompasses this. Other translations of this passage are in a scholarly and readable translation by Crosby and Skilton, and for a good presentation of Tibetan versions, see Wallace 1997.
9. The word *viveka* is sometimes translated as solitude. It has been rendered as seclusion, as this meaning seems associated with the description of *jhānas* as 'born of seclusion', meaning more a seclusion of the senses and the body, rather than being alone.
10. The word for assemblage is *paṃkti*, used for collections of five elements, and so the five aggregates.
11. This refers to a story where the Supuspacandra is tortured to death by a king for teaching liberation; he had embarked on his teachings even though aware of his possible fate. After his death a number of miracles confirmed his *bodhisattva* status.
12. I am grateful to a reading class with Professor Paul Harrison at SOAS for work on this.
13. The word *sukha* has been translated throughout this anthology as 'happiness', the fourth *jhāna* factor. In this context the word is usually translated as bliss, so the usual translation has been retained for the Land of Bliss, though the word 'happy' is used sometimes descriptively.
14. These are given within Chinese versions of the text as 'cool, clear, sweet, light, soft, free from odour, free from disease, refreshing and invigorating' (Gomes 1996: 16). See also Williams 1989: 251–8 on this *sūtra*.
15. I am grateful to Dr Richard Hayes for discussion about this work.

16. For a translation of the entire work, see Sharma 1997, and see, for Kamalaśīla, Williams 1989: 196ff. For an excellent introduction to Tibetan calm meditation see Lamrimpa 1992.
17. These points were raised during Florin Deleanu's teaching stay in Oxford.
18. See Strong 2001: 41–3 and Shaw 2009: 127–30.
19. See Tucci 1971: 3 n.21 for *kale* on the basis of a Tibetan variant: 'at the time of meditation', rather than *bhavanbalena*, 'through the power of his meditation'.
20. The five limbs are the head, two arms and two legs.
21. This is the same word as *anumodana*, to transfer merit.
22. This probably means some kind of cushioning.
23. Instructions regarding the eyes vary according to the type of practice: most concentration practices have the eyes shut. Here, where the external object is an important aid, the eyes are half open, as in the first stages of *kasiṇa* practice, which also employs an external object (Vism IV 28). Practitioners sitting in meditation sometimes just open the eyes for a moment in the practice to see the world around, or a shrine if there is one.
24. See Harrison 1978.
25. This refers not to the distinction between form and formless meditations, but that between mind and matter.
26. The first of the five aggregates (*skandha/khandas*), literally 'heaps', is *rūpa*, 'form', or matter. The next four, of feeling, identifications, formations (*saṅkhāras*) and consciousness, are without form, that is, mind (*nāma*).

BIBLIOGRAPHY

Pāli texts used are the Pali Text Society (PTS) and the *Chaṭṭha Saṅgāyana Tipitika* CD-ROM

Pāli texts

A	*Aṅguttaranikaya*
Ap	*Apadāna*
Asl	*Atthasālinī*
D	*Dīghanikāya*
DA	*Sumaṅglavilāsinī*
Dhp	*Dhammapada*
DhpA	*Dhammapada-aṭṭhakathā*
DhS	*Dhammasaṅgani*
Ja	*Jātaka*
	(where the number of the story is given, J: e.g., J 539).
M	*Majjhimanikāya*
MA	*Papañcasūdanī*
MP	*Milindapañha*
Nidd	*Mahāniddesa*
Patis	*Paṭisambhidāmagga*
S	*Saṃyuttanikāya*
Sn	*Suttanipāta*
Th	*Theragāthā*
Thī	*Therīgāthā*
ThiA	*Therīgāthā-aṭṭhakathā*
UdA	*Udāna-aṭṭhakathā*
Vin	*Vinaya*
Vism	*Visuddhimagga*

Pāli Translations

Bodhi, Bhikkhu. 1995. *The Great Discourse on Causation: The Mahānidāna Sutta and its Commentaries*. 2nd ed. Kandy: Buddhist Publication Society.

— 2012. *Connected Discourses of the Buddha*, 2 vols. Somerville, MA: Wisdom/PTS (CDB; trans of S).

— *Numerical Discourses of the Buddha*. Somerville, MA: Wisdom/PTS (NDB; trans. of A).

Burlingame, E. W. 1921/1990. *Buddhist Legends: Translated from the Original Text of the Dhammapada Commentary*. 3 vols. Cambridge, MA: Harvard University Press/ PTS (BL; trans of DhpA).

Ehara, N. R. M., Soma Thera, and Kheminda Thera, trans. 1977. *The Path of Freedom (Vimuttimagga) by Arahant Upatissa*. Kandy, Sri Lanka: Buddhist Publication Society, 1977.

Hare, E. M., and Woodward, F. L, 1934–6. *The Book of Gradual Sayings*. 5 vols. London: PTS (GS; trans. of A).

Horner, I. B. 1964. *Milinda's Questions*. London: PTS.

Luk, C. 1964. *The Secrets of Chinese Meditation*. Maine: Samuel Weiser.

Ñāṇamoli, Bhikkhu. 1991a. *The Path of Discrimination (Paṭisambhidāmagga)*. Oxford: Pali Text Society.

— 1991b. *The Path of Purification (Visuddhimagga)*. 5th edition. Kandy: Buddhist Publication Society (Vism trans.: this edition cited by section-heading).

— 1998. *Mindfulness of Breathing: Buddhist Texts from the Pali Canon and Commentaries*. Kandy: Buddhist Publication Society.

Ñāṇamoli, Bhikkhu, and Bodhi, Bhikkhu. 2001. *Middle Length Discourses of the Buddha*. Boston and London: Wisdom/Pali Text Society. (MLDB: trans. of M)

Norman, K.R. 1992. *Group of Discourses (Sutta-Nipāta)*. Oxford: PTS.

— 1997. *Poems of Early Buddhist Monks*. Oxford: PTS (trans. of Th).

Pruitt, W. 1998. *The Commentary on the Verses of the Therīs*. Oxford: PTS.

Rhys Davids, C.A.F. 1974. *Buddhist Psychological Ethics*. 3rd edition. London and Boston: PTS/Routledge Kegan Paul (trans. of DhS).

Rhys Davids, C. A. F., and Tin, P. M. 1958. *The Expositor*. Edited and revised. 2 vols. London:PTS (trans. of Asl).

Rhys Davids, C. A. F., and Norman, K. R. 1997. *Poems of Early Buddhist Nuns* (trans. of Thī). Oxford: PTS.

Rhys Davids, T. W. 1890/1925. *The Questions of King Milinda*. Oxford: Clarendon.

Rhys Davids, T. W. and C. A. F., 1959/1977. *Dialogues of the Buddha*. 3 vols. 4th edition. London: Pali Text Society (DB: trans of D).

Roebuck, V. *The Dhammapada*. London: Penguin, 2010 (trans. of Dhp).

Soma Thera. 1981. *The Way of Mindfulness: translation of the Satipaṭṭhāna-Sutta of the Majjhima-Nikāya, its commentary and other excerpts*. 5th edition. Kandy: Buddhist Publication Society.

Walshe, M. 1987. *Thus Have I Heard: the Long Discourses of the Buddha: Dīghanikāya*. London: Wisdom (trans. of D).

Woodward, F. L. 1930. *The Book of Kindred Sayings*. Vol. V. London: PTS (trans. of S V).

Sanskrit texts and translations

Batchelor, S. trans. 1979. *A Guide to the Bodhisattva's Way of Life (Shantideva)*. Dharamsala: Library of Tibetan Works and Archives (Tibetan).

Covill, L. 2007. *Handsome Nanda by Aśvaghoṣa*. New York: New York University Press (Sanskrit text used).

Crosby, K., and Skilton, A. 2008. *The Bodhicaryāvatāra*. Williams, P. ed. Oxford: Oxford University Press.

Gomes, L. O. 1996. *The Land of Bliss: the Paradise of the Buddha of Measureless Light; Sanskrit and Chinese Versions of the Sukhāvatīvuyha Sūtras.* Honolulu: University Press of Hawaii.

Müller, F. M., and Nanjio, B. 1883. *Sukhāvatīvuyha Sūtra: description of Sukhāvatī, the Land of Bliss.* Oxford: Clarendon.

Sharma, P. 1997. *Bhāvanākrama of Kamalaśila.* 1997 New Delhi: Aditya Prakashan.

Shastri, H. 1939. *Saundarananda Kāvya of Ārya Bhadanta Aśvaghoṣa.* Chakravarti, C. ed. Calcutta: Royal Asiatic Society of Bengal.

Tucci, G. 1971. *Minor Texts: Third Bhāvanākrama of Kamalaśila.* Vol. 3. *Rome: Istituto Italiano per il Medio ed Estremo Oriente.*

Vaidya, P. L. 1960. *Bodhicaryāvatāra of Sāntideva with the commentary pañjikā of Prajñākaramati.* Darbhangha: Mithila Institute.

Wallace, V. A and B. A. 1997. *A Guide to the Bodhisattva Way of Life.* Ithaca, New York: Snow Lion (Tibetan).

Dictionaries

Cone, M. 2001/2010. *Dictionary of Pāli,* 2 vols. Oxford/Bristol, Pali Text Society (DP).

Monier-Williams, M. 1899. *Sanskrit-English Dictionary.* London (SED).

Rhys Davids, T. W. and Stede, W. 1925. *Pāli-English Dictionary.* Chipstead: Pali Text Society (PED).

Trenckner, V. et al. 1924–. *Critical Pāli Dictionary.* Copenhagen.

General bibliography

Appleton, Naomi, Sarah Shaw and Toshiya Unebe. 2013. *Illuminating the Life of the Buddha: An Illustrated Book from Eighteenth-Century Siam.* Oxford: Bodleian Libraries.

Aronson, H. B. 1980. *Love and Sympathy in Theravāda Buddhism.* Delhi: Motilal Banarsidass.

Bizot, F. 1993. *Le Bouddhisme des Thais.* Bangkok, Thailand: Editions des Cahiers de France.

Bronkhorst, J. 1993. *The Two Traditions of Meditation in Ancient India,* Delhi: Motilal Banarsidass,

Brown, K., Warren, R., Richard, M., and Creswell, J. D. 2007. 'Mindfulness: Theoretical Foundations and Evidence for its Salutary Effects.' *Psychological Inquiry,* 18:4, 211–37.

Buddhadāsa Bhikkhu. 1989. *Mindfulness with Breathing; unveiling the Secrets of Life (a Manual for Serious Beginners)* Bangkok: The Dhamma Study and Practice Group.

Collins, S. 1990. *Selfless Persons: Imagery and Thought in Theravāda Buddhism.* Cambridge: Cambridge University Press.

— 1998. *Nirvana and other Felicities: Utopias of the Pali Imaginaire.* Cambridge: Cambridge University Press.

Cousins, L. S. 1973. 'Buddhist *Jhāna*: its Nature and Attainment According to the Pali Sources.' *Religion* 3. Autumn: 115–31.

— 1983. 'Pali Oral Literature'. In P. Denwood and A. Piatigorsky, eds. *Buddhist Studies Ancient and Modern.* London: Curzon Press, 1–11.

— 1984. '*Samatha-Yāna* and *Vipassanā-Yāna*". In *Buddhist Studies in Honour of Hammalava Saddhatissa*, Gatare Dhammapala, R. F. Gombrich and K. R.Norman, eds., 46–68. Nugegoda, Sri Lanka: Hammalava Saddhatissa Felicitation Volume Committee.

— 1985. 'Buddhism'. In J. R. Hinnells, ed. *Handbook of Living Religions*. Harmondsworth, Middx.: Penguin, 278–343.

Cox, C. 1992. 'Mindfulness and Memory: the scope of *Smṛti* from Early Buddhism to the Sārvastavādin *Abhidharma*.' In J. Gyatso, ed. *The Mirror of Memory: Reflections on Mindfulness and Remembrance in Indian and Tibetan Buddhism*. Albany: State University of New York Press, 67–108.

Crosby, Kate. 2013. *On Traditional Theravāda Meditation and its Modern-Era suppression*. Hong Kong: Buddha Dharma Centre of Hong Kong.

— 2014. Theravāda Buddhism, Continuity, Diversity and Identity. Hoboken, New Jersey: Wiley Blackwell.

Dhammasami, K. 1999. *Mindfulness Meditation made Easy*. Penang: Inward Path.

— 2000. *Different Aspects of Mindfulness*. Penang: Inward Path.

Dennison, P. 1996. 'Na Yan: an Introduction'. In *Samatha: Insight from a Meditation Tradition*, Llangunllo, Wales: Samatha Trust 2: 16–18.

— 1997. 'Na Yan: Continued'. In *Samatha: Insight from a Meditation Tradition*, Llangunllo, Wales: Samatha Trust 3: 19–23.

Dhammadhāro, Ajahn Lee. *Keeping the Breath in Mind: Lessons in Samādhi*. Geoffrey DeGraff trans., Rayong, Thailand (undated: talks from 1956 to 1960).

Gethin, R. 1992. 1992a. *The Buddhist Path to Awakening: a Study of the Bodhipakkhiyā-Dhamma*. Leiden/Koln/New York: Brill.

— 1992b. 'The Mātikās: Mermorization, Mindfulness and the List.' In J. Gyatso, ed. *The Mirror of Memory: Reflections on Mindfulness and Remembrance in Indian and Tibetan Buddhism*. Albany: State University of New York Press, 149–72.

— 1998. *Foundations of Buddhism*. Oxford: Oxford University Press.

Gombrich, R. F. 1996. *How Buddhism Began: The Conditioned Genesis of the Early Teachings*. London and Atlantic Highlands, N.J.: Athlone.

— 1997. 'Religious Experience in Early Buddhism', *Eighth Annual Lecture, British Association for the Study of Religions*.

— 2009. *What the Buddha Thought*. London: Equinox.

Gorkem, N. van. 1975. *Abhidhamma in Daily Life*. Bangkok: Dharma Study Group.

Guneratana, Mahathera H. 1985. *The Path of Serenity and Insight; an Explanation of the Buddhist Jhānas*. Delhi: Motilal Banarsidass.

Halkias, G. 2013. 'The Enlightened Sovereign; Buddhism and Kingship in India and Tibet'. In S. M. Emmanuel, ed. *A Companion to Buddhist Philosophy*. Malden, MA/ Oxford: Wiley-Blackwell.

Hamilton, S. 1996. *Identity and Experience: the Constitution of the Human Being According to Early Buddhism*. London: Luzac Oriental.

— 2000. *Early Buddhism: a New Approach: the I of the Beholder*. London: Curzon.

Harrison, Paul. 1978. '*Buddhānusmṛti* in the *Pratyutpanna-Buddha-Saṃmukhāvasthitasamādhi-Sūtra*.' *Journal of Indian Philosophy*. 6: 35–57.

Harvey, P. 2013. *An Introduction to Buddhism; Teachings, History and Practices*. Revised edition. Cambridge: Cambridge University Press.

Hinüber, O. von. 2000. *A Handbook of Pāli Literature*. Berlin: Walter de Gruyter.

Lamrimpa G. 1992. *Śamatha Meditation: Tibetan Teachings on Cultivating Mental Quiescence*. A.Wallace trans., H.Sprager intro. Ithaca, New York: Snow Lion.

Masefield, P. 2004. 'Milinda'. In Buswell, R., ed. *Encyclopedia of Buddhism*. 536–7. 2 vols. New York: Macmillan, 2: 536–7.

Norman, K. R. 1991. 'The Pratyeka-Buddha in Buddhism and Jainism'. *Selected Papers of K. R. Norman*. Vol. 2. Oxford: PTS, 233–49.

Nyanaponika, Thera. *The Heart of Buddhist Meditation; a Handbook of Mental Training Based on the Buddha's Way of Mindfulness*. London: Rider, 1962.

U Pandita Sayadaw. 1992. *In this Very Life*. Somerville, MA: Wisdom.

Pradhan, A.P. *The Buddha's System of Meditation*, 4 vols, New Delhi: Oriental University Press, 1986.

Rahula, W. 1967. *What the Buddha Taught*. Bedford: Gordon Fraser.

Saddhatissa, Ven. 1971. *The Buddha's Way*. London: George Allen and Unwin.

Sayagyi, U Chit. 1993. *Buddhism as a Way of Life and Other Essays*. W.Pruitt assisted. Chippenham, Wiltshire, UK: Sayagyi U Ba Khin Memorial Trust.

Shaw, S. 2006a. *Buddhist Meditation: an Anthology of Texts*, London: Routledge.

— 2006b. *The Jatakas: Birth Tales of the Bodhisatta*. Global Classics Series. New Delhi: Penguin.

— *Introduction to Buddhist Meditation*. London: Routledge, 2009.

Snyder, S., and Rasmussen, T. 2009. *Practicing Jhānas: Traditional Concentration Meditation as presented by the Venerable Pa Auk Sayadaw*. Foreword by Ven. Pa Auk Sayadaw. Boston, Ma: Shambala.

Strong, J. S. 2001. *The Buddha: a Short Biography*. Oxford: Oneworld.

Swearer, D. K. 1973. 'The structure of Buddhist meditation in the Pāli *suttas*'. *Philosophy East and West*. 23: 4, 435–55. Honolulu: University Press of Hawaii.

— 'Thailand'. 2003. In *Encyclopedia of Buddhism*, 2 vols. Robert Buswell, ed. New York: Macmillan. 2: 830–6.

Swearer, Donald. 2004. *Becoming the Buddha: The Ritual of Image Consecration in Thailand*. Princeton: Princeton University Press.

Tiyavanich, K. 2003. *The Buddha in the Jungle*. Chiang Mai: Silkworm.

Tolkien, J. R. R. 1975. *Tree and Leaf; Smith of Wootton Major; the Homecoming of Beorhtnoth*. Reset edition. London: George Allen and Unwin.

Vajirañāṇa, Mahāthera. 1975. *Buddhist Meditation in Theory and Practice*. Kuala Lumpur: Buddhist Missionary Society.

Williams, P. 1989. *Mahāyāna Buddhism: the Doctrinal Foundations*. London/New York: Routledge.

Wonglakorn, P.A. 2010. *Dhammayātrā on the Sacred Land of the Buddha*. Thammasapa and Bunluenthm Institution: Bangkok.

Wynne, A. 2009. *The Origins of Buddhist Meditation*. London: Routledge.

Yamabe, N. 2003. 'On the School Affiliation of Aśvaghoṣa: "Sautrāntika"or Yogācāra"?' *Journal of the International Association of Buddhist Studies*, 26, 2:225–54.

Yamaben, N., and Sueki, F. 2009. *The Sūtra on the Concentration of Sitting Meditation. Translated from the Chinese of Kumārajīva*. Taisho Volume 15:614. Berkeley, California: Numata Center for Buddhist Translation and Research.

Zacchetti, S. 2003. 'The Redisovery of Three Early Buddhist Scriptures on Meditation: A Preliminary Analysis of the *Fo-shuo-shi'er-men-jing*, the *Fo-shuo-jie-shi'er-men-jing*, translated by An Shigao, and their Commentary preserved in the newly found Kongo-ji Manuscript. *ARIRAB*, Soka, Japan.VI (March), 251–99.

Internet resources

(sites accessed 5 October 2013)

Dhammadhāro Ajahn Lee. 'Basic Themes'. Thanissaro Bhikkhu trans., *Access to Insight*, 23 August 2010 (unpaginated): http://www.accesstoinsight.org/lib/thai/lee/themes.html

Eliot, T.S. 1922. 'The Waste Land': http://www.poetryfoundation.org/poem/176735

Mahasi Sayadaw: http://www.accesstoinsight.org/lib/authors/mahasi/progress.html (The Progress of Insight (*Visuddhiñāṇa-katha*) by The Venerable Mahasi Sayadaw, Nyanaponika Thera trans., 1994–2011).

Spiritual Biography by Maha Boowa Nanasampanno (1870–1949), Bhikkhu Dick Salaratano trans. (undated): http://www.buddhanet.net/pdf_file/acariya-mun.pdf

Norman, K. R. 2005: 'The Origins of the Āryā Metre': http://www.ancient-buddhist-texts.net/Textual-Studies/Prosody-Articles/Norman-Arya-Text.htm

Rowlands, M. 1982. *Abhidhamma Papers*: http://www.samatha.org/publications

Some suttas and chanting

Buddhanet: http://www.buddhanet.net/audio-chant.htm

Aditta-Sutta: Palichanting.org

Mora-paritta (peacock protection): Ven. Jandure Pagngnananda Thero: http://www.youtube.com/watch?v=kSj0KKIUfe4

Rathavinita-Sutta: podcast, *Bhāvanā* Society's site (2007): http://bhavana.us/mp3/Rathavinita.mp3

Pali Chanting in the Theravada Buddhist tradition: http://www.buddhanet.net/pali_chant.htm

Piyadassi Thera (1999–2013) *The Book of Protection: Paritta; Foreword by V. F. Gunaratana*: http://www.accesstoinsight.org/lib/authors/piyadassi/protection.html

Samatha Chanting Book, Samatha Trust, Llangunglo, Wales: http://www.samatha.org/publications